The Procurement Value Proposition

The Procurement Value Proposition

The rise of supply management

Gerard Chick
Robert Handfield

KoganPage

LONDON PHILADELPHIA NEW DELHI

First published in Great Britain and the United States in 2015 by Kogan Page Limited

2nd Floor, 45 Gee Street
London EC1V 3RS
United Kingdom
www.koganpage.com

1518 Walnut Street, Suite 1100
Philadelphia PA 19102
USA

4737/23 Ansari Road
Daryaganj
New Delhi 110002
India

© Gerard Chick and Robert Handfield, 2015

ISBN 978 0 7494 7119 4
E-ISBN 978 0 7494 7120 0

British Library Cataloguing-in-Publication Data

A CIP record for this book is available from the British Library.

Library of Congress Cataloging-in-Publication Data

Chick, Gerard.
   The procurement value proposition : the rise of supply management / Gerard Chick, Robert Handfield.
      pages cm
   Includes bibliographical references and index.
   ISBN   978-0-7494-7119-4 – ISBN   978-0-7494-7120-0   (ebk) 1. Industrial   procurement.
2. Purchasing.   3. Business logistics.   I. Handfield, Robert B.   II. Title.
   HD39.5.C475 2015
   658.7'2–dc23

                                                                              2014036687

Typeset by Amnet
Print production managed by Jellyfish
Printed and bound by CPI Group (UK) Ltd, Croydon, CR0 4YY

CONTENTS

03   From global trends to corporate strategy 51

04   Five game changers: their impact on procurement and supply management 77

08   The dawn of procurement's new value proposition: innovation, collaboration and focus 173

09   The future: from strategic procurement to value procurement 197

The following supplementary materials to Chapter 11 are available to download at **www.koganpage.com/pvp**

- PowerPoint slides covering innovation debates on talent, visioning and risk.

PREFACE

We see a new vantage point on modern business. One that highlights interrelationships between specific business units and the broader economic, social and market systems in which we all live.

The current view on business tightly restricts the business model within which an organization operates. Often short-term goals are the immediate focus. Business decisions seldom consider the power of supply side management and its impact on economic, social and environmental systems. Smart procurement in modern businesses can ensure that resources are in place to absorb the growing middle-class and consumer demand portended by globalization. Corporate decision makers also tend to overlook the destabilizing effects created by disparities in wealth and the corresponding inability of people to satisfy their fundamental needs – because of their corporation's desire to continuously reduce cost. Today an alternative perspective on business is emerging. It is one that is informed by an understanding of the dynamics of modern business in global markets with global consumption.

In 2008 we held an executive summit with a group of CPOs from major UK businesses on the status of the supply base in light of the emerging financial crisis at that time. We found that there were significant challenges that existed in preserving the financial health of suppliers, and that firms weren't really doing enough to try to support suppliers.

Since then things have actually worsened. In spite of this, when we met up again in 2012 we discussed some of the positive issues we saw for procurement, such as the increased importance and impact of the profession in a time when liquidity (the degree to which an asset or security can be bought or sold in the market without affecting the asset's price) was low. The importance of good procurement practice had become critical: we saw the role of the supply management leader growing in organizations both in a strategic sense and in its centricity to organizational performance.

As supply management moves away from being a cost-reducer (only), it will play a much more important role in value-adding activity and influencing business strategy. This central involvement will become all the more important as major trends start to hit business and subsequently procurement, including increased corporate social responsibility, technological advances, global geopolitical and macroeconomic change, demographic changes, changes in supply and demand patterns and the shift in the economic centre of gravity from West to East. It was from this discussion in 2012 that the germ of an idea for this book was conceived.

The aim of this book is to contemplate the value proposition to the business of contemporary procurement and supply management. Business organizations are going through rapid external and internal organizational changes for the reasons given above.

Much of the foregoing points to the increased as well as changing nature of the risk we face in business today. That said, we must avoid risk becoming the responsibility of a few more or less isolated individuals within organizations; instead it is important that risk awareness becomes integrated into the fabric of the business: where all processes, including purchasing and supply chain management, should take into account the need for risk awareness.

Value and what it means is the key purchasing and supply chain management challenge we seek to address in this book. If purchasing and supply chain managers are to embrace this challenge they have to change the ways they operate. This requires new ways of thinking about supply structures and processes, and new skills and competencies.

As a result, the very future of procurement – as a function within organizations, as a process that spans organizational boundaries and as a profession – raises important concerns for both organizations and the procurement practitioner. This book considers the practice of procurement and supply management in the modern era and how this might shape the next generation of procurement professionals.

The value proposition of procurement is examined in terms of its changing focus set against changes in business contexts, purchasing strategy, organizational structure, role and responsibility, system development and skills required to work in the profession. Consideration has been given, too, to geographical contexts and differences highlighted between the United States, the UK and China.

It is worth pointing out at this juncture that some of the ideas presented in this book have been kicking around for quite some time, although the conditions under which they might flourish have yet to materialize in more than a handful of organizations. The hope is that – with all that has been accomplished in procurement over the past few decades – the time for these ideas may finally be coming.

It follows from the above that the integration of procurement across the business is not the responsibility of a few but rather a challenge that must be embraced company-wide. You don't have to be a 'procurement convert' to believe in the theme of this book – as the realization of value is not purely about the challenges of getting an enterprise to realize its economic potential, but also about a range of social and economic challenges outside the organization.

It is for this reason that the book is intended as a *starting point* for those interested in the future of procurement – a trigger to establish discussion and debate regarding procurement's value and stimulate future conversation about what the next generation of procurement practice might look like. We hope, too, that this book will play its small part not only in educating, but also changing the mindsets of current and future purchasing and supply chain management professionals.

Gerard Chick MSc
Chief Knowledge Officer
Optimum Procurement Group

Robert B Handfield PhD
Bank of America University Distinguished Professor of Supply Chain Management,
North Carolina State University
Director of the Supply Chain Resource Cooperative

ACKNOWLEDGEMENTS

We wish to thank all of the individuals who work in the procurement area all over the world. This book is dedicated to you and your pursuit of excellence. The work here is a culmination of ideas you have brought to us and shared, and as such, represents more than just a sum of the parts.

I would particularly like to thank Ian Sillett who told me a long time ago that I could do something like this if I put my mind to it – so I did! Naturally I want to thank my family Jo, Jake and Luke and my wife, Andrea who pushed me along when I could have easily stopped (GC).

To Sandi, Simone and Luc, and to the memory of my baby brother, Carlo (RBH).

Introduction

Procurement has a history that is linked in the core concepts of centralization, volume leveraging and cost reduction. The earliest traces of this can be linked to materials management. Charles Babbage's book on the economy of machinery and manufacturers, published in 1832, referred to the importance of the purchasing function. Babbage alluded to a central officer responsible for several different functions in the mining sector: 'a materials man who selects, purchases, receives, and delivers all articles required'.[1]

By 1866, the Pennsylvania Railroad had given the purchasing function departmental status, under the title of Supplying Department. The purchasing function was such a major contributor to the performance of the organization that the chief purchasing manager had top managerial status.[2]

The comptroller of the Chicago and Northwestern Railroad wrote the first book exclusively about the purchasing function, *The Handling of Railway Supplies – Their Purchase and Disposition*, in 1887. He discussed purchasing issues that are still critical today, including the need for technical expertise in purchasing agents along with the need to centralize the purchasing department under one individual. The author also commented on the lack of attention given to the selection of personnel to fill the position of purchasing agent. In Europe, organizations in the European coal and steel community in 1951 began exploring centralization of coal purchases to drive greater leverage.

These early insights evoke a situation that is still not uncommon to what we see today. Although procurement has certainly evolved from its early roots, it still faces challenges in terms of executive recognition, talent management and organizational challenges. Modern enterprises are faced with a massive new set of challenges, including the forces of globalization, increased risk, complex supply chains, and the spread of government regulation on decision making, not to mention the tremendous strain of man's presence on the earth's natural resources. This book will seek to document not only what the future holds in store for the materials buyer, but also how this role is likely to emerge as critical to the future.

Our central thesis is that those organizations who are better able to position procurement as a core business function, with direct responsibility to the chief executive officer (CEO), will be able to drive a more competitive lever for change, and adapt more readily to the rapid forces of change in the current global environment. In the way that Charles Darwin identified that organisms better able to adapt to their environment ultimately survived, so organizations that embrace complexity – and manage it through more rapid responses, improved market intelligence, greater adoption and translation for internal stakeholder requirements, and adaptive capabilities – will survive.

Faced by these issues many businesses have turned to procurement, looking for solutions to these burgeoning problems. As a consequence of this responsibility, procurement as a business discipline has grown exponentially since the 1980s. Many organizations across the private and public sectors worldwide have elevated procurement to a strategic business role; the emergence of the Chief Procurement Officer (CPO) is manifest recognition of the rising profile of procurement. The trend towards outsourcing of non-core activities has clearly had a positive impact on the discipline, as a large proportion of value addition to the business comes from the supply base and many organizations have woken up to this fact and manage their procurement function accordingly.

However, the elevation of procurement to a strategic business function is a relatively recent development and for many businesses procurement remains a low priority. Here procurement remains focused on gaining low prices from suppliers, regardless of whether the business strategy is focused on low cost or not. So, although procurement in some organizations has become more sophisticated, there remains much scope for improvement in the discipline.

Another interesting development is that an increasing number of people choose a career in procurement; however, as recently as the mid-2000s this was by no means the case. Procurement was often seen as a backwater, a somewhat dubious choice for a career. It can be argued too that the emergence of supply chain management has played into the hands of procurement, which is seen as a critical link in the supply chain. In other ways, however, the role of procurement in relation to supply chain management is all but clear: some people regard purchasing as an integral part of supply chain management whereas others regard it as complementary but separate.

Procurement executives today are being asked to bring more to the table in this era of globalization and outsourcing capabilities. Many are being asked to push procurement in directions that represent new business models and approaches. And yet many feel torn between delivering the traditional demands of procurement – supply assurance and cost reduction – while frustrated knowing what the real potential of a world-class supply management organization is capable of delivering.

In an effort to explore 'the art of the possible', this is not a book with a primary focus on procurement and supply management techniques or practice, but a book that identifies and discusses the value proposition offered by contemporary procurement to the sustainability and development of the business it serves. In effect, this book is about change. And because change is constant, we acknowledge that the story is still being written. The inclusion of case studies focusing on organizations that are moving through procurement transformation are thus not depicted as 'best practices', because in a sense the story is still being written for each of these companies and their managers. Rather, the case studies provide a snapshot of organizations in transition, in a continual phase of movement, alignment, flux and adoption to the multitude of shifts that are occurring in each of the ecosystems they populate. And because change is so fundamental to the ideas presented here, we hope to provide a view of how to think about change, and how procurement needs to change. This is not so much an evolution of procurement, but a suggestion of what procurement may look like at some point in the future. Not every organization will get there. Some may founder, or remain stuck. But in the end they will all change to some extent. What we hope to provide here is a roadmap for navigation to this change.

Structure of the book

Book overview

As shown in Figure 0.1, the book is divided into two parts:

FIGURE 0.1 Book overview

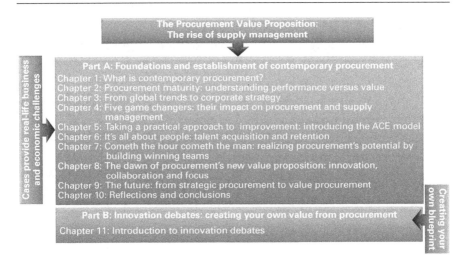

Part A: Foundations and establishment of contemporary procurement

The chapters in the first part of the book focus on how, since the 1980s, procurement has matured as a strategic business unit (SBU) – transforming itself from the low-level clerical service it once was into the creative professional team that today brings value to the business and the customer.

As the point of departure, Chapter 1 (What is contemporary procurement?) begins by tracing the development of purchasing from a principally administrative, tactical service within organizations to a managerial, strategic, value-adding function. We introduce the implications of supply chain management for purchasing and conclude with an overview of how this impacts the structure of the rest of the book.

Chapter 2 (Procurement maturity: understanding performance versus value) is designed to offer some insights into how procurement has evolved; we introduce a maturity model to help the reader understand at what level of maturity different organization's procurement functions are capable of operating at. Here we examine how the value of procurement is delivered into the business in terms of the service mix: ie how procurement performs. We look at what levels of capability we have today and to what extent it needs to change, allied to how well an organization can execute efficient and effective procurement. We also investigate the importance and nature of purchasing strategy and explore different purchasing organizational structures, skills and competencies. In Chapter 3 (From global trends to corporate strategy) we examine how a procurement executive's ability to read trends accurately in a rapidly changing business setting can make all the difference between surviving or going under. We assess too the impact of emerging macroeconomic, social, environmental and business developments against the needs of a business. We ask whether the trends detailed in the chapter are in some way self-predicting; and what contribution procurement professionals can deliver to the business. Taking both internal and external procurement dimensions into account, we examine the five widely accepted key trends that dominate the business world today, and consider what the really good procurement organization does to maintain competitive advantage.

Chapter 4 (Five game changers: their impact on procurement and supply management) evaluates the big issues affecting business today. We explore the way in which procurement is structured and how procurement will increasingly find itself managing virtual networks of suppliers, stakeholders and internal customers, drawing on powerful new social media channels to communicate. We discuss why it is important that this technology does not come at the expense of face-to-face relationships because of their importance in establishing solid supplier connections. Alongside this, we look at the debate regarding the battle for talent.

We highlight why businesses can no longer afford to downplay the strategic role of procurement, and develop an understanding of the impact of the game-changing phenomena that have brought this about – and how procurement can offer the wider business opportunities to take advantage of some of them. Clearly not every procurement organization is at the same level of maturity, so we consider three levels of capability, as identified in Chapter 2 in terms of the achiever; the value-adder and the leader.

Part A continues on a pragmatic note with Chapter 5 (Taking a practical approach to improvement: introducing the ACE model). Here we introduce a model to work with in association with the maturity ladder to plot procurement's future. Whilst we continue our focus on how the issues discussed in Chapter 4 have changed the face of global supply chain management (SCM) we contemplate what options are available to those leading procurement set against the ACE model – via the three dimensions of the model's aspiration, capability and execution and what they might offer to the ambitious procurement leader. In Chapter 6 (It's all about people: talent acquisition and retention) we begin our examination of talent as well as mindset and skill sets. In Chapter 7 (Cometh the hour cometh the man: realizing procurement's potential by building winning teams) we contemplate how procurement has changed, the different levels of procurement maturity that exist today and the consequent impact on the people, talent and creativity needs of procurement. All too often we hear that we can't find the people 'out there' to take on this new role. Clearly these people are available, because other parts of business such as finance or marketing can find people with the qualities required to work in the contemporary business world.

Procurement's journey from 'also ran' to core business capability matches the way in which the business landscape has changed since the 1980s and 1990s. Procurement began to change as the customer moved to the centre of the business universe and corporates such as Apple, Wal-Mart, Amazon and Zara gained dominant market positions largely by building and operating supply chains that outstrip the competition.

Part A concludes by focusing on the role of innovation in procurement. The first part of Chapter 8 (The dawn of procurement's new value proposition: innovation, collaboration and focus) discusses how purchasing can facilitate product development and innovation through the involvement of suppliers. The second part of Chapter 8 discusses what procurement might become and offers six signposts to the future. In Chapter 9 (The future:

from strategic procurement to value procurement) we contemplate how an implicit view of value does not allow practitioners to fully understand which elements of value must be achieved to sustain relationships, or the complex commercial and operational tensions that exist in transactional exchange. We argue that much of the current thinking tends to overemphasize the operational and underplay the commercial interests, which exist in business relationships. We discuss the importance of understanding the supplier's needs and wants as well as an understanding of the sources of supplier value, arguing that this could help buyers to manage a whole range of buyer–supplier interactions and develop them to gain strategic competitive advantage. We discuss too that it is necessary for the buying organization to understand what it is that suppliers want from them other than more revenue. Some suppliers, for example, might want demand stability and are prepared to improve their performance to get this. In Chapter 10 (Reflections and conclusions) we spend some time building on these insights to understand where we are likely to go in the next decade.

Part B: Innovation debates: creating your own value from procurement

Part B is more practical in nature than Part A. It considers how companies can implement some of the ideas in this book, by using both the procurement maturity ladder and the ACE model to examine 'the art of the possible' within their organization in order to explore new forms of supply chains and the need to engage with a range of network suppliers and stakeholders.

How to use this book

The structure of this book is designed such that the chapters can be read either sequentially in the order they appear, or the reader can opt to be more selective by dipping into topics of specific interest at their choosing. Throughout all the chapters in this book, we have sought to address what we perceive as the prime challenges facing procurement today in terms of understanding and developing value to both the business and, ultimately, the customer. Each chapter highlights specific issues or practical examples from industry and we have adapted major case studies to demonstrate core themes and concepts in each chapter.

As noted, we have woven stories of procurement change into every chapter, in the form of brief case studies. These provide not just examples of what we mean by change, but also provide some important practical examples of how to get started. Each case is not a success story – many of the companies are in transition, or faced with seemingly insurmountable obstacles. But they all provide a window into the mind of how progressive procurement executives are moving in the right direction. Finally, we feel it worth signposting the fact we have included blog posts from http://scm.ncsu.edu/blog/ in our book. We think this introduces a live element. A problem we perceive is that it is very difficult to get senior executives to devote themselves to opportunities with the potential to bring real change. However, by introducing the blog address we hope to generate a robust flow of new procurement management ideas.

What does the future of procurement look like to you? Today, it would seem that every CEO has a point of view about the strategic worth and/or direction of procurement. The blog gives us and you an opportunity to innovate and engage. Everyone has a voice. This is your opportunity to help shape the future of procurement and its impact on business. So come on and join the debate.

Notes

1   Babbage, C (1832) *On the Economy of Machinery and Manufactures*, Charles Knight, Pall Mall East.

2   Fearon, H (1968) History of purchasing, *Journal of Purchasing*, February, pp 44–50.

PART A
Foundations and establishment of contemporary procurement

What is contemporary procurement?

01

Procurement began with various dubious roots. In the late 1980s, one of the co-authors regularly attended purchasing conferences at an organization known as the National Association of Purchasing Management.[1] The meetings served largely as a social function for a lot of buyers to get together, sit at the bar and tell war stories. Someone listening in on these conversations was likely to hear people discuss how they had 'got a great price' from a supplier, after they 'threatened to go with someone else', followed by guffaws and other discussions. Many of the buyers who attended these conferences had been promoted as a result of working in a warehouse, in an administrative assistant role, or even as an assembly-line worker. If one were to attend a supply management conference today, one would meet a very different type of individual, and engage in a very different set of conversations.

This chapter traces the development of purchasing from a principally administrative, tactical service within companies to a managerial, strategic, value-adding function and introduces the implications of supply chain management for purchasing.

The emergence of procurement as a profession

Modern societies have for some time articulated the division of expert labour into various 'professions'. These professions – of which medicine, accountancy and law are obvious examples – are found, on analysis, to meet certain common criteria. It is generally accepted that there are seven criteria that need to be satisfied in order to describe an activity as a profession. The first six of these are:

- The members of the profession are engaged in the performance of a service, which is vital to society.
- Their performance is based on a specialized and codified body of knowledge.
- Those who enter the profession must first undergo a programme of broad general education as well as further education and training for a career in the speciality.
- Candidates for the profession undergo an examination to test their qualifications to enter the practice.
- The profession promulgates a code of ethical conduct for members and makes arrangements to enforce compliance to this code.
- The profession offers a secure career to its members.

The seventh relates to a licence to practise. Whilst the first six criteria can be satisfied by the existence of organizations such as the Chartered Institute of Purchasing and Supply (CIPS) – who provide for all six points through their charter and via their standards, qualifications and certifications – it is the seventh criterion that remains to be achieved. In the United States, the Institute for Supply Management (ISM) has a similar focus on engaging in all of the first six elements, but not the seventh.

That said, at no time in its 80 years has CIPS or its members seen so many opportunities for creativity and leadership via professional procurement. Doubtless this will apply to ISM in the United States and NEVI and others in Europe. Some of these opportunities can be seized and realized by individuals, but more usually they require a team effort under some professional sponsorship.

For a body of specialists to be accepted as professional requires that they meet their obligations to society at large with respect to that specialty. No one wants to become a professional through self-appointment. The deep-down satisfaction comes when others regard one as having earned the status of professional through one's deeds.

Within the terms of the criteria outlined above, one can decide whether a case can be made for professionalism in procurement. However, while procurement has undoubtedly come a long way – and paraprofessional it may be – it still has far to go if it wishes to be seen in the same light as medicine or the law.

The emergence of procurement as an academic discipline

When compared with other business and management professions such as marketing, finance or human resource management, procurement is relatively new. Whilst the origin of supply management is closely linked with the birth of the company itself, it was viewed by academe as being of little interest as it appeared to require little or no skill.

Supply chain management (SCM) as a concept was born at the beginning of the 1980s. At that time research and teaching in the field was almost non-existent. Some of the early academic programmes in supply management were created by Hal Fearon at Michigan State University and Arizona State University, where these early programmes were called 'Materials Management'. Both of these universities also created executive programmes in this area.

In the period 1992–99, a group of like-minded academics at Michigan State University created an initiative called the Global Procurement Benchmarking Initiative, and created a series of studies that focused on leading procurement practices.[2] These technical reports were largely focused on documenting what organizations were doing, and classifying these strategies into *basic, moderately advanced* and *most advanced*. Out of these early studies were derived many of the maturity models that formed the basis for procurement consultancies at Accenture, AT Kearney, IBM, McKinsey, Booz & Co and others.

Since the mid-1990s, the growth of both teaching and research has been exponential. In 2014 SCM is making the change from being an emerging research field to becoming a consolidated one. The importance of an academic perspective on SCM and, more to the point, the role of procurement within it, is that it ensures that any possible gaps between research and practice can be minimized.

The 1970s saw the publication of the first real textbooks on procurement, the most notable being England (1970), Lee and Dobler (1971) and Baily and Farmer (1977). From a pedagogic perspective, these can be seen as the foundation stones of procurement as an academic subject, which in itself affords the subject the gravitas required for a 'profession' to be taken seriously.

By the 1980s and early 1990s books and articles were published that really sought to promote procurement as an important business function and therefore as a worthwhile academic field of study. In particular, writers across Europe and North America argued for the position and status of procurement as a function, rather than a service, within organizations and that it should be elevated in status accordingly.

It is in no small part that this lack of academic credibility of procurement and supply management until relatively recently reaffirms that its practise for some considerable time had been little more than a clerical service, focused predominantly on obtaining the lowest possible prices for goods and carrying out low-level, mundane tasks such as record keeping. Today, more than 50 universities in the United States and more than a dozen in the UK have supply management curriculums.

Early developments towards modern procurement

Around the same time as procurement began to evolve as a field of academic study in the late 1980s and early 1990s companies had embarked on changes in industrial organization, in particular the advent of 'outsourcing'. Businesses began moving non-core competencies and other activities that they previously performed in-house to third-party service providers in an effort to reduce cost. This trend had major implications for procurement because it meant that strategically important resources or complementary competencies had to be sourced – and purchased – from specialized suppliers.

As the business landscape began to change so did inter-company relationships, principally due to globalization and rapid developments in new information technologies; and with this change came the need for the proper management of the supply side. Consequently, the position and status of the procurement function within organizations was elevated again. People developed various maturity models, with some portraying procurement as a reactive, passive and tactical service, whilst others portrayed it as an advanced, integrative, strategic function.

Procurement becomes supply (chain) management

Peter Kraljic's publication in the *Harvard Business Review* in 1983, 'Purchasing must become supply management', was pivotal in the rise of procurement from a tactical service to a strategic business function. His key message was that procurement should focus more on high-value and high-risk supply items and that these called for 'supply management' rather than 'purchasing management'. This is a theme that has since been the subject of much debate and, in some parts of the world, most notably North America, procurement is now frequently referred to as supply management or simply 'supply'.

The rise of supply chain management is in many ways a natural extension of this development. Adding the word 'chain' to 'supply management' may seem trivial but is, in fact, significant. The inclusion of the concept of chain hints at the multidisciplinary genesis of supply chain management, most notably the inclusion of concepts such as Porter's value chain (strategic management) and channel management (marketing and distribution).[3]

As procurement metamorphosed into a professional function, it became more deeply involved with changes in industrial organization. The introduction of 'outsourcing' of non-core competencies and other activities formerly performed in-house is possibly the most prominent. This trend towards outsourcing has accelerated; since the mid-2000s or so outsourcing has been an integral part of globalization as companies have looked to low-cost countries for cheaper sourcing. Outsourcing reflects a deep trend; moreover, outsourcing is part of a wider change process of industrial reorganization in which companies focus on what they do best and connect to the rest through a network of business relationships.

Technological innovation is now happening at such a rapid pace that companies can no longer do everything in-house. Today businesses have little choice but to outsource, principally because the most critical resources are intangible and knowledge-based.

The dawn of the modern era: procurement as an enabler and value adder

What is without question is the fact that today many organizations see their supply function as a key driver of competitive advantage. Procurement is at the heart of supply chain management, but SCM shifts the focus from direct relationships between buyers and suppliers towards entire end-to-end supply chains. In many organizations procurement is now an integral part of the supply (chain) management function, focused on the management of the part of the upstream, supplier-focused supply chain (sourcing).

Whereas the focus of procurement is clearly on supplier relationships, the focus of supply chain management is on the wider business system that includes several layers, or tiers, of suppliers, sub-suppliers, customers, distributors and so on. In some ways supply chain management has absorbed a number of business functions involved in the process of supply, including procurement, operations, logistics and distribution management.

In 2014 the proportion of value across many industrial sectors that stems from the supply chain is almost 80 per cent and in many companies the outsourcing ratio can be greater than 90 per cent. The consequence of the outsourcing trend is that companies become heavily dependent on the performance of their suppliers and therefore need to make sure that suppliers are effectively managed, as if they were an extended part of their own company.

As a central function to working with suppliers, procurement plays a key role in the management of supplier relationships. This role is not only a matter of cost reduction, although saving money remains a priority for any procurement organization, but it is also about ensuring that the need for a range of criteria – including for example quality, delivery, innovation and service – are being met by suppliers.

Moreover the changes witnessed since the mid-1980s have brought a new complexity. The need to procure complex performance requires not only deep collaborative relationships with suppliers, often spanning multiple decades, but also an understanding of how complex outcomes are articulated over time through a combination of contractual incentives and collaborative relationships, requiring new skills and competencies from procurement people.

It is against this backdrop that the elevation of purchasing – from a passive low-level organizational service to a strategic function with corporate visibility and influence – needs to be understood. The rise of the executive board position of the chief procurement officer (CPO) is symptomatic of this trend. Companies are increasingly realizing the importance of improving their knowledge and competence in procurement. They realize that they need to start filling this knowledge gap and to develop fundamentally new ways of thinking about procurement and its potential contribution in order to ensure sustained competitive advantage in an increasingly competitive global business landscape.

Purchasing's legacy

It is worth reflecting again on where procurement has come from and what the procurement 'industry' at large comprises. Many people still think that procurement, rather like buying or purchasing, is nothing more than some form of professional 'shopping'. This view could not be further from the truth. Procurement has many components: for example, the main types of spend that naturally require different responses. In Table 1.1 the three principal types of spend – direct procurement, indirect procurement (which includes the procurement of goods not for resale) and retail or goods for sale – have been outlined and set against the variables, which help to differentiate the role of procurement in each.

TABLE 1.1　The three principal spend types in modern procurement

Variables	Indirect Spend	Direct Spend	Retail Spend
		Spend Type	
Number of suppliers	High	Low	Medium
Value of transactions made	Low	High	High
Number of transactions made	High	Low	Low
Number of stakeholders	High	Low	Low
Does procurement own the spend?	No	Occasionally	Yes
Number of requisitions made	High	Low	Low
Business focus/ drivers	Operationalizing the business	TCO	Gross margin
Potential for unauthorized spend	Yes	No	No
Number of spend categories	High	Low	Medium
Procurement's focus	Internal: stakeholders External: supply market	Supply market	Supply market
Source of value	Changing internal behaviours	Supply market	Supply market

What is clear from Table 1.1 is that procurement is much more than a simple transaction process between buyer and seller. In fact, procurement does not own the internal stakeholders' budgets. As can be seen, in many cases procurement will not 'own' spend at all. Nor does it run the business unit/function it is procuring for. More often than not, the primary role of procurement is to provide stakeholders with fact-based proposals on how to better manage their spend based on reality, procurement's expertise and the good practice methods their professionalism brings.

In fact, procurement is often seen as the poor relation of other business functions and, when it comes to those in indirect procurement, something of an even lesser status. This is partly because procurement is a prisoner of its heritage. As has been outlined above, procurement is in its relative infancy, and as yet has not reached intellectual maturity. Journal articles and books on procurement were rare prior to the 1980s and, as a consequence, there was little to promote procurement as an important business function and therefore as a worthwhile academic field of study.

However, there is an immediate need for businesses to view procurement differently. Those who are already enlightened recognize that it is the essential activity that enables a business to run. Furthermore, the hubris over what is 'best-in-class', and who we can benchmark ourselves against to see if we are too, is as pointless as it is misguided. Today it is far more realistic for businesses to understand what is needed for them as a distinct and individual organization.

As has already been noted, until relatively recently the position and status of procurement as a function, rather than a service, within organizations endorses that its practise in the eyes of many was and is little more than a clerical service, focused predominantly on obtaining the lowest possible prices for goods and carrying out low-level, mundane tasks. This has meant that procurement has remained ill-positioned in many businesses; that it has for many years remained unappreciated and its true value has remained unrecognized. This low status has blighted the reputation and attractiveness of procurement and, as a result, as a profession of choice it fails to attract the best talent.

Compounding this lack of clarity of what a procurement organization should look like is the constant change going on in the world we live and work in. As will be seen later in the book, this change is panoptic – none of us is immune – whether it be due to technological advances or the impacts of globalization. As a result, the pressures on procurement are increasing and frequently as we will see that these pressures are conflicting.

Towards procurement's value proposition

The ultimate measure of procurement's value will be its ability to support the company's overall business strategy. This will require some procurement organizations to make far more than incremental changes. There will need to be a change in procurement's priorities from cost reduction/avoidance only to proactively expanding the scope of its spend influence in order to ensure that a company-wide good-practices-driven procurement process is in operation.

Unquestionably, the goal of raising procurement's spend influence indicates that many procurement groups, having reached the upper limit of cost reductions possible within their current remit, are looking to take on new spend categories in an effort to unearth additional savings and further demonstrate their value to the business.

The aspiration of procurement to expand its influence is not a new one. In fact it is the root of the deepest frustration amongst most CPOs and their teams; and whilst leading-edge businesses no longer treat procurement as intermittent in nature but rather as part of the natural business cycle, there are many more that do not. These organizations still see procurement as tactical or low-level work.

To address this misconception let us reflect on an explanation of why procurement is strategic – one that was given in a presentation made in 2008 by Rob Morgan, CEO of Morgan Smith Ltd, who suggested the simple equation below as a way of articulating procurement's value proposition to business:

$$P = \frac{R - C}{A^u}$$

What this represents is that profit equals revenue minus costs divided by assets used. This very simple equation seems to encapsulate precisely how and why good professional procurement is critical to all businesses. However, the perennial debate regarding how procurement tangibly benefits the business continues to rumble on.

If one reflects on the above it makes perfect sense; it is quite simple really – if procurement impacts the profit-and-loss account (P&L) and the business's cost of goods (COG) then it follows that it has a very real value to business and it demands that businesses realize that they need very good people working in their procurement organizations. In fact, if we reflect for a moment on the reach of people working in procurement today:

- they operate globally;
- they communicate and collaborate inside and outside of their business;

- they have a direct (and often immediate) impact on the P&L;
- many are fully responsible for the activities of the categories they manage and how they impact operational and/or capital expenditures;
- they are increasingly expected to be 'students of their industry', because it is their understanding of the marketplace that businesses value most – deciding when to go to market to source a product or service is ultimately their responsibility.

The impact of this could be critical. These people are on the front line – a decision they make can swing a budget by £100 million. This is very important work, strategic in nature, which requires working with a wide range of stakeholders and also calls for an adjustment to the skill sets of procurement people – as not all of these skills are currently within procurement's areas of expertise.

Procurement's starting point is its ability to capture and understand the total volume of spending that falls under its purview. This sounds like an obvious statement, but in fact it is a mystery to many organizations. That's right – many companies do not fully understand the full measure of their external spending, and cannot identify who they are spending their funds with. In the case study below, we look at one of the first companies to realize this, and how this led to the roots of what is now known as strategic category management. The story also emphasizes how small the role of technology is in this effort. The individuals in this case study were using 'green screen' technology. Today's technology certainly would have made their life easier – but it was the understanding and leadership in this case that made the difference for Ford Motor Company.

CASE STUDY   Pioneering category management at Ford Motor Company

Steve Zimmer was the architect of the Extended Enterprise concept pioneered by Chrysler during the years 1989–98. The origins of the Extended Enterprise started well before this period, however, and began with the early work that Steve did while he was a senior purchasing buyer at Ford Motor Company.

Steve described his experience to us over a pizza in Detroit:

When I first started at Ford in the early 1980s I was working with Jack Hughes on plastic parts. I was involved in inventory control area on what they used to call 'residual parts', which were leftover parts that you ended up trying to sell into the service parts organization. They had all these computer systems to help analysts try to figure out what to do with it. This was my first exposure to the part number mentality with a bunch of analysts. Ford had a lot of rejects and I worked with a guy who had programmed it for years, and I realized how crazy the part number system was. So I flowcharted the whole thing and found that there were loops in the system that didn't work – and made changes. Unfortunately I eliminated several people's jobs in the process! But they didn't know what to do about it at Ford. So I started to do programs on how to handle it, and in three months I was laid off.

Later I was rehired and brought back into purchasing. Jack Hughes sought me out because during this period in the 1970s, price controls were coming in due to the extreme shift in the cost of oil that America was experiencing. Suddenly, overnight, Ford Motor was exposed to over US $400 million of economic exposure for pricing. This impacted transportation costs, resins, chemical feed stocks, and a whole bunch of other areas. Buyers were being told to just make this cost increase go away, but of course they didn't have the tools to do so. So I started to try to project the economics around these cost increases, using some of the ideas I had developed while working in the part number space.

The first thing I did was I interviewed buyers and tried to get an idea of which parts were made of what material, and the relative level of exposure they had to oil prices. I learned quickly that it wasn't all that accurate, and the information was highly dependent on the buyer. So then I got the forecast of material projections and labour and did some projections. I looked at exposure versus budget, and most of it was on an annual basis. I figured out you could meet exposure by either resisting or deferring it, and was able to come up with a way to put a value on deferment. This allowed buyers to use some combination of deferral and resistance that would equal the same outcome. For instance, you could do a 50-day resistance combined with a 90-day delay, and it would get you there. I took this and then developed a 'must pay list' for every buyer of material. They thought I was crazy, but I assured them that this would work!

But understanding exposure wasn't enough, as my boss came to me and said we were under attack from petrochemicals, and we had to deal with it. We needed to know what was the leverage available. So I talked to a few people and tried to understand where the raw material was coming from in the third or fourth tier of suppliers. I needed to find out the types of plastics we were buying, and I couldn't get that information – but we needed it! So I sat down with all of the Ford parts and ran programs on them. This was awful – you had to use punch cards to find out what the parts were made out of and where we were buying stuff. I had boxes of punch cards! But I was able to map out the value chain back to petrochemicals, and was able to derive weights that were then pushed back onto part numbers. I recombined the data and understood where they were getting the parts. My boss said we needed to get contractual control over our supply chain, so we started to leverage out buys at the petrochemical level, and started writing contracts with the big petrochemical companies. Eventually we did the same thing with zinc and steel. Later, when I worked at Chrysler, we were the first automotive company to leverage the steel buy. Chrysler didn't have the leverage that Ford or GM did – and so they leveraged it and got them to ship steel directly into the suppliers.

What happened then was that this whole exercise got me thinking about commodities, *not* parts. And Ford was spinning off a new heavy truck de-partment, with a new 9000 truck. For the buyers who bought parts this new low-volume truck would have more exposure than other products out there on material price variance. But how could I get all the parts and consolidate them in a way that made sense to measure exposure? The only way I knew how to do this was to dive down into the bill of materials – and do a cross-tab. Fortunately, Ford was one of the few car companies at that time that had a decent commodity coding system for each part number, with a prefix that described the car the part was attached to, the function of the item and the suffix that, to a certain degree, described engineering levels, colour and ma-terial. This was the first intelligent database system I had seen, and it allowed me to do a few things.

What I would do is to start with the commodity description that the part code was associated with. Say it was transmission, followed by assembly, etc. I arbitrarily adopted a simple language to group the parts. If the part code was 'trans-assy' – that meant it was an assembly, and belonged in the transmis-sions category. Although there were thousands of part codes, I was able to work it down to 200 specific groupings of parts. And then I compared this grouping to a list of the buyers for each part. This allowed me to see if they were assigned to the right people in a way that made sense, and in some cas-es, I was able to recategorize the buys into a logical grouping by buyer. I had to have a conversation with the buyers to let them know that 'I've miscategorized your buys, and I'm going to add some parts to your list of managed parts'.

Once I did this, I was able to take a look at a 'deck' of the current buy for a commodity group for Ford's production buy. I started by looking at no more than 10 commodity groups, and looked at the production buy across these commodity groups. With the data organized this way, I was able to see that

I could consolidate the number of suppliers by commodity, the value of the buy for the group, using data that no one had ever seen before! This was really exciting! Then I created a matrix of around 35 existing buyers, pulled all the heavy truck stuff out of it, and ran summaries of the data. I could then start to see how many commodities I was dealing with, and was able to reload the commodities to a smaller group of buyers with broader responsibilities that might cover more than one commodity. This was tricky, as I had to consider the workload. For example, just the two groups of engines and transmissions might be too much for one buyer, so it had to be measured in terms of the complexity of the commodity group.

The other big advantage to working with commodity groups was in transfer of ownership if a buyer left the company. Historically, if a buyer gives responsibility of a part to another, we had to fill out forms and transfer all the parts over one by one. With the new system, transferring to a new buyer was easier because we knew what commodity group all the parts were attached to.

Later at Chrysler we were able to do the same thing, to drive strategic alignment by commodity code by buyer, and identify the highest value of business. But this was a lot more complicated, because the data cleansing at Chrysler was much more laborious. At one point we had 12,000 non-production categories, many of which were duplicates of other MDM numbers.

This story told by Steve Zimmer holds several key points that merit discussion:

- Prior to launching any type of major procurement transformation initiative, there is a need to really understand the discipline of what you are buying. The discipline involves beginning to understand and build better data on what suppliers are doing, so that you can establish the right type of business driver you are asking them to deliver to!

- Once you understand your buy, you can begin to organize it around similar categories of products and services, which then allows you to study the behaviours and markets for those categories. Conducting category analysis studies helps procurement executives to discover the cost drivers, and begin to establish ways to take out costs that cross multiple part numbers and purchases. For stampings, Ford used to get quotes on one part at a time, with no concept of 'press loading'. They would bid and source only one part at a time! In such cases, the material cost doesn't change, so the only advantage one can derive is to load the presses at a given supplier efficiently to drive the best productivity and reduce set-up costs.

- Once you understand the variance in cost and productivity drivers, you can begin to understand risk. Supplier risk is a function not only of single sourcing situations, but also of the extent to which you are exposed in the tier 2 level of supply to material price variance. By looking at supplier volumes across categories, Steve could also see if they were giving too much business to one supplier given their capacity load. These types of thoughts on cost drivers and risk didn't come from just the buying activity, but came from understanding the data, differentiating the strategy and establishing the optimal approach to source each category.

A final thought: an important moment came when we asked Steve Zimmer about the importance of trust in supplier relationships. He thought a moment, and then responded: 'I don't like to use the word trust – I prefer the word *expectation*. Trust comes and goes, and there is a lot of variation in the way trust evolves across cultures. In the United States people will trust you early but be easily disappointed and not come back. In Europe they may not trust you at all, and only much later begin to approach something like trust. In other cultures in Asia, trust may never really occur.' By really understanding what it is you are buying, you are able to set the expectation of the supplier that drives the relationship. Trust is a function of people meeting expectations, which in turn builds the relationship, not the other way around. You can look back at supplier relationships and you trust those that met the expectation and the commitment.

Conclusions

In this chapter we outlined the reasons why procurement is no longer simply an administrative or clerical responsibility, but a critical and strategic priority for companies. In particular, we emphasized the importance of the trend towards outsourcing: as companies have outsourced a high proportion of production and service activities, procurement plays a key role not only in cost reduction but also in value creation. In many companies the outsourcing ratio is around 70–80 per cent, in some cases even higher, so reducing purchase costs has a direct and significant impact on the bottom line.

Furthermore, by helping to ensure that product materials, ingredients or components, as well as services, are purchased at the right quality and the right time, procurement contributes significantly to the competitive advantage of the company. Ensuring that procurement makes such a contribution to the company requires an understanding of procurement as a strategic value-creating function and not simply a service whose sole aim is to save money.

Having touched on outsourcing and globalization as two of the issues that have brought procurement to the fore, there is a third issue: sustainability. This is a rapidly emerging concept with strong implications for procurement. In fact, the trend towards sustainability looks set to transform the ways in which we think about, design and manage both procurement processes and supply chains.

It must be pointed out that sustainability refers to three dimensions: the social (people), environmental (planet) and economic (profit) – where profit is not made at the expense of people and/or the planet. The sustainability challenge is real: regardless of one's personal feelings towards climate change, the planet's resources are in decline, placing increasing pressures on companies to reduce carbon emissions, recycle or reuse, and to develop green technologies. Moreover, the current model of extensive reliance on global low-cost country sourcing is not sustainable, as demonstrated by frequent media reports.

In conclusion, it is interesting to note that when tackling three of the biggest issues confronting contemporary business, which have indeed brought procurement to the fore – outsourcing, the increased use of technology and globalization – many organizations have in their myopia simply succeeded in managing cost out of the company only to manage risk in. It is in light of this that we decided to embark on the undertaking to produce this book, which looks at procurement's journey and its current impact on business.

Notes

1 Today that organization is known as the Institute for Supply Management.

2 This group included Robert Monczka, Robert Handfield, Ken Petersen, Gary Ragatz and David Frayer.

3 Porter, M E (1985) *Competitive Advantage: Creating and sustaining superior performance*, Simon & Schuster, New York.

Procurement maturity
Understanding performance versus value

02

In Chapter 1 we looked at the origins of procurement, along with some of the early approaches to spend analysis and the development of appropriate categories as a basis for strategic sourcing. These approaches provide some guidelines into the roots of the current radical shift under way in procurement, as well as some of the pioneering efforts to build strategic capability.

This chapter is designed to offer some insights into how procurement has evolved. We introduce a maturity model to help the reader understand the levels at which different procurement functions are capable of operating at, and the journey of change that organizations move through as they improve. This relates back to our idea of change as a core necessity for success. Procurement needs to change, and a refusal to do so will most surely result in its demise.

Here we look at the value of procurement to the enterprise; how this value is delivered into the business in terms of the service mix – that is, how procurement performs, its level of capability; what level of capability we have today, or need to change; and how efficient and effective procurement is in the execution of its role.

Today's global marketplace is perhaps best described as unpredictable: increased exposure to shocks and disruption risk pervades economies, financial markets and supply chains like never before. Complexity exacerbates the problem; even minor mishaps and miscalculations can have major consequences as their impacts have almost immediate effect. Some of the biggest changes occurring in today's global environment were enumerated by Handfield *et al* in a study of global supply chain executives in Europe, North America, Brazil, India, China, and Russia.[1]

Organizations continue to grow their supply chain global footprint

Organizations in multiple sectors are continuing to pursue global growth strategies that focus on expansion into new regions. In particular, the focal BRIC countries (Brazil, Russia, India and China) represent major targets for expansion, but with them come a host of new problems that enterprises have little to no experience in dealing with in terms of logistics capabilities. Major growth strategies are driven by economic realities, currency movements, government regulations, or access to existing logistics networks. With globalization, the need to partner with local logistics service providers becomes an imperative. Such providers understand domestic transportation issues, and can plan to develop long-term solutions to complex local distribution challenges.

As companies expand globally, so does supply chain complexity

Globalization of organizational supply chains is continuing to expand as organizations seek growth markets in the BRIC countries, which has proven to be a lucrative target but has also changed direction. Globalization is now increasingly linked to labour costs in countries such as China, as well as fuel costs and regulatory shifts, which are in turn driving a dramatic impact on where companies source, where they produce, and the complexity of processes required to sell to the customer.

This complexity is occurring in many forms. First, products are becoming more complex, as organizations need to create more diverse sets of options, packaging designs and logistics arrangements. Customers increasingly want customized solutions, and require specific logistics delivery requirements. This means that companies need to have more facilities in more countries, with more suppliers, greater diversity in product and packaging needs, more e-commerce and other market channels, and more part numbers.

Complexity is also occurring due to increases in local delivery requirements. In many emerging countries, there is a massive expansion in small neighbourhood stores, which brings a strong challenge to distribution networks. Small stores translate into an increase in deliveries and a decrease in size of truckloads. Layer on top of that the spread of urbanization, the economic uncertainty, military conflicts and political volatility, and you have a powerful set of possible complicated interactions to contend with.

Increased globalization brings increased risk of supply disruption

The rise of global markets and the decline in 'cheap' labour costs are profoundly influencing where companies source, produce, and the complexity of their processes and operations. Risk is accelerating, and every two weeks companies encounter some sort of logistics problem as a result of volcanoes, wars, tsunamis or other complications. Another major source of risk is the unreliability of global logistics channels, especially the challenges associated with ocean freight lines, which are becoming increasingly unreliable. Labour issues at ports, ships with greater capacity, port capacity and multiple other issues are driving executives to worry about the status of their shipments and whether they will reach their destinations in time to meet customer requirements.

Regulatory requirements are a big part of complexity

As the global footprint of organizations worldwide expands, by far the biggest trend that emerged in all of the interviews (undertaken by Handfield et al)[2] was:

- the increasing complexity of logistics and supply chain regulations;
- protectionist policies;
- product regulations;
- compliance to customs;
- trade;
- local content issues;
- security requirements.

As the private sector seeks to expand its growth in emerging countries, there is increasing pressure economically in these countries to levy import codes and product restrictions to drive revenue and protect local industries. The barrier of regulatory issues is a shifting target that is continually changing, yet the fines and penalties for non-compliance are on the rise. These regulations render it more difficult to meet increasing customer requirements for reliable product delivery, and make it challenging to be able to plan using normal lead times, inventory requirements and scheduling. Multiple interviews by Handfield *et al* reveal the complex and shifting nature of government regulations, making it more evident than ever that 'the government is part of every supply chain!'

Logistics network redesign and customization

Many of the companies interviewed in the study noted that outsourcing is on the rise and, as this occurs, increased customization of delivery service and logistics service requirements are on the rise. Customers are relying more on third parties not just to deliver products, but also for increasingly value-added activities. Similarly, manufacturers are being asked to develop customer-specific logistics solutions, and must be able to develop elaborate systems to deal with different customer requirements globally.

Challenges in supply chain and logistics infrastructure

An increasing number of companies note that logistics infrastructures have not been upgraded in many years, and are beginning to show signs of wear. Similarly, the growth and migration of individuals to major urban areas is straining infrastructure, and as companies grow their footprint in emerging countries they are finding that the infrastructure was never there to begin with. A movement of shops from rural areas to the suburbs and urban centres is under way in many cities, yet the numbers of bridges and roads into the city is fixed. In countries such as India, for example, there simply is no logistics network available – just a series of cities separated by small roads and a small railway.

Increasing sustainability pressure

As the global footprint of organizations worldwide expands, by far the biggest trend that emerged in all of the interviews was the increasing pressure to drive sustainable logistics solutions, reduce carbon footprints and other pressures. Proactive companies are looking to sustainability as a source to exploit competitive advantage not just for their brand, but for operational improvements and inefficiencies in the supply chain. One example is that operators of the largest truck fleets in the United States are in the process of converting their fleets to natural-gas-powered trucks. Experts predict that the total fleet of trucks could increase by 30 per cent or more in five years, as the cost of these trucks comes down by 10–20 per cent.

What does this mean?

The importance of these trends leads to the conclusion that understanding and mapping out your supply chain will be more important than ever. You will need to know who is in your supply chain. Who are your supplier's suppliers, and who is distributing your product, particularly in emerging countries? This is often difficult to grasp, and requires a systematic analysis of who the players are in your network, their relationship to one another, and competing interests that may not always be aligned with those of your sustainability initiatives.

You will need data systems to collect and consolidate technical information on your suppliers and their process inputs and outputs in the supply chain, to be able to construct value stream maps, life cycle analysis, carbon footprints and other required documents. Current systems are often unable to do so. Organizations are beginning to exploit new mobile technologies and social media to compensate for the inability of current enterprise resource planning (ERP) systems to capture what is happening in your supply chain.

You will need both internal parties and external parties (customers) to value the transparency and efficiencies that are gained, and be able to place a return on investment (ROI) on the benefit of complying with sustainable requirements. In the case of some areas, such as labour and human rights violations, this is increasingly tricky to do.

Can procurement embrace complexity?

To some extent, contemporary procurement practice (as described in Chapter 1) is faced with more challenges than ever before. Not only must executives drive a relentless pursuit of innovation and operational excellence, but they must also do so in the face of risk, volatility and massive global complexity in the supply chain. Ironically these increased levels of complexity in modern business have presented an unheralded opportunity for procurement to evolve its value proposition to the business; shrewd procurement leaders have used the prevailing conditions to drive change within procurement and across the enterprise.

That said, this is something of a double-edged sword. On the one hand, global supply markets have never offered so many innovations to those willing to embrace them. On the other, there is only so much that procurement can do with limited time and decreasing budgets, which makes achieving the demands for year-on-year cost savings increasingly difficult. Of course, there have been many organizations that have not been sitting idle. These organizations have reinvested any or all of their hard-won efficiency gains into capabilities that are focused on delivering procurement effectiveness. One of the key capabilities that emerges in the face of this complexity is the value of building a 'networked economy'. This refers to the ability to effectively create the right set of partners in the network, and together to create a seamless and integrated channel for the free flow of information, products and services. In the modern ecosystem, it is the 'best supply chains' that win, not the individual organization. And this is where procurement has the ability, like never before, to lead the charge and herald early success in this new era.

Defining procurement performance and procurement value

Efficiency and effectiveness are the two dimensions of procurement performance. Against these dimensions one can understand what makes a procurement organization a leader in the field or, conversely, a laggard. One can also apply a similar notion to define procurement value. For top-performing procurement organizations, the attainment of this leading practice is not in any way temporary. Rather it is a continuous journey, as the bar keeps getting raised on existing performance in a desire to maintain competitive advantage. There is always something new, a challenge, which requires procurement practitioners to develop newer and more strategic sources of value that procurement (and the supply markets) can deliver. Increasing value is very different from simply setting new targets on the same old measures – and this is a very important factor.

Value – the holy grail for procurement

Value is arguably the most overused term in business today. It is therefore important to clarify its definition and its relevance to both procurement and the enterprise. In Peter Drucker's celebrated book *Management: Tasks, responsibilities, practices* (1974), he says: 'The final question needed in order to come to grips with business purpose and business mission is: "What is value to the customer?"'

This in itself is possibly the most important question business leaders can ask themselves, and yet it is the one that is asked least often. A possible reason for this is that business leaders usually think that they know the answer. In their rather narrow view, value is frequently what they define as quality. This definition is incorrect and Drucker goes on to say: 'The customer never buys a product. By definition the customer buys the satisfaction of a want. He buys value.'

So value is, in essence, utility – that is, the total satisfaction derived from a good or service. Whilst the utility a customer derives from a good or service is difficult to measure, we can assume that consumers will strive to maximize their utility. The term value has to some extent been diluted as it is frequently used loosely and in a number of contexts; but there are a few things we can be certain about – value is relative to an alternative, ie value cannot be judged in isolation. Value is composite and decomposable; value can be analysed into a set of value drivers.

If we look at value in business-to-business relationships it tends to be economic in nature. If we look at this economic value aspect, we can ascertain that value is measureable and quantifiable. For example, economic value can be seen as cost or revenue. A useful way to quantify economic value is shown in Figure 2.1 in a simple economic value model.

There should also be a mapping from the value metric (the way in which the customer gets value) to the pricing metric (the way in which the seller charges for value). For example, the value of a can of paint may derive from the area covered, while the price is far more likely to be quoted in volume.

Value management has become a hot topic in the business world. Advocates proclaim that value creation and capture is the holy grail – its goal

FIGURE 2.1 Simple economic value model: $P = \dfrac{R - C}{A^U}$

	Positive Value Drivers	Negative Value Drivers	
Unique economic advantage	Capital assets	Cost	Unique costs
	Cost	Defects/Failures	Differentiation Value
	Revenue		
	Cost of Next Best Viable Substitute	Economic Value	

to ensure sustainable and profitable revenue growth for the organization. Value management relies on multiple streams of information from inside and outside the organization. Both internal and external perspectives are necessary. Information about customers, competitors, demand, offers, costs and production constraints are all used in value management, and procurement is well placed to make this part of its contribution to the success of the organization. Put simply, value management delivers profitable growth and it does so because innovation is focused on products and services that provide value to the customer.

Executives recognize that supply management must adopt a more strategic approach that targets performance beyond simple cost savings. To some extent, the field of supply management has become more enamoured with strategic sourcing, to the exclusion of the most important party in the supply chain: the internal customer. As one CPO we interviewed at a major oil and gas company emphasized:

> Procurement has got too hung up on being 'world class.' Procurement is simply a set of tools on a tool belt, but the real wave of change involves understanding the business well enough to apply the tools that will drive the most effective model for each of the operating groups and geographies we are in. We have a strategy that is focused on ticking the boxes around applying the tools. But we are too focused on getting an answer, rather than an outcome that matters to our stakeholders. We want to create nice 2 × 2s to label our suppliers, rather than generating and delivering a coherent strategy that defines how we work with them to meet our business needs.

This characterization of procurement recognizes a new set of value drivers that go beyond cost savings: understanding internal customer requirements, and codifying these requirements into a coherent statement of need that can be understood by the external supply market.[3] In a sense, this is a type of *'congruent capability'* in that it enables procurement to link internal and external parties that are mutually dependent on one another. Congruent capability is what an executive we interviewed was referring to when he identified the ideal of creating a 'virtual integrated company' where 'the existence of suppliers is an explicit outcome of a strategic decision to buy versus make. Implicit in this decision is the question of whether an organization is willing to manage the standards, discipline, execution, fixed capital investments, etc of the 'make' decision, versus the sourcing, negotiation, contracting and supplier signals associated with the 'buy' decision.' As the primary boundary-spanning interface between the internal and external domains of the enterprise, purchasing has an exclusive mandate to ensure congruency in performance outcomes between the stakeholder's expectations and the supplier's resulting performance.

The types of congruent contributions that procurement is capable of providing include:

- product innovation and technology development;
- knowledge sharing and new process capability development;
- multi-tier supplier integration;
- mitigation of supplier risk;
- supplier performance improvement and capability augmentation;
- supplier financial disruption avoidance;
- sustainable supply chain improvements.

Supply management leaders are unanimous in their call for an evolutionary approach to procurement transformation, through the improved alignment of internal stakeholder requirements with an emerging and growing global supply base. Procurement is expected to deliver innovation often from the supply base and this is reflected in the end product or service. Any innovation that does not provide additional value relative to the best alternatives is in essence money wasted. But there remains the perennial debate regarding how procurement tangibly benefits the business.

Many people in supply management and for that matter in the wider business community still lump value and performance together, but they are very different things indeed. Procurement can perform extremely well on a very narrow value proposition. As we know only too well in many organizations, procurement is only measured on purchase order processing and tactical negotiations, which is seen as decidedly average across a spectrum of high-impact procurement processes. So which is better?

To get better value, do you need to spend less or perhaps ensure that more of your expenditure is conducted wisely and brings with it the value that then creates competitive advantage? Procurement value is therefore defined by procurement-led improvements that safely tap supply market power to increase spend value, which is about getting more out of the expenditures you make with your supply base.

Businesses and their CPOs have two choices they can make to maximize their expenditure value through their supplier expenditures. First, they can simply decrease spend magnitude by reducing consumption as well as total cost of ownership (TCO). TCO includes prices, other landed costs, capital costs and the cost of procurement. Second, CPOs can increase the utility they and the business derives from spend to better support stakeholder objectives.

Utility (and thus value) are defined then in the eyes of the customer. These customers include budget holders, requisitioners, shareholders, regulators, suppliers and procurement staff. For procurement to improve spend value, it must improve the value of the services it delivers to the enterprise in order to help it safely tap supply market power to support its mission and create strategic advantage.

Procurement value is simply about offering and executing high-impact procurement services that tangibly and, probably more importantly, visibly increase the value of the procurement team's spending. So, for procurement, efficiency and effectiveness is paramount in defining its performance. And of course it is on this that expectations are built.

If the CEO was to ask you 'how much might that price cost the business?' could you answer?

Procurement has for some time been very conservative within the 'business'. Its practitioners in the main tend to be reactive in mindset and need to move into a more forward-looking posture. They must develop their commercial skills and better manage working capital, enterprise process sourcing (how capability should be delivered, ie make versus buy) and tapping supply markets for innovation. Supply assurance and purchase cost reduction are where many practitioners operate and are the foundations for value management, but procurement practitioners need to evolve to produce greater value by getting more involved in stakeholder processes earlier. They must also become tech savvy too. The best procurement people will have well-developed skill sets in process capabilities supported by technology. The use of analytics will move procurement beyond the 'commoditized' technology offerings they utilized traditionally. These bimodal procurement professionals will move the function beyond supply-sided strategic sourcing to earlier and deeper involvement in stakeholder processes.

Contemporary businesses are receptive to procurement taking on more challenging categories of expenditure and responsibilities that give a step change in performance. However, procurement needs to earn the right to move into these categories and this comes from building reputation and developing sustainable improvements. Procurement practitioners need to sell the procurement value proposition, develop capability and execute to improve performance as the procurement value proposition relates to the alignment of capability and performance.

Figure 2.2 sets out a maturity model for procurement and supply management. As the capability of the procurement organization moves up the ladder, so its role and value proposition increases accordingly – moving from 'laggard' at the very bottom of the ladder where the function is focused on low-level tactical activity to a 'leader' role where the procurement organization directly influences corporate strategy.

FIGURE 2.2 Procurement maturity ladder (procurement's role and value proposition)

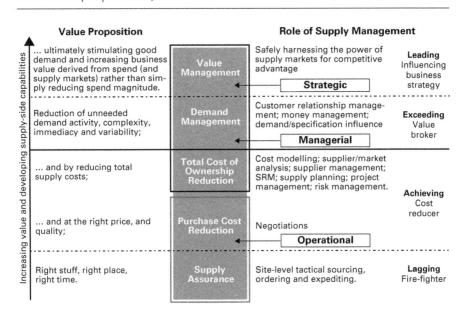

The right stuff

The procurement maturity ladder categorizes the role of supply management at four different levels of performance. It equates each level of performance to certain attributes and articulates the value proposition of procurement to the business at each performance level. This is set against value proposition on the left-hand side, and role (performance and capability) on the right-hand side: we can evaluate and identify the increasing performance levels of procurement and its value to the business as it climbs the ladder.

The levels of performance and capability accumulate as the procurement organization evolves from the lowest level of the clerical role, engaged in sourcing, ordering and expediting, where the primary role of procurement is supply assurance through to value management role where procurement is directly influencing the business strategy and is harnessing the power of the supply markets for competitive advantage. As procurement moves from one classification to the next, it takes the attributes of the former with it. Thus a top-performing procurement organization would carry out all of the procurement roles, deftly applying them and increasing the functions value accordingly.

It is true to say that there are many procurement organizations that operate in the lower box in Figure 2.2. They carry out the very basic roles of procurement: to obtain the right things, at the right time and right place for the right price and right quantities and quality. To many people in business this is the accepted view of procurement; nothing more and nothing less.

Procurement value proposition has come about as procurement and its role in businesses has evolved. Its value is defined in terms of generating more value for monies spent on suppliers. This is typically achieved by either less expenditure or deriving greater impact from the monies spent. Doing so requires that procurement offers a set of services that are valued by stakeholders. To define levels of value, we have a scalar of five principal value propositions:

- supply assurance;
- cost reduction, which covers two aspects:
  - purchased costs;
  - total costs;
- demand management;

- value management – where procurement teams are tapping supply market innovation to support the strategic objectives of the business.

What is apparent is that the best procurement organizations focus on generating value instead of generating transactions. It is often said that the largest cost in procurement is the opportunity cost of not freeing up staff to perform higher-value activities. The question then becomes: how do procurement organizations move away from the transactional activities to spend more time on higher-value activities? This question brings into play one of the fundamental questions in procurement: the make versus buy decision. It raises too questions around how procurement is actually measured. Is procurement measured on its diverse value contributions or simply on reducing spend magnitude?

Procurement's aspiration to move up the ladder has to be deliberate and it must be sustained. As the business begins to expect more from procurement it has to continue to deliver. At the same time, chief executive officers (CXOs) are likely to give the CPO and the procurement organization increasingly more latitude in the transformation. However, it is not just about giving and getting more of the same thing. As procurement's services evolve, so will its role and its brand.

While brand management might seem a little far-fetched, procurement is a professional services organization and needs deliberately to create and execute against the promise of its brand. Otherwise, the brand will be created on prejudice, perception will become reality, and procurement may well find itself doomed and lapsing back to its historic role.

The differences in the brand 'promise', or role, of a new procurement organization makes it difficult to compare an internal satisfaction score across businesses, simply because the services offered are highly likely to be different. A business where people are saying that procurement is excellent because it scrambles well or places purchase orders (POs) well is far worse than a business where the prevailing view is that procurement is doing a good job on its broad array of strategic supply services. In other words, internal satisfaction is an effectiveness performance measure focused on quality set against a service level – not the quality of the procurement service portfolio itself. So, in a very real sense, it is limited.

This evolution is not an easy process, especially when procurement's desire to perform higher-value activities will undoubtedly conflict with peoples' perceptions of what it should or can do. Many businesses do not want procurement to move beyond its 'accepted' role – the 'table-banging' negotiator or buying stationery. They don't want procurement to play a role in demand management, specification management or continuous improvement activities.

Some obvious examples of strategic projects for which procurement support should constantly be called upon to add to its arsenal of capabilities include:

- pre-merger planning;
- post-merger integration;
- asset rationalization;
- product/service design rationalization, and so on.

This expansion of procurement's circle of influence should occur across the whole business, including operating units, regional groups, functional partners, senior management, regulators, suppliers, and for the benefit of procurement staff too. After all, stakeholders are not just budget holders.

To reiterate: this process has to be a continuous evolution and there are many barriers to push through. The biggest of these issues tends to be procurement's ability to create an operating model that allows it to evolve its value proposition and create substantive change in its own organization. Turf wars are another major barrier. Immediately you cross the line into processes that other functions within the organization are performing – the in-fighting begins. In fact, this issue gets more complicated with the emergence of global business services organizations that are continuously pulling more processes inside them. Examples include procure-to-pay (P2P) transaction processes, analytics, continuous improvement – and even procurement is occasionally being turned over to them.

How should we measure procurement's performance?

One single and rather compelling metric of procurement performance is procurement return on investment (ROI). This can be expressed as the ratio of traditional expenditure cost savings as a percentage of spend with suppliers divided by the annual investment in procurement processes.

Another way of measuring procurement's performance might be to look at the impact of maverick spending, which can be described as a 'yield' loss on the business's negotiated savings figures in any year. In doing this we must of course assume that the procurement organization is not overstating its savings. This could be a possibility if procurement is unable to track savings to the bottom line; but a good procurement organization should be equipped to do this. Doubtless people will squabble over this issue, claiming that it simply isn't worth the effort when considered against attracting new deals. However, to improve procurement's credibility with budget holders an increase in terms of the validity of procurement's claimed savings would not go amiss.

Finally, in terms of quantitative measures, which these measures invariably are, measuring spend influence is perhaps the favourite. Another very important issue relating to the quality of procurement's spend influence will clearly be dependent on when they become engaged in the spend cycle; a loss of leverage, and thus business impact, because of 'late-stage' procurement involvement is fairly common in most businesses.

However, times are changing and procurement is increasingly influencing new spending areas. In fact, the economic downturn that began in October 2008 and the cash-strapped years that followed gave procurement an opportunity to bring greater influence in new spending areas and perhaps, too, to develop new policies that were not possible before.

Looking forward

Whether in one's personal or professional life, we all need a vision of where we will be or where we want to be in five or ten years' time; and the same holds true with procurement as a function. Procurement in the future will likely be substantially different to what it is today. To ensure this, one's vision for procurement must be clear and achievable. Moreover, procurement's visibility, credibility and resilience within business are critical, if it is not to be subsumed into or by another strategic business unit (SBU).

Increasingly the work of the procurement professional is knowledge-based, virtualized and globalized. The idea of 'everything as a service' will make its way into these internal end-to-end processes via a clear trend towards global business services (GBS) organizations – to which procurement may have to some day report or, as is more likely, complement. The deliberate design of these value chains requires a vision, a service delivery strategy and a supporting service delivery model. It will be incumbent on procurement professionals to demonstrate that they have the associated capabilities not only to ensure that the vision can be implemented but also to signal to the rest of the business that they are the natural owners of this aspect of the value chain.

As procurement broadens its vision, rethinks its strategies, tunes its service delivery models and shores up its capabilities, it needs to do so while continuing to execute and also to perform this transformation as efficiently and effectively as it can.

In the case study that follows, we identify the trajectory taken by one organization, Biogen Idec, as they sought to improve value and transformed themselves into a new procurement capability.

CASE STUDY   Motivation for change – Biogen Idec's transformation to world-class supply management[4]

Many organizations have begun to create centralized supply management organizations to improve leveraging of spend and improve alignment with executive stakeholder objectives. Targeted first in the automotive sector in the 1980s, sourcing has spread rapidly through a number of industries including electronics, pharmaceuticals, oil and gas, financial services, insurance, but still has a few remaining holdouts in the biopharma sector. Not only are these organizations younger in maturity than their 'big-pharma' counterparts, but they also face imposing challenges in the form of good manufacturing practice (GMP), a complex clinical trials process that is global in scope, temperature-controlled environments, and complicated manufacturing processes.

The first wave of strategies typically identified by these organizations embarking on strategic sourcing is often targeted at cost reduction through volume consolidation and leveraging of an organization's total spend, followed by supply-base reduction and longer-term contracting. Yet as organizations mature, executives recognize that supply management must adopt a more strategic set of value propositions beyond leveraging spend for cost savings. Moreover, supply management is now being asked to build rapid insight into customer requirements, and translate this rapidly into product offerings with increased reliance on outsourced capabilities in the supply chain.

In 2009, Biogen Idec (BIIB) underwent a major shift in the way it operates its supply chain. What began as a 'grass-roots' transformation effort produced strong early results in the form of cost savings (an initiative that was deemed important by its executive management team). As the effort grew, however, it produced exemplary results beyond simple cost savings, sustaining the momentum and moving the organization to higher levels of process performance. This was accomplished with comparatively little automation of the process, but focused instead as stakeholder engagement as a critical enabler of improved supply chain performance.

In June of the same year, an assessment of supply chain maturity was performed across the Production, Operations and Technology (PO&T) group at Biogen, and significant opportunities for improvement identified. Supply chain processes were deemed to be at an ad hoc level, with resulting inefficiencies and uncontrolled spending prevalent in many parts of the organization. A summary of the current state was reviewed by the leadership team who agreed that there was no way to go but up. Specifically, the following observations were made in six critical process maturity components:

- *Governance*: at the time of the gap analysis, there was a lack of formal executive oversight of major sourcing and supply chain initiatives. Sourcing was largely disengaged from stakeholders, and were brought in at the last minute to 'paper deals' manually. Suppliers typically worked closely with stakeholders to drive specifications and pricing, with little engaging of supply chain teams in market analysis or cost management.

- *Procure to pay*: less than 40 per cent of spend was actively managed and properly contracted, there were some very basic metrics to track spending or savings, which had the potential to overlook significant leakage and maverick spending. Approvals typically took in excess of 45 days, due to lack of due diligence around documentation and manual systems, contract compliance and an ongoing issue at board meetings.

- *Category management*: a small number of category strategies was under way, but formal category management (CM) processes had not been rolled out. Senior category managers (SCM) had little opportunity to demonstrate the value of market insights and rationale for supply base optimization, as there were few resources available to draw on. Finally, while supply chain risk was informally recognized, few metrics or contingency planning were in place to drive risk management activity, and planning meetings were rife with firefighting activity.

- *Supplier relationship management*: with little governance and no formal governance mechanisms, it was not surprising that supplier selection and evaluation occurred on an ad hoc basis by stakeholders. Inconsistencies in selection criteria, relationship owners, lack of market price benchmarking, and informal performance measures led to poor business decisions and exposure to contracting risks. A large supplier base had developed, causing an explosion in the workload for managing the suppliers.

- *Performance measurement*: no formal key performance indicators (KPIs) were employed to track supply chain performance around critical processes such as spend under management, supplier performance, contracting status, cost savings, visibility of service level metrics, or multiple sourcing agreements with suppliers across sites.

- *Talent management*: because of their high workload, SCM associates were often stuck on transactional activities. Not only was the function under-resourced, but despite their hard work associates received derisive reviews from their business partners due to disruptions and late deliverables. In addition, new people entering the team were in some cases cast-offs from other business partners, and there were no formal career path development activities occurring.

When it came to execution, several steps were taken to add structure and discipline, with the underlying theme that sourcing, in a decentralized form and in concert with good business processes, could yield a lot of value and transform the supply chain. These actions are documented below.

Governance and stakeholder engagement

A PO&T leadership meeting in July 2009 established a road map for delivery of results aligned around core deliverables. A sourcing council was formed within the operations group that focused on all direct materials and services – direct here being defined as any material or service being utilized within the process and production. Three working groups (raw materials, change management officers (CMOs), and distribution/logistics) were established to drive category strategies. The decision was made to establish a decentralized but dedicated direct (GMP) focused sourcing organization, with team members placed in proximity to stakeholders for maximum interaction and dialogue. A consistent sourcing approach was developed to ensure that strategies were data-driven and aligned with stakeholder expectations.

Recognizing the need to drive stakeholder engagement, a supply chain mission statement was established and communicated through 'road shows' with stakeholders. The message was that supply chain's objective was to work more closely with functional groups to reduce costs, reduce risk and maintain compliance. A two-tiered structure was established, with one group focused on strategic sourcing, and another on procurement transactions and analytics.

The biggest change, however, was the active application of sourcing council involvement on supply chain policies and processes. Major supply chain projects were reviewed quarterly by the sourcing council to ensure that projects were sanctioned and resourced appropriately.

A major change in the way that the supply chain engaged with stakeholders involved a culture of data-driven business case development. Stakeholders were engaged in major sourcing decisions, and supply chain associates adopted a culture of bringing relevant data to the table to establish sourcing and planning decisions. In every sourcing decision, market intelligence, spend forecasts, contract data and technical requirements were systematically applied to build a convincing rationale in support of decisions. Although there was some resistance to the structure imposed by a sourcing governance framework, it quickly became clear that early supplier engagement was beneficial to the business teams. Today, technology development and other units voluntarily bring category managers 'into the loop' early in the project initiation stage, as they see the benefits of this approach. One of the important change management principles that supported this was that all benefits (cost, etc) achieved by the team were directly attributed to the business unit, not the sourcing team, and savings were validated by finance for presentation to senior leadership. Finally, suppliers are now much more willing to work with BIIB sourcing teams, and have gone so far as to recognize that 'BIIB's request for quotations (RFQs) are the clearest and easiest to work from in the industry!'

Procure-to-pay systems

One of the most important changes that occurred to drive improvement was the use of a PO recommendation memo, which is a standard template that captures the essential justification, fair value and rationale for the purchase. All purchase orders and requisitions that do not require vice president (VP) signature authority are routed to a single individual tasked with recording and tracking the amount. This has led to significant reductions in approval lead times, as approval levels have been raised given the increased confidence in the approval process and documentation. Physical copies of contracts are now sent to an individual who sorts them through an intelligence nomenclature that allows quick retrieval. As a result, mid-year reviews and reports for business managers who wish to track spend against contract are now easily produced and are accurate. In addition, 100 per cent of spend managed and under contract. PO memos capture rationale and due diligence, and approvals are routed quickly in less than 15 days. Contracts are reviewed, catalogued and tracked against actual spending, and reports generated for business directors on a timely basis.

Category management

Coming out of a 3Q 2009 short course, a handbook was used as a guide for teams to begin the category management development process. Category teams were formed in GMP, Technology Development, and Distribution/Logistics. The handbook provided guidelines to assist the team in the core steps of business requirements development; technical requirements; supplier evaluation; and supplier selection and sourcing strategy. A standard set of strategy templates was developed presenting the current situation, analysis and business case. As the number of sourcing projects increased, stakeholders were asked to engage and participate in strategy development. With supply chain bringing believable and accurate spend data and technical requirements to the table, stakeholders' confidence in their ability grew, to the point where they now actively seek out PO&T for all major sourcing initiatives. All sourcing projects are supported by a strong business case, and major strategies are reviewed by the sourcing council. The business case is comprised of spend analytics, vendor risk analytics, additional market intelligence, 'should-cost' models and vendor continuity reports. One of the two biggest additions during this process was the development of market intelligence resources, including outsourcing partner Beroe and access to six new market databases. Whereas in the past supply assurances were based on the relationship, selection (a function of the supplier's marketing strength) and tribal knowledge, and price was proposed by the supplier, the teams became much more proactive in building strong negotiating positions and buy-in based on solid data and analytics. Once selected, new suppliers are vetted in partnership with a rigorous qualification process. For suppliers with an above-average risk profile, contingency plans are integrated into contractual terms and conditions, or alternative redundancies identified.

Supplier relationship management

Supplier selection is developed by category teams led by sourcing specialists, based on business requirements and fair value, not on relationships. Supply chain is actively engaged in the early stages of project identification and specification, with market-based price and cost data employed to ensure fair value. Should-cost models and supplier scorecards are used to govern the supplier relationships after contract sign-off.

Performance measurement

Client-focused metrics are established and tracked for all sourcing engagements. Spend against contract budget is regularly communicated to business partners. Metrics include rolling spend, cumulative savings, per cent on preferred suppliers, number of projects, business impact, fair value assessed, and supply risk. P2P metrics around PO compliance and supplier performance is also tracked. This visibility and transparency has created significant benefits, most importantly that senior leadership feel that supply chain is in a managed, controlled state and that discipline has been used in the way that teams make decisions.

Talent management

PO&T associates have been augmented significantly with highly qualified technically proficient people, and former associates have expressed a renewed *esprit de corps*. Associates are less focused on transactional activities and instead are engaged on strategic management of critical outsource relationships, cost management, and risk monitoring and control. Several individuals have been recognized as high potentials across the organization, and senior leadership has formally acknowledged the contributions of the team to BIIB's competitive future.

To summarize

Supply chain at BIIB underwent a significant transformation in its critical processes. Current validated savings (effective September 2010) exceed US $9 million and current avoidances exceed $4 million, amounting to almost $15 million of savings on managed spending of $150 million.

Some conclusions

Procurement's value proposition to the business is inextricably linked to performance and capability. Capability enables better performance, as well as adding value. The impact of value and performance on the business requires procurement to maintain a high profile and the appetite to deliver ever-broader services.

It is also critical that procurement treads carefully. Misalignment or the possibility of disintermediation will create very real issues across the organization. Procurement's vision of its high-value proposition without the requisite level of performance and the right relationships is nothing more than an empty promise. Well-developed procurement capability without the requisite performance levels is an opportunity missed and money down the drain.

For procurement, to exist in a space where a low level of value to the business is all that is expected of them might appear safe or even comfortable today. However, there is a real possibility that if this situation were to remain the same then, before very long, procurement will tomorrow become a commodity – and possibly redundant the day after that.

If we contemplate a scenario of performance without capability then the usual outcome is characterized by unsustainable heroics, which are neither scalable nor repeatable. The best procurement organizations of the future will have the greatest relative strength in core process capabilities – supported by high-impact technology to support high-impact processes.

Both the business, and procurement, want activity shifted to higher-value propositions, but current measurement systems and metrics do not encourage this. Many procurement organizations execute well to the traditional metrics, such as purchased cost savings and supply assurance goals, but are still considered decidedly mediocre when it comes to higher-value services. The greatest capability gaps are in working capital management, involvement in the business 'process sourcing' decision, and in tapping supply markets for innovation.

Finally, there is a clear need for procurement's operating model to catch up with the times. Frankly, the typical procurement model has become stale. With no historic permission, no mandate or accountability, and weak IT support, there is a clear need to push beyond a basic supply-centric, 'n'-step procurement methodology. Customer and demand management adoption is critical to procurement realizing its potential and delivering value, as is earlier and deeper involvement in stakeholder processes, including involvement with external suppliers. It is fair to say that spend analysis, cost modelling and strong procurement 'execution' capabilities are the prerequisites of a value-adding procurement organization.

In this chapter we explored the concept of value, and identified how procurement can move up the ladder to go beyond cost savings, and drive towards true value improvement. In the following chapters we go on to depict how global trends are leading to profound changes in the thinking behind corporate strategies. We then discuss the drivers of the shifts in global business, which we call the 'game changers'. These are essentially creating an entirely new set of rules for playing the business game. We also introduce a practical approach to change, using the ACE model, because in this game, doing nothing is a decision that some may choose to take – and that is a decision that will ultimately cause you to lose the game.

Notes

1 Handfield, Robert *et al* (2013) *Trends and Strategies in Logistics and Supply Chain Management*, BVL International, Berlin.

2 The interviews referred to were undertaken by Handfield, R *et al* (2013) *Trends and Strategies in Logistics and Supply Chain Management*, BVL International, Berlin; plus some work undertaken by Gerard Chick whilst at CIPS.

3 Handfield, Robert (2013) The future of procurement, Research Brief, published by KPMG Procurement Advisory Group, KPMG International, October.

4 Ganguly, Joydeep *et al* (2011) A textbook transformation: how Biogen Idec overhauled its supply chain, *Supply Chain Management Review*, May/June, pp 28–35.

From global trends to corporate strategy

03

C learly there has been a 'procurement revolution' since the mid-1980s and the function has moved from being transactional in nature to the strategic organizational tool it is today. There are operational trends impacting procurement such as stronger cross-functional working, which naturally increase strategic visibility; and whilst procurement acts as the main interface with supply markets we must also develop an understanding of what has come into the mix via challenges from without, what we might call *global trends* and how they impact procurement. We will look at these global trends from the standpoints of either adopting a 'let's just get through it' mindset, or anticipating them and 'taking a chance' on the future.

In this chapter we look at how a procurement executive's ability to read trends accurately in a rapidly changing business environment can make all the difference between surviving or going under. But how do you assess the impact of emerging macroeconomic, social, environmental and business developments against the needs of a business? Are the trends, detailed below, in some way self-predicting? And what contribution can procurement professionals deliver to the business to ensure the sustainability of the enterprise they serve?

The key global trends

Taking both internal and external procurement dimensions into account the five widely accepted key trends that dominate the business world today are highlighted in Table 3.1.

TABLE 3.1 Five key global business trends

Trend	Potential for Impact
Increasing focus on impacts of corporate social responsibility	Corporate social responsibility will grow in importance for all organizations. Changes in demographics and global consumption patterns will impact the triple bottom line and have significant impact on green, social and financial strategies.
Burgeoning technological advances	Technological innovations will continue to grow and at an ever-quickening rate, impacting all that we do in society and business.
Global geopolitical and macroeconomic change	There has already been a shift in global markets. These market changes alter demand and consumption, which in turn creates increased pressure on the availability of raw materials and other resources.
Changing demographics	Changes in demographics – be they declining birth rates, ageing populations or migration patterns they will have high-level impact on the availability of skilled and/or affordable labour.
Shift in the economic centre of gravity	Demand in the mature markets in the developed economies of the world is slowing down, whilst in developing markets and economies it is quickening pace and strong growth is being created.

These global trends are a pointer to the fact that existing procurement models may have reached their 'use by' date. Consequently, the first step in understanding how procurement will deliver to the business in the future is to fully understand how the procurement landscape is shifting around us, often more radically and quickly than we might first realize. Given globalization, ever-increasing logistics costs, increasing levels of risk and complexity, and the perennial issue of rising labour costs, could it be that now is the time for a major rethink regarding procurement and supply management strategy?

Where will any future global sourcing benefits come from, given all the above? These global trends are the 'game changers', which keep today's business leaders awake at night. Just as 'cheaper, faster, better' has been their mantra for some time, these changes are a clear message about the need to understand and focus on uncertainty, the level of which we can expect to increase. A crisis on the other side of the world can now spread very quickly across the globe, creating unnerving turbulence. What's more, this change is occurring across a backdrop of continued volatility across the supply chain, impacting nearly all industries; swings in the prices of commodities and currency shifts are unprecedented in many markets. On top of this are the opportunities and threats of a complicated global regulatory and tax environment.

The story of procurement since the early 1980s mirrors the wider business landscape. During this time, the profession has risen steadily to hold a strategic function, playing a critical role in helping businesses manage both direct and indirect spend and acting as the guardian of supplier relations.

The impact of globalization and technological advances has only served to further both the cause of procurement and its perception in the wider business world, with suppliers' health and other risk-related issues increasingly seen as its prime responsibility, if not its unique selling point.

The next several decades promise to be even more significant. Having established its credentials, the profession will need to evolve and demonstrate the real benefits it can bring in a wide range of areas to add genuine value to business as a whole. Risk will increase in importance; corporate social responsibility (CSR) will be tied up with security of supply; and procurement will need to draw on market knowledge, supplier relationships and the use of new technology to identify major threats to a business.

The wider political and economic environment will become even more relevant to global organizations in this context. Recent events such as the Arab Spring that began in 2010 and the Japanese earthquake of 2011 have highlighted the risks of an ever-more interconnected landscape, while increasing logistics costs and concerns over security of supply will mean procurement professionals must compete to become customers of choice with key suppliers. How amplified will this be in the future?

The way in which procurement is structured and perhaps even where it is based will change, too. With teams spread around the globe, procurement will increasingly find itself managing virtual networks of suppliers, stakeholders and internal customers, drawing on powerful new social media channels to communicate. But it is important that this technology does not come at the expense of the face-to-face relationships that will be so important in establishing solid supplier connections.

Alongside all of this, procurement must continue to compete for talent and aim to recruit the best and the brightest people. Organizations will face competition not just from within their own countries but from the emerging economies, and talent that is attracted into the organization will expect – and be expected – to be mobile.

The five game changers

Let's now take a closer look into each of these issues and their impact on business and on procurement, which cannot be ignored. They are game changers because they impinge on the very nature of business around the globe and are profoundly affecting both the way we work and where we work.

Corporate social responsibility

Since the mid-2000s, growing concern about the future of our planet and the inherent inequalities of an increasingly globalized economy has driven the corporate social responsibility (CSR) agenda firmly to the top of the list of boardroom priorities.

In this age of mass communication and heightened consumer awareness, organizations can no longer afford – either financially or in terms of reputational damage – to become embroiled in damaging environmental practices or child labour scandals, and the boundaries of responsibility now stretch well beyond the walls of any individual corporation.

The focus on CSR, though, now goes beyond how an organization is perceived. Increasing demand for raw materials from emerging economies and the impact of government legislation means organizations that fail to conduct themselves in an environmentally friendly and ethically sound manner face significant risk to the bottom line. They will also struggle to recruit an ever-more aware generation of talent.

Thus far, genuine attempts to reduce carbon emissions or introduce socially responsible methods of doing business have been interspersed with 'green wash' and 'box ticking'. But the future will be different, and the current generation have become more interested in the whole supply chain and the social, economic and environmental issues that surround it.

We sense a distinction between issues that are creating barriers to economic growth as a result of resource constraints, and ethical issues, which are still at an early stage in terms of their impact on the corporate world. Whilst there is some overlap, the 'ethical' activity is being led primarily by consumer sentiment – people don't want to think about other people doing nasty things in sheds somewhere in the supply chain. Environmental behaviour is largely being driven by legislation and regulation to its resource costs. The drivers are very different; they won't go away, but they may morph or change in the future:

- On the environmental side, the increasing scarcity of oil and other raw materials is likely to have a huge impact on organizational strategy. Already China sources around one-third of its oil from Africa and is rapidly acquiring mining rights for other valuable assets such as uranium, tin and coal. The emergence of natural gas in parts of the world may temporarily relieve the pressure but, with biofuels and renewable energy still some way off reaching their potential, the battle for resources is only likely to increase over the next two decades.

- In the field of social responsibility, what is seen as acceptable in the UK may be viewed differently in other countries. Our point of view could well 'cost' a family elsewhere, as our ethical standpoint could take an earner out of the labour market. Issues such as these are likely to become even more prominent and contentious in the future, as new sourcing destinations emerge and more economies industrialize.

- We sense too that the social and economic impacts of trade are likely to become intrinsically linked, particularly as the prospect of low economic growth looks set to continue. This could lead to greater pressure from consumers, media, shareholders and even governments for more local sourcing, as was seen in the recent debate over the award of the contract in the UK to manufacture trains for a new Thames Link contract to the German business Siemens.

The implications for the profession regarding CSR are significant. Procurement will increasingly be required to take ownership of this entire issue, helping to outline the threats for boards and other stakeholders, working closely with PR and marketing teams to ensure there is sufficient communication and transparency around the issues, within the organization and externally.

Procurement has to be the voice of 'commercial conscience', remaining impartial in terms of articulating its view to the business so that people can make decisions with all of the facts at hand. Indeed, procurement will need to strike the right balance between outlining the risks and benefits attached to policies or choices of supplier to the wider business, ensuring continuity.

Establishing just how important CSR is to the organization – rather than something that fluctuates depending on the economic climate – will become a critical feature of procurement's role and focus. This requires clear policy setting at board level. Increasingly, this means working with suppliers and alerting and influencing them to work with their own supply chains. If procurement only works with the first-tier suppliers it will simply fall away further down the supply chain. Procurement will have to:

- play a prominent role in spearheading industry-wide initiatives to drive up standards across entire supply chains;
- develop key performance indicators and utilize benchmarking tools such as the Dow Jones Sustainability Index or the Carbon Disclosure Project;
- monitor and assess the performance of suppliers and those further down the chain.

These are critical features of procurement's role. An increasingly important role in the coming years will be the lobbying of government and other bodies to match their own efforts with legislative action that will further drive behavioural change.

New technologies

Nowhere is the pace of change likely to be more visible than in the field of technology. Already today there are a number of new devices and applications – from smartphones, tablets and embedded chips through to the continually evolving use of social media – that are helping to revolutionize the way in which businesses operate.

A new internet-savvy and technically confident generation is already entering the workplace, while countries such as China and India are able to develop applications and technologies without the hindrance of legacy systems, which have acted as a brake on progress in the West.

Technology itself, however, is just the beginning. As new hardware and applications emerge, so too do innovative ways of working, whether in the form of remote working, virtual networks of partners and suppliers based all around the globe, or increasingly automated supply chains.

With this, too, come challenges, not least the issue of making sense of the torrent of information now freely available on the internet and the need to protect the business against reputational risk, in an era where one person armed with nothing more than a smartphone can wreak untold brand damage in a matter of minutes.

The use of social media in particular has the potential to revolutionize existing practices, in terms of how the profession interacts with potential recruits and within the business, but also in helping practitioners to develop new sources of supply from anywhere in the world. For all the talk of a generational divide, many experienced professionals already use platforms such as LinkedIn, while today's graduates – and tomorrow's future business leaders – now use such technologies as their primary means of communication.

We sense that the potential exists to develop entire virtual networks that could be a means of both sourcing new suppliers for low-value items and encouraging innovation from partner organizations. Increasingly, these are likely to be located in the fast-developing economies, which at the time of writing are demonstrating significantly higher rates of year-on-year growth in innovative products and services.

New systems as yet undeveloped will emerge to facilitate the exchange of information between organizations, while procurement will need to develop closer working relationships with other functions, including research and development, sales and operations. Against a backdrop of more open relationships with suppliers around innovation, procurement will also be required to play a role in safeguarding intellectual property and identifying the potential for industrial espionage.

The use of such technology, however, will not negate the practice of due diligence carried out on suppliers. In fact, suppliers are likely to find themselves under far greater scrutiny than ever before, with performance and price just one criterion on which they are assessed, alongside others related to CSR measures and those focusing on financial health. Here, too, technology and the amount of information freely available online can help procurement to monitor and assess potential suppliers, with the potential to share information across organizations and possibly entire supplier networks.

This can cut both ways, however, and in an era where resource constraints and the wider economic climate could see an increasing shift in power towards suppliers we will see procurement organizations competing to become customers of choice. Factor in, too, the growth of outsourcing, tighter integration, and heavier reliance on the shrinking supply base and we will see that they will gain far more leverage in future buyer–supplier relationships. Instead of them selling to you, it may be you selling to them – procurement will have a new challenge – to remain attractive to key suppliers.

We sense too that procurement will become part of the trend towards more remote and virtual networks. As organizations establish country and regional hubs across the world, potentially relocating functions to major sourcing hotspots, will a global, virtual, procurement team be a requirement in the future? Will the next generation use technology and communication strategies to work across boundaries and across borders?

Technology (including social media applications) will also play a prominent role in the way in which organizations and procurement professionals handle risk, giving them greater access to information so they can map out and assess the dangers they face and make informed judgements on what strategy to follow. The use of systems with 3-D, 4-D and 5-D information modelling, mapping the supply chain and understanding the financial and economic risks, will become increasingly the norm.

Finally, as procurement continues to become a more strategic part of the organization and takes on more responsibility for managing virtual networks and risk, it becomes apparent that some of the lower-value activities will either be picked up by technical solutions or outsourced. And yet whatever tools that technology may create to help procurement professionals and organizations in general, they will only complement, and not replace; as procurement becomes pivotal to organizations, the need to develop personal relationships with executives, internal customers and external suppliers will increase in importance.

Globalization: risk

The increasingly globalized nature of many markets has featured largely since the mid-1990s and is likely to continue. New sourcing markets will emerge during this time, while the current emerging economies will become established destinations, as well as powerful consumers in their own right. Operating such a global supply chain – set against an increasingly protectionist stance by many governments and the constant spectre of political uncertainty – will create a heightened exposure to risk, and one that will require a fundamental shift in approach for procurement functions.

No longer will it be sufficient to look at risk mitigation and devise business continuity plans for specific events; instead, the focus will shift towards proactive risk management, using market intelligence and supplier relationships to make strategic assessments around risk and reward, and balancing the need for security of supply with the merits of low-cost sourcing and remaining competitive.

The growing demand for raw materials and commodities from emerging economies, and an increasing global population, will bring its own challenges for procurement. But the increasingly interconnected economy and supply chain will also bring other threats, with the potential for supply disruptions from a range of economic, political and natural issues.

Events triggered in 2010 such as the Arab Spring, the eurozone crisis and the ash cloud, followed in 2011 by the Japanese earthquake and subsequent tsunami, along with the growing threat to oil supplies from the Gulf all serve as reminders of just how vulnerable entire supply chains are – and highlight the need to develop strategies that will allow organizations to respond swiftly to events, as well as minimizing the impact of unforeseen occurrences.

Some of the above events were predictable, or at least slow burners; others, such as the ash cloud and earthquake, less so. In the current economic landscape, and in an age where social media allows the mass mobilization of large numbers with very little notice, though, there is another emerging risk that procurement needs to be aware of – social and political unrest. Many chief executives see risk management as the 'stay awake' issue. The impact of supply will be judged by how well it manages contingency and risk, and how well supply chains are designed. This is where the real leaders of tomorrow will come into their own: by getting better at identifying the risks that a business faces and deciding the level of risk they want to take, which is about procurement becoming part of a strategic discussion.

We have seen examples of organizations failing to take a balanced view in the past, in particular the decision by organizations to manufacture inland rather than on the coast of China, due to lower labour costs. These decisions were made without recognition of the risk in their reliance on internal road, rail and electricity provisions. Management maturity is required in making these decisions, based not only on the benefits of lower costs – but on recognition of time factors, quality and service.

These issues point to an underlying pressure for a broadening of skill sets and a deeper understanding of the business landscape. Crucial to success in the future will be:

- the depth of supply chain knowledge in terms of geographical location and political constraints;
- quality;
- financial health;
- ability to withstand unexpected events and environmental or social factors.

This begs the question of just how far down the supply chain it is possible to see. In the future, it could be the case that contracts will be developed for long-term performance and the creation of strategic partnerships, which effectively incentivize the supply chain. Procurement must broaden supply chain horizons, developing a deeper sense of how it operates and how it delivers benefits for the longer term:

- The complexity in globalized supply chains is likely to lead to a greater emphasis on multiple sourcing plans as a mitigation strategy in the next 20 years to 2034, as all supply chains are now susceptible to turbulence. This is something that was brought into sharp focus by the impact of the earthquake and tsunami in north-east Japan and the floods in Thailand in 2011.

- As part of our attempt to manage price volatility, procurement is likely to find itself having to take on far more responsibility for – and develop a greater understanding of – financial tools to help manage risk, such as hedging against commodity and currency fluctuations on the markets.

- The constantly evolving landscape and greater prominence of supply chain risk will fundamentally impact the relationship between procurement and suppliers in years to come, particularly where there is high demand and a shortage of supply. For example, organizations could find themselves faced with a supply base choosing partners they wish to work with based on the attractiveness of the relationship. In some industries, this could even lead to direct investment in the supply base to ensure supply.

For many businesses today, the issue of risk is a defining one. The profession and its role in the globalized age brings with it opportunities as well as threats. Procurement must pick up responsibility for supply chain risk and make this its professional unique selling point (USP), demonstrating that it adds tangible value to organizations.

Demographic changes: talent

Global demographic trends will have huge implications for businesses over the next two decades, as Western nations face ageing populations and developing economies emerge as hotbeds of talent. Recruitment and talent management will be the single biggest issue for most organizations, and competition will increasingly come not only from the same country but all around the globe, and China and India in particular.

The organizational requirement for global sourcing and managing a network of international suppliers, as well as a growing need for diverse teams to be based on the ground in far-flung locations, means that the procurement professional will be impacted by this trend more keenly than most. The skills required to cope with the demands faced by procurement over the next 20 years are likely to change, increasing in complexity, with greater analytical and technical requirements accompanied by an increased need for expertise in the softer skills:

- Procurement professionals will need to be competent internal networkers, data analysts, developers of global supply bases and attractors of innovation, while category management will require an entrepreneurial streak and strong leadership skills. The transactional skills of procurement's 'back-room boys', on which the function was built, will become correspondingly less important, being subsumed by technology or performed by outsourced providers.

- On the softer side, the profession will need people who are culturally aware, collaborative and innovative, and have strong leadership teams capable of transgressing functional, national and virtual boundaries. Leadership development programmes will need to reflect this demand, and job rotation within organizations will become an important learning tool as procurement becomes more firmly embedded within the business.

- With 'generation Y' now firmly established in the workplace, many in leadership roles, procurement will need to appeal specifically to this talent pool. A willingness to countenance flexible or remote working, with reduced travelling time and opportunities for a better work–life balance, will be more important than in the past, while salaries will need to remain competitive to entice top candidates who will be starting out in their working lives with more debt than any generation in the past.

- The profession needs people who are specifically focused on a career in procurement; it needs to lure top graduates away from investment banks, consultancies and law firms by raising the profile of the profession beyond the corporate world. Perhaps one of the solutions to attracting this generation into the profession comes in the form of one of the challenges it must confront as an issue going forward. This is a generation that has been brought up on environmentalism and CSR, and being able to influence that aspect of business will be a powerful pull.

- Another factor for individuals coming into the profession is likely to be the opportunity to travel and work overseas. This is something that will fit in with the increasingly globalized nature of the profession and also act as a core part of the development process for young talent – and this will become an important requirement in the future, from both an individual and organizational perspective.

We sense that the likelihood to live and work abroad will increase in the next 20 years. Given the opportunities in the emerging markets and the current state of the UK economy people will have no option but to consider working in China, Brazil or India, because this is where the jobs will be. This shift to working outside the UK or Europe will require a cultural and generational mindset shift as the profession evolves with the times, thus adding another dimension to the way we do business, particularly regarding cultural aspects.

Yet while this desire for international exposure will work well for those businesses that can offer it, and have a genuine requirement for it, it could potentially make the challenge of recruiting talent even tougher for those that are unable to do so. This could require some innovative thinking on the part of procurement organizations, such as establishing talent programmes with other businesses in similar industries but in different geographies.

However this plays out, managing virtual teams will inevitably be a more prominent part of the procurement function's role, as a means of interacting with internal stakeholders, suppliers and staff. This is where the relationship skills will come to the fore, and it is here that procurement will need to excel.

Working in an increasingly globalized environment will create a need to build talent pools around the world. Here, the challenge for procurement will be to strike the right balance between a local presence and international direction, as well as creating an environment that can compete for talent at a local level and where a diverse workforce can flourish.

An interim solution could be to develop a pool of talent recruited from around the world, which will have a rolling brief and be sent to various countries for a number of medium-term stints during their careers. In the longer-term, the emergence of and competition for procurement professionals in markets such as Asia, the Far East and Africa is likely to be every bit as pivotal and intense as developing home-grown talent.

Two key demographics for the spotlight are: first, the West's ageing population and the East's skills shortage. Operating a global team will bring with it its own challenges, such as managing a much younger workforce, and one with different views around what the function is and how it should operate. Second, the profession has to contrast established and emerging markets in terms of the demographics. Fundamental is the need to establish the profession in the developing economies with the same gravitas it has in the developed economies.

The shift in the global economic centre of gravity

The emergence of powerful new economies based predominantly in the East has been the most significant change in the global economic landscape since the mid-1990s. Today we can argue with some certainty that the real centre of economic gravity no longer sits in the West – the economic downturn triggered in 2008 has only served to accelerate the shift, which will continue to dominate both the political and economic landscape over the next 20 years.

China is already the world's largest manufacturer and most estimates predict it will overtake the United States as the biggest economic power in the world at some point in the early 2020s. Other powerful economies include the world's third biggest in the shape of Japan – as well as India and Russia, while Brazil recently overtook the UK as the world's sixth biggest economic powerhouse. The overall shift to the East is undeniable and, with seven of the so-called 'next 11' (N11) – Bangladesh, Indonesia, Iran, Pakistan, Philippines, South Korea and Vietnam – tipped to follow Brazil, Russia, India and China (the BRIC nations) also based in this part of the world, the direction of travel is undeniably one-way.

This shift will inevitably have a profound impact on procurement, in terms of both sourcing strategy and how – and where – the function is set up. The emergence of these new economies as viable customer markets will have an effect, too, with procurement increasingly tasked with securing supply into as well as from such countries, using its local knowledge to help build sales operations.

Procurement will need to be better informed about the wider environment in which it operates. It will need to be more aware of the implications of the shift in economic power and understand how to manage and forecast future shifts. Over the next 20 years procurement will need more rounded individuals who can understand the strategic implications in the medium as well as the short term.

Up to now, the East has largely been viewed by the West as a source of low-cost materials, goods and services. In the future, though, these markets will change, with improvements in quality matched by higher costs, borne mainly out of increased labour rates. Chinese labour rates are already rising sharply, especially in the coastal areas, although for now they remain well below levels in the West.

With events such as the Arab Spring generating a newfound confidence in these parts of the world, the pressure for better pay and working conditions will, quite naturally, increase in the coming decade. This could be problematic for procurement, if its aim is to establish security of supply matched with low costs. As the emerging markets become more mature, so too will those behind them. The N11 will take over as the major low-cost sourcing hotspots.

Working on the basis that low-cost country sourcing is all about labour rates, as countries win more and more business, they will also start to lose their competitive advantage. This is already happening in China and South America. So, in 20 years – where next, Africa? This constant process of evolution means that procurement must be ready to respond to shifts at short notice, even factoring in exit strategies once relationships have run their course in a particular country.

The availability of raw materials is another issue for the future, particularly as emerging economies themselves increase their own consumption and look to buy up sources of supply. There will be more people demanding more food, more water and using more natural resources. An increasing scarcity of vital raw materials – oil in particular – will have profound implications for organizations in terms of pricing and security of supply, and for the very nature of the relationships between procurement and its suppliers.

Alongside the continued evolution of the East is an increasing trend to consider sourcing – or manufacturing – certain products and services closer to home. In part, this will be driven by politics – a legacy of the economic downturn and high levels of unemployment, as well as the decline of manufacturing in traditional destinations. More significant, though, will be the growing issue of rising fuel and logistics costs, coupled with higher wage rates in the emerging economies and stagnating labour costs in the West. In the longer term, organizations in the West may have to look to rebuild their intellectual property, particularly in areas such as manufacturing and engineering.

Operating in global markets has implications for both the structure of procurement and the practical aspects of managing suppliers and internal customers. On the supplier side, procurement will be required to develop much more of a network mindset, where strategy is likely to be devised centrally but local knowledge will determine ways of working on the ground. Procurement will need to be wary of suppliers potentially becoming competitors, but at the same time must seek to develop closer working relationships to become the customer of choice, as well as the foundation for innovation.

Procurement will find itself operating in a more strategic role:

- Advising internal customers and stakeholders on sourcing and outsourcing strategies and drawing on the knowledge of local cultures and quality standards.

- It will need to be at the forefront, more proactive in delivering ideas around what should be outsourced, and perhaps what should be insourced to reduce risk.

- It will contribute to strategy setting, rather than just being the receiver of strategy; it will thus become part of the fabric of the organization.

Procurement's strategic posture will be to link product and service development to supply chain capability to source and deliver with a deep knowledge of geographical and cultural nuances. The skills that a procurement professional will develop should be transferable to other areas of the organization, creating more attractive organizational assets.

This applies to procurement's role in the emergence of new markets as sales channels for businesses as well as sourcing destinations. Deep local knowledge and relationships will be crucial in helping to identify opportunities and establish operations in heavily localized environments.

The profession of the future will need to be able to interact and operate seamlessly across many environments. There will be a need for different skill sets for different regions and different engagement strategies.

There is strong evidence that procurement's involvement in such fast-paced markets could lead to the emergence of two types of purchasing function: one that operates in a mature, non-growth marketplace, where procurement's role is to drive out costs; and another in a rapidly growing market to support the supply of goods and services into that marketplace, rather than from it, providing access to capacity. This would require very different business models and it raises the question as to whether one procurement activity can cover both.

The shift from West to East is likely to create a constantly moving environment for global businesses, and procurement professionals will need to be able to respond effectively. Procurement's position at the heart of such activity, however, should only serve to make the function more strategic and offer more career opportunities to its practitioners.

External impacts: what procurement must do today and in the future

From the points made so far, clearly we can see that procurement will encounter expanding risks and extended supply chains. The locations of suppliers for both physical and virtual goods and services, as well as the geographic location of internal procurement staff and facilities, may have growing and significant total cost and risk implications. Today, when it comes to managing supply chains on a localized basis (eg Southeast Asia), such activity is pressuring organizations, even those that are less resource-constrained than most.

For procurement's leaders there is recognition too that supply risk factors are increasing year on year and they relate not only to supplier financial stability and price, but also to supply assurance, customer perceptions and regulatory concerns. As scrutiny of business practice increases, there is also a requirement for procurement to understand the implications of its corporate responsibility and sustainability for purchasing and the supply chain. Technology is increasingly enabling businesses to do this in real time in order to predict and forecast outcomes, factoring into account a range of cost, compliance, transfer prices and other inputs.

Given these converging risks as well as increased organizational expectations and requirements, traditional procurement is trying to press today's hot buttons as well as dealing with longer-term and more strategic opportunities.

Leading procurement organizations are already looking to develop their own advanced capabilities, such as leveraging suppliers as important sources for innovation, employing advanced commodity management tactics and focusing on currency and foreign exchange in partnership with other parts of the business. These boundary-spanning multilevel programmes will be critical in developing broader risk, sourcing and working capital management strategies to drive not just procurement-led savings and compliance but also company-changing strategies.

Developing corporate and procurement strategy to meet the challenges

To meet the challenges outlined in this chapter, businesses will have to supplement internal efforts with reliance on external expertise and capabilities to drive enhanced market intelligence and analytics (especially in non-core areas). Procurement for its part will need to build a new level of trust and transparency within the broader business in order to facilitate innovation and develop their ability to successfully manage internal and third-party relationships.

New sources of information are already available in 2014 that were not there only five or six years ago. As a consequence we are seeing something approaching data overload for some, and intelligent supply-chain-bliss for others. Across categories and supply chains, available datasets for input and analysis continue to increase by an order of some magnitude. Businesses that do not have competency in managing information and intelligence today may fall increasingly further behind tomorrow, creating gaps that will become tougher and tougher to close.

For those leading new procurement functions, a near revolution will likely have to occur. Many of today's fundamentals will obviously remain: category sourcing, baseline procurement systems, human resources management, purchasing performance, and knowledge management.

Over and above this, procurement will need to offer a new operating approach to optimize localization (ie regional enablement) and global support. Decisions around centralization and execution may vary between businesses, but the need to define functional and organizational structure will always remain as part of overall processes, category sourcing, leadership, and execution roles – just as it is today. Such structures not only will enable procurement to support internal customers (and their needs) at more defined and localized levels, it will also enable insight and action to adjust for balance of trade questions that might arise with customers.

Let's say that on a localized basis a procurement organization opts to support global marketing with a shared, data-driven infrastructure that supports a macro-view of activities all the way down to local planning. Such a structure would enable a global marketing organization and agencies of record (and local teams and local agencies supporting execution) to collaborate on improving measured outcomes across all media planning. But the same business might take a hybrid approach for direct procurement categories, via centralized supplier management data collection in support of local – in country – procurement teams (including supplier quality and development resources).

As with traditional change management activities, leadership and stakeholder engagement will remain essential, but with a new, finance-centric alignment. So procurement will still need to engage other business colleagues, ranging from those responsible for profit and loss as well as those in functional roles such as legal, IT, human resources, marketing, engineering, design, customer service, manufacturing and so on. So, in essence, procurement will need very quickly to enlist change management tactics within the function, with finance partners and across the business.

Finally, the foregoing may create the distinct possibility that who *works in* procurement' will be different to who '*does* procurement', and this potential outcome is in itself a critical nuance. At the extreme, maybe half or more of the procurement function could be comprised of those carrying out procurement responsibilities as part of a rotating assignment.

Procurement's responsibilities for innovation, automation, compliance and value-capture approaches (including systems that report on performance) will remain, as will collaboration, benchmarking, measurement, and reporting processes and tools. But given the expanding definition and scope of procurement, these elements will grow to encompass additional areas, such as embedding previously internally focused environmental, health and safety (EHS) team members in continuous external-supplier development activities.

CASE STUDY   The Footwear material sustainability index

The case of how a company, referred to as 'Footwear' in this study, adopted a material sustainability index that would capture the knowledge inherent in their supply base on sustainability, and integrate that intelligence into its product design decisions, is a case in point of how technology can be leveraged to drive sustainable outcomes when procurement puts its mind to work on solving these kinds of problems; this was a 10-year journey in the making.

When Footwear began to think about a sustainable supply chain, they recognized that sustainability was a criterion that competed with other concerns: price, performance, quality, technology, functionality and, most of all, consumer preference. In 1998 the vice president of sustainability at Footwear, and others in his organization began thinking about how to create a tool for Footwear product-creation teams to select environmentally better materials from better suppliers, and to drive the right decisions that would benefit the business, as well as the environment.

The team began trying to understand the impact of their products on water, waste, toxics and energy. They knew they couldn't look at everything, so they focused on the impact of their products overall. For athletic apparel, material is 60 per cent of Footwear's footprint, with manufacturing making up 25 per cent, transportation 7 per cent, and retailer/services the remainder. So it was clear that to make a difference, the impact had to be on materials. Unfortunately, this involved impacting parties who produced the materials before they reached Footwear, and this implied impacting the decisions of others in the supply chain. But the decision was more complicated than that – they also had to influence people who designed Footwear's products, made decisions on the types of materials used, as well as the people who selected the suppliers to buy these materials from.

The goal: a single numeric indicator

The goal of creating a sustainability index was ambitious from the outset. Footwear sources over 80,000 materials from 14,000 suppliers, which determines 60 per cent of the environmental impact (as well as 60 per cent of product cost), and needed one tool for product-creation teams to make better decisions. We know that their decisions impact on material sustainability. When the vice president of sustainability's project started in 1998, Footwear and their leadership handed him and his team a mandate to make their products more sustainable. The team had tried to develop life-cycle assessments at that time, when they began exploring alternative materials for their products such as bamboo, hemp and others. They began constructing early life cycle assessments (LCAs) on spreadsheets, and realized quickly how complex these calculations were.

Footwear had also dabbled in sustainability programmes in 1998. They had developed a list of restricted substances, a water impact programme, carbon footprint and recycling programmes, and manufacturing waste-reduction programmes. The team recognized that the suppliers' effort in these areas were measured but rarely impacted designers' decisions, as the results were held off to the side and never tied back to business decisions. They also recognized that including those pieces in the management systems information (MSI) was important, to ensure that material suppliers received credit and visibility for those programmes relative to their competitors' when it came to sourcing decisions. Whatever system was used had to reward suppliers not just for quality, performance and price, but also amplifying and consolidating efforts that Footwear cared about and wanted to encourage their suppliers to pursue, in a fair and equitable manner.

What started out as a simple effort resulted in three major efforts over a 10-year period. The first two efforts were discarded until the current MSI format was deemed successful. Several guidelines were applied in developing the MSI that are applicable for any organization seeking to develop a sustainability index for their supply chain.

First, don't become a data collection machine. The VP of sustainability and his team recognized from the outset that life-cycle analysis and other means of developing sustainable data required complicated chemical engineering capabilities and biomaterial science capabilities, which are not always easily found in an apparel company. Some companies seeking to build sustainability programmes insist on measuring 'cradle to grave, end to end' carbon footprints. The problem is that you often don't know who your supplier's suppliers are, and tracking down this type of information is highly complex.

The VP of sustainability notes that:

> We actually didn't worry about LCA too much – we just went off the best publicly available information. Our team tried to model a supply chain that was the most representative of what we believed was in our supply base. If we were measuring a Taiwanese polypropylene producer – we didn't care whose process it was. There was a life-cycle assessment built into the MSI, which is a proxy for that material supply chain.

In other words, Footwear didn't attempt to get a measure that was precise, but one that was 'directionally correct'. The VP of sustainability notes:

> If a supplier doesn't like the number we came up with, we encourage them to come up with a better one. To do so, they have the opportunity to open up their supply chain, and show us the nodes and the six other suppliers that go into their finished product, and the environmental impact at each node. By opening it up to the apparel industry, we also recognize that updates through collaboration with the community is part of continually improving the MSI.

This also drives more visibility and transparency into those variations.

Second, use an index that represents 'a thesis on sustainable materials'. The MSI is not an absolute measurement. The VP of sustainability describes it as 'a thesis on the way we need to evaluate materials, and as such, is always open to debate'. By that he means that the MSI is cradle-to-gate index. An index takes information and applies a value system to it that produces a numerical value that is not tied to any single impact. The number is unit less, and represents a complex set of value attributions that are also driven by publicly available data. Using the best available public information was key, as Footwear recognized that they could not do primary data generation. Lots of chemical engineering studies exist on life-cycle assessments, so the team decided to simply pull the best available information they could find and apply it to their supply chain in a framework that is transparent, and understood by as many people as possible. Although the MSI was LCA-inspired, the data limitations drove them to use indicators that were the best available ones – and that was a starting point that was deemed 'good enough.' The MSI is *not* an LCA, but instead complemented traditional LCA tools to make them understandable to 'the common man'.

The index was constructed in a straightforward manner. It begins with key materials, 50 per cent of which are life-cycle based. Of the remaining points, 25 per cent are those that impact that base material, which is where biomass-derived materials can be used to improve the base material impact. The final 25 per cent of points are based on supplier-driven activities that they are engaged in that act as a proxy for differentiation of the supply chain. If a material supplier is engaged in a biomass material programme, has eliminated toxic materials and has a zero-based energy programme, they will receive extra points in this category, and Footwear's index makes the assumption that there is a lower impact overall. So if Footwear has 50 polyethylene suppliers – each has an individual own score based on their differentiated sustainability programmes (including labour and human rights policies), and that is what modifies the base polyester core.

The index does not yet go beyond the tier-one primary material supplier into tier-two suppliers, but the recognition was that Footwear had to start with the group with whom a commercial relationship was with. If the index could be directionally correct and enable the people making design decisions to have a high degree of decision-making power that would reward the right behaviours, it isn't as important that it be precise.

Finally don't forget about the dreaded trade-offs, because all sustainability decisions require them. Most often, this involves paying a higher price relative to consumer preferences. It has been well established that consumers are typically unwilling to support sustainable products with equal performance at a higher price. So how could Footwear trade off price?

In fact, the decision-making process made by Footwear's designers involves a number of factors. When designing new products, Footwear product design teams are fighting off multiple trade-offs, including not just costs, but quality, delivery performance, the 'feel' of the material, the innovation piece, the functional performance of the material, and consumer preferences. In this context, sustainability is one of eight different factors that go into the material selection decision. So to make it easier to include, it was important to make the MSI simple. Having it boil down to a single number was about as simple as you can make it. But behind that number, the right information needs to be available and feeding into it.

The MSI was the third iteration of a materials assessment tool, and represents multiple trial-and-error learning occurring over a 10-year period. Although it is only a single number, it represents the underlying science-based material score, greenhouse gas emissions, litres of water, yield per acre, and multiple other metrics that are mashed together into an index in a clear and transparent way.

The second section of the MSI includes material environmental indicators, such as chemistry, water conservation, organic content (eg pesticide free, etc). These are areas where the team felt there was a clear consensus from the scientific community of what constituted an improvement over currently used standard base materials. The environmental footprint of that material is thus implicitly included in the MSI, and spans more than 50 materials with many different supply chain maps. In each case, the team tried to use a single representative supply chain to derive the score, with the understanding that the metric could be revised as more information became available.

The last section included supplier practices. Suppliers were coming to the procurement team, saying 'Hey we have renewable energy programmes and the lowest level of restricted substances, restricted water treatment and other programmes you have told us that you care about. But your designers are not dialled into all of this effort that we've made to be more sustainable!' So that is where certifications come in. For example, the leather working group has an industry-specific audit where if suppliers achieve bronze, silver or gold status, they get points for that on the MSI. Location-specific programmes pull into an indicator that assigns value to that material.

Example: virgin polyester

Consider for instance three suppliers who all have a base MSI score of 24. All three provide virgin polyester material. However, supplier A is 'washout' on sustainability programmes in the third section of the MSI; the company is not engaged in green chemistry, continue to use restricted substances, and do not have a documented clean water initiative. In this case, the MSI is reduced to 12. Supplier B participates in all of these programmes, and is assigned an additional 17 points, receiving an MSI of 41. Supplier C is using recycled polyester in addition to compliance with programmes, and thus is scored an additional 12 points for an MSI of 53. In each case, the team is adjusting the MSI to provide incentives for suppliers to do the right thing. Suppliers have autonomy to invest in these programmes, and are given a frame of reference by which to judge the return on them in terms of the value of their business to Footwear. They can decide 'is it worth the additional 5 points to make this capital investment or business decision?'

Rolling up scores

The VP of sustainability emphasized that 'Across Footwear, product groups now all have a sustainability index target for all new products.' The MSI index is driven by material scores associated with that particular product (eg running shoe versus apparel T-shirt, etc). Scores for every material show up in the bill of materials. In evaluating the product design, the design team now have a way to consider trade-offs between different materials and different suppliers that consider the sustainability impact. This simply wasn't there before. Now it is much more than lip service and the team can consider the sustainability index as one more parameter that must be considered in the trade-offs made between price, performance, functionality etc. The team can game the parameters to come up with the best optimal score, all the while going for the margin.

The VP of sustainability says:

Because of the work we've invested into the MSI, we have been able to jump in with a sustainability impact that doesn't screw up business processes associated with product design and development, yet impacts business outcomes and decisions in a meaningful way. We have also been able to meaningfully impact suppliers' business strategies and attitudes towards sustainability. We are in our tenth season of the MSI. In our sixth season, we began to see for the first time that suppliers were coming to us and telling us what their score was going to be before we even audited them! They know what they have to do to get a better score, and are acting on it. Every material now has a score that has driven a whole new level of competition in the supply base. We tell suppliers the range of scores for the materials they provide and where they fall in that range! The ones that are business savvy know if lower scoring won't help them, and know what they have to do to target a given product score that will give them more business when product designers are making decisions (all other elements being competitively equal).

Labour and human rights

Footwear also has a group that is involved in assessing the labour and human rights (LHR) component of the management systems information, but there is also a team that will make universal sourcing decisions. In 2005 the company decided to disclose publicly the factories that make its products. Most retailers and clothing brands refuse to disclose where their goods are made, citing competitive reasons. But in addition, Footwear attempts to reduce its exposure to countries where it considers factory conditions to be risky, including Bangladesh. In 2012 a factory in Bangladesh burned to the ground due to unsafe working conditions, killing 112 workers. Wal-Mart and Sears apparel was discovered in the facility, although both companies claim they had pulled out of the factory the year before. It is possible that one of their other suppliers was subcontracting to this facility.[1] At Footwear, only eight of the 896 factories it worked with in 2011 were in Bangladesh. 'Bangladesh for us has been on our high-risk country list, so unlike many suppliers we kept our footprint there very limited', says Footwear's vice president of sustainable business, in an interview: 'While many companies moved there due to low costs, we chose to go in a different direction.' She also notes that: 'Across a fragmented supply chain are you sometimes going to have problems? Yes. You have to judge your system by how quickly and effectively you can respond.'[2]

Conclusion

Efforts by procurement to make a bigger contribution to strategy continue, but sometimes at the cost of misunderstandings between procurement and the rest of the business. And yet procurement has much expertise to offer, which can provide substantial financial benefits. New vision and capabilities are needed. Procurement leaders might well ask not what their business can do for them; rather what they can do for the business.

This journey may start with finding new ways to build trust within the business by procurement extending an empathetic but challenging hand to work with spend owners to improve business outcomes through new exploration of demand specifications, buying decisions and supplier engagement. Or perhaps it will start with procurement assuming a risk management role that takes into account commodity, currency, political, regulatory and other emerging areas that bring both threat and opportunity. These early steps must quickly proceed beyond singular initiatives to address the future outcomes. Key will be procurement's role and impact on financial performance, risk management, supplier relationships and its impact on customer satisfaction.

Procurement must approach these issues in the knowledge that incremental changes will not do. Procurement must earn the trust of the business to fully succeed. And, in doing so, it must embrace a vision that goes far beyond the thinking of today, leveraging creativity and know-how to change not just the function from within, but the overall business value that procurement can deliver.

In developing and deploying procurement's true value proposition to the business, everything it has learned and practised still counts. However, procurement transformation, lessons from the past and classic maturity model thinking must be put in context. Modest changes in capability and thinking can help but will not bring the value that modern business demands. Procurement must progress and, as George Bernard Shaw put it so eloquently, 'Progress is impossible without change, and those who cannot change their minds cannot change anything'.

In this chapter we have looked at practical ways in which we can assess the procurement organization and what good organizations do. In Chapter 4 we consider the shifts discussed above in more detail and look at what has brought this wholesale change about. We also look at how the very notion of business and the organization has changed, before setting up a discussion around how we might practically approach these changes and offering some ideas regarding what procurement can do.

Notes

1 Bustillo, M, Wright, T and Banjo, S (2012) Touch questions in fire's ashes, *Wall Street Journal*, 30 November, p B1.

2 Bustillo, Wright and Banjo (2012) p B6.

Five game changers

Their impact on procurement and supply management

04

Increasingly businesses are directing more and more of their budgets towards a complex web of global suppliers to help deliver on their business strategies. According to some industry reports as much as 70 per cent of corporate revenue is directed towards externalized, supplier-driven costs. In 2011–14 alone it is estimated that companies have increased their external spend as a percentage of revenue by nearly 4 per cent. As a result, the role of procurement has been brought into very sharp focus.

And yet as has already been mentioned, procurement doesn't register on the C-suite's radar in a manner proportionate to its growing importance within the organization, and most procurement departments are neither ready nor empowered to take on their new responsibilities. Given the ever-increasing logistics costs of globalization, increasing levels of risk and complexity and the perennial issue of rising labour costs, now seems a good time for a major rethink on procurement and supply management strategy.

The story of procurement since the mid-1980s mirrors the wider business landscape. During this time, the profession has risen steadily. The impact of the economic downturn triggered in 2008 has only served to further both the cause of procurement and raise questions regarding its perception in the wider business world. The next several decades promise to bring even more significant change. Having established its credentials, procurement needs to evolve and demonstrate the benefits it can bring in a wide range of areas to add genuine value to business as a whole. Risk will increase in importance, CSR will be tied up with security of supply, and procurement will need to draw on market knowledge, supplier relationships and the use of new technology to identify major threats to a business.

The way in which procurement is structured – and perhaps even where it is based – will change too. With teams spread around the globe, procurement will increasingly find itself managing virtual networks of suppliers, stakeholders and internal customers, drawing on powerful new social media channels to communicate. But it is important that this technology does not come at the expense of the face-to-face relationships that will be so important in establishing solid supplier connections. Alongside all this, the profession must continue its battle for talent and aim to recruit the best and the brightest.

One thing that is for sure is that leaders can no longer afford to downplay the strategic role of procurement. To understand why this has happened we will look at the game-changing phenomena that have brought this about and how procurement can offer the wider business opportunities to take advantage of some of them. Clearly not every procurement organization is at the same level of maturity, so we will consider them against the three levels of capability identified in Chapter 2 in terms of the *achiever*, the *value-adder* and the *leader*.

Game changer no. 1: corporate social responsibility (CSR)

The world's bio-capacity is becoming increasingly unbalanced. Global warming and pollution, the result of industrialization and greenhouse gas emissions, ever-increasing water consumption and levels of cropland fertility are changing or at least shifting regionally. As a consequence we can be sure that energy costs will rise, even if liberalization of energy markets does result in price decreases in the short term in certain regions (eg natural gas and electricity in Europe and the United States). But it is our dependence on unstable regions that will grow in the medium to long term – and price increases are likely to be the outcome.

The increasing levels of demand for energy will undoubtedly raise prices and force exploration for new resources – for example, deep-water oil exploration. However, the risks associated with this are becoming increasingly obvious – a recent example is the monumental incident off the coast of the southern United States following the explosion on BP's Deepwater Horizon Rig in 2010. Clearly the exploration for primary raw materials such as oil and gas will become more challenging as resources decrease. Renewable raw materials as an alternative source are already being considered but their wide use will only be seriously exploited if they prove to be more competitive in the markets than fossil raw materials and/or they can offer technical advantages – the cost of their recovery notwithstanding. Finally, it is becoming increasingly clear that gas will be the fastest growing primary energy source.

What we can take from this is that increasing energy costs and general risk aversion will create a shift in energy demand and a focus on renewables. Nevertheless, usage of renewable energy will increase slowly due to the energy transition lag.[1] Biofuel utilization will be driven by regulation, most probably leading to price increases as production is limited by cropland availability for food production in many regions. Renewable energy sources are most likely to become significant beyond 2030. A demand-driven focus on renewables is not foreseeable until 2020 but may become a bigger issue in the decade that follows, as the availability of fossil fuels diminishes. Whilst renewables are most certainly on the business agenda and driven by increased awareness of CSR, its ranking might well change in the light of the Fukushima disaster of 2011 and help speed up the transition time.

Never have environmental challenges been so present in public awareness as today. The trend towards ecological and social responsibility, which was once the preserve of a few zealots, has gained tremendous speed in the 21st century and will grow in focus and impact over the next decade to 2024.

The importance of requirements related to CSR has increased over the last few years, mainly driven by growing consumer awareness and extensive legislative requirements (compliance). Environmental issues are clearly of concern to consumers and this concern will increase in importance over the next 10 years or so.

There will also be an increased awareness concerning the social impacts of these changes as consumers understand the holistic nature of the sustainability agenda. Already there has been some reaction: Supplier Diversity, Localism and Big Society in the UK, and legislation in both the United States and China. This will result in a combining of environmental protection with social and economic development – and a better understanding of the triple bottom line.[2] This shift is also being triggered by a new generation of consumers who are much more aware of the impacts of climate change and will assert their demands for even greater social progress. One only has to look at the rising middle class in the developing economies, who conform to Western consumption patterns, yet are paying an increasing level of attention to sustainability-related issues.

This trend is clearly event driven. In a world where information spreads faster than ever before, catastrophes such as Fukushima have far more impact on the environment and society than their immediate environs. As a consequence of the social media tools available to us, social injustice is revealed more quickly and more often. Consequently, incidents such as Deepwater Horizon or Fukushima create greater immediate awareness and, behind the immediate reaction, much deeper changes in trust and opinion.

In the world's fastest growing economies legislation is changing very rapidly and huge reforms are planned. Legislative changes can be introduced overnight, making it almost impossible for organizations to foresee them and even harder to react accordingly. For China, whose markets are cost driven, players will be forced to respond to sustainability issues very quickly due to the potential of adverse effects on both domestic and foreign consumption. However, this situation could stabilize as the high-growth markets increase in maturity, and one can reasonably expect that China particularly will reach legislative stability and maturity regarding both environmental and social aspects of CSR by 2020. Whether it is at a level comparable to the United States and Europe in that timescale remains questionable.

For most organizations the impact of this change in emphasis on CSR is twofold. On the one hand, the consumer demands transparency regarding production conditions and the environmental footprint of products. On the other, young 'socially literate' talent is attracted to organizations that offer the best working conditions and are associated with a 'green' or sociably responsible image. Organizations can no longer afford to ignore environmental and social issues. They can choose one of two paths to deal with this growing need: they can be defensive and avoid risks related to social and environmental issues, or drive differentiation by embracing them. The latter radically changes both the structure and focus of the organization, with tremendous impact being placed on the value chain;[3] increasingly we see the most advanced organizations embrace a strategy that reads: Sustainability = Innovation.

CSR is no longer the sole responsibility of a corporate function or the mantra of the Marketing Department. Procurement now plays a central role in championing it through its responsibility for the environmental and social integrity of the supply base, thereby directly ensuring the organization's brand value. Indeed both consumers and the media are very quick to blame organizations for the transgressions of their suppliers. Furthermore, the challenge is increasingly coming from within and procurement will have to accept its responsibility in this regard and demonstrate its know-how in handling these often brand-critical responsibilities. For efficient communication and transparency regarding these topics, procurement professionals will need to work closely with both PR and marketing departments. Additionally, sophisticated monitoring systems will be needed to assess suppliers' compliance and to understand legislative evolutions all around the world.

A special focus on suppliers located in developing/high-growth markets with unpredictable legislative environments is very important, and keeping up with a growing body of suppliers in these markets – many of which will require very specific audits – can be expected to be a major challenge. Moreover, the speed of change in these high-growth markets makes early warning systems pretty much ineffective and leaves supplier audits as the only feasible solution.

However, this approach will not be enough, as supplier relationship management (SRM) incorporates many CSR themes and, for first-tier suppliers, the danger often lurks at the margins of the supply chain. We know too that organizations will remain responsible for problems that appear anywhere in the chain, despite best efforts to eradicate danger. We also know that organizations with the most significant brand value and customer proximity are always to blame. CPOs must take on responsibility for compliance at all levels in the supply chain but they don't have – and never will have – the capacity to keep track of them all. So how can it be possible to control and assess the compliance and performance of thousands of suppliers on a regular basis? What is certain is that it will be of paramount importance for procurement professionals to engage more and more in initiatives designed to cover entire markets by establishing binding standards. By 2024 we will almost certainly see leading procurement organizations in the role of lobbyist, lobbying governments and participating in the legislative effort to diminish risks that cannot be covered internally.

How should procurement organizations respond to this increased focus on CSR?

For those organizations working at the traditional end of the procurement spectrum, the *achievers*:

- They should be closely monitoring the CSR-related aspects of SRM and the development of adequate risk mitigation stratagem. This is a must-do. Furthermore, the supply base and value chain must be re-evaluated and aligned with the organization's CSR policy in order to seize competitive advantage opportunities emerging from developing supply markets.

- They should also consider looking at critical suppliers beyond tier one in an effort to understand the full depth of supply. CSR has to become part of the daily routine of both category managers and strategic buyers. SRM has to provide criteria and methods to facilitate the integration of CSR in supplier qualification, approval and evaluation.

- For organizations procuring in Asia-Pacific, keeping track of regulatory changes will be key.[4] This will require both efficient warning systems (knowledge transfer, escalation systems and defined reaction planning) as well as close relationships with suppliers.

- At the next level of maturity, that of the value-adding procurement organization, supplier development with a specific focus on CSR will be of paramount importance. Suppliers must be classified in terms of levels of (CSR) risks. Supplier development activity might simply be target setting or actively helping suppliers to reach the necessary levels of compliance to work in your supply chain. A high-performing or strategic supplier with difficulties in embracing CSR has to be supported, as losing them could be disastrous.

- CSR in the procurement organization needs C-suite support. To create organization-wide transparency and uptake of CSR, procurement as a function must become part of corporate machinery with a place on the board regarding CSR issues and be fully involved in top management decisions. Optimization of environmental and social issues has to be designed in cross-functional processes, for example in optimizing waste management or carbon-reduction initiatives. Here, procurement has to go hand in hand with operations, linking suppliers' manufacturing with the internal operations of the organization.

- Finally, reporting has to include CSR-related KPIs so as to track procurement's achievements and value generation. Some examples include the percentage of spend covered by sustainability assessment, the percentage of suppliers with a potential sustainability risk, the percentage of suppliers in high-risk countries, or of suppliers not complying with your organization's code of conduct.

When we get to the top of the pile, amongst those procurement organizations seen as the practice *leaders*, the picture changes again. Here procurement has to:

- Promote industry-wide approaches and standards across the whole supply chain.

- Monitor the evolution of regulation and involvement in political decision-making processes. This is becoming crucial for leading global corporates.

- Report on CSR topics in ways that must be both transparent and reliable – for internal and external audiences. This will enhance the organization's competitive advantage, enhance its brand and position it as a reliable and responsible organization. Consumer awareness will be driven by recognized indices and certification – such as the Dow Jones Sustainability Index. Serious CSR activity requires real investment, which will have payback in the long run. Baselines in measuring procurement's success have to be adjusted accordingly when decisions and commitment in favour of CSR investment are made.

- Finally, procurement has to contribute to carbon-reduction calculations across the supply chain, using support and external data from suppliers. In major supply markets, procurement needs local CSR (regulations) expertise and has to be in country and as close as possible to decision makers.

A global perspective on CSR

The CSR focus changes as we move around the globe. The United States considers itself as the 'differentiator' in all matters CSR and that it is they who will define tomorrow's standards. Supplier Diversity has long been part of business in the United States encapsulated in law, and diversity and inclusion have long been part of the procurement role – the social inclusion aspect has an equal weighting in the United States to environmental considerations.

In Europe, and particularly the UK, sustainability – once considered a fad – is now taken very seriously. Europe leads the world in developing green supply chains. In the UK, legislation is being developed regarding this: the Carbon Bill, the Equalities Act and the Remedies Act will all impact directly on supply chains. Sustainability will drive innovation for smart organizations – via small and medium enterprise (SME) engagement or through green applications where there are advantages to be gained. Procurement here has to play a leading role in CSR activity. Procurement will be the external interface for CSR.

Finally, turning our focus to Asia-Pacific, we will see CSR but with a premium price tag. Their ability to become 'green' quickly will be limited by financial imperatives. SME engagement and other socially focused initiatives are being developed to drive internal consumption patterns and reduce dependence on exports. However, limited CSR awareness in a cost-driven environment today limits CSR potential via procurement, but this will change over time.

Game changer no. 2: technological advances

The proliferation of innovation in recent years from the developing economies has seen a speeding up of innovation cycles globally and an increase in pressure to perform on businesses in the developed economies. The developing economies will make enormous investments in education and technological advances in order to close the gap between them and the developed economies. Today, developing economies have a significantly higher rate of year-on-year increases in innovative products and services than the developed economies.

The growth of research and development (R&D) expenditure and intellectual property (IP) filings in Asia-Pacific across all industries reflects a significant shift in where the new ideas are coming from. The old notion of 'heads' in the West and 'hands' in the East is rapidly fading. Developing economies will soon become the main destination for R&D activity and the global lead in innovation. China experienced very strong growth in the 2000s, closing the gap on the United States and Japan in patents ownership. It is significant too that IP violations and industrial espionage is widespread around the world, and protectionism is growing in significance. It is also important to recognize that, as productivity and innovations in materials and services grow, an eye needs to be kept on price increases and an understanding of the potential impact they might have.

Disruptive innovation will trigger new products and fundamental improvements in productivity and IT and data communication.[5] Internet applications play a vital role almost everywhere today, but there will be continuous developments in IT and communications and a similar growth in usage in all walks of life. Growing coverage and access to the internet across the globe will encourage greater use of social media and web. 2.0 applications in areas of the world that as yet do not use them. These social innovations will translate to business applications, enabling ease of use, standardization, as well as ERPs, information and communications technology (ICT) processes and so forth. As a consequence, the financial and economic impact of IT will increase and at the same time there will be higher demands placed on our ability to extract the important data from increased information flow.

Advances in technology will become increasingly tied to organizational success, especially in high-growth markets. The fact that many developing economies are not burdened with legacy systems means they can establish themselves with state-of-the-art technologies, often developed by them and bypassing the turgid development cycles that have characterized the catch-up strategies in Western economies. It is not too bold to suggest that China is likely to dictate and lead in specifications of the future.

This situation will boost demand for innovative products – with the innovation often being derived from local sources hungry to satisfy the voracious appetite of developing economies, which in time will reach critical mass; given, too, the entrepreneurial spirit, and the indifference to high workloads prevalent in the developing economies, this furnace of innovation is stoked for the higher generation of ideas and greater developments. The established markets might still have the edge today, but over the next decade efficiency gains in the developing economies will catch up and eventually outstrip the West.

Finally, information and knowledge exchange will speed up and be facilitated by technological advances. Absolute transparency will become a must for complex organizations with the mantra 'adapt or die' becoming universal. Social networking, via communications channels yet to be defined, will enable the establishment of innovation networks far removed from the internal R&D activities of the organization, building on the growing phenomenon of open innovation.[6] This is likely to change the way that people work together; indeed new information and communication technologies are creating some of the biggest shifts in human behaviour and fundamentally changing the way we live, work and interact. Location is not a limitation; people are increasingly connected to the global network not because of their geographies, but in spite of them.

As all organizations strive to be more innovative, so the role of the procurement professional becomes more entwined in the creative activities associated with it. Depending on the depth of the organization's value chain, procurement will become a significant player in securing a continuous flow of innovation. According to Holger Schiele at the University of Twente in the Netherlands, at the beginning of the 2000s more than 80 per cent of organizations depended on external partners in order to remain competitive – and this trend continues. Procurement's role will be to work with suppliers on the development of innovations via their relationships and to secure cooperation to bring the innovation from the supply market into the organization. This in turn can only work if procurement has strong ties between R&D, Sales and Operations and is brought in at an early stage of new projects. Procurement, for its part, needs people with new skills – a significant characteristic of the new supply professional is the extent and depth of his or her knowledge: they will become 'students of their industry'. They will know everything of their supply markets – the science, economics, law and politics – on a global scale.

Procurement too will need to play a major role in promoting the organization's image in the supply market. Lean organizations rely on innovative suppliers to compete in supply markets and it is becoming increasingly important to be the preferred customer of your key suppliers. As supplier cooperation is critical to develop successful innovation sourcing strategies, so traditional price-oriented and global-sourcing strategies are becoming less effective than innovation-oriented cost-saving strategies. Since the 1990s the move from closed to open innovation models has facilitated innovation-oriented cost-saving strategies and this innovation typically occurs between manufacturers and their suppliers. There is evidence too that the largest savings potential in the purchasing volume of a typical modern industrial firm stems from innovation-oriented strategies; early supplier involvement in new product development has become critical in increasing the impact of co-creation strategies.

To enable this, a tremendous amount of information in real time will have to be filtered through procurement and shared effectively across the organization. A category manager's ability to network effectively will be as important as the processes developed within the organization to capture and analyse supplier relationships. This can be achieved through mechanisms such as virtual exchange networks, and software developers are increasingly enhancing social networking platforms into equivalent business applications.

How is procurement responding to advanced technologies?

For those organizations working at the traditional end of the procurement spectrum, the *achievers*:

- They will need to take a leading role in bringing innovation from the supply market. Early involvement in projects is critical.
  Organizations need to reposition themselves to facilitate this via

cross-functional working, with procurement developing its knowledge and understanding of internal customer requirements and operating as a networker and integrator.

- A prerequisite for this evolution is an enhanced level of skills and competencies in procurement – which is an absolute necessity to develop credibility inside the organization. Procurement professionals need to become business savvy – professional; polished; intelligent; respected; influential; persuasive; visionary; strategic; sharp; global; collaborative.

- The increased possibilities brought about by the technological developments will free up procurement professionals to focus on more strategic tasks – promoting these value-adding efficiency gains will be an important aspect of procurement's forward focus.

For the *value-adders*:

- Market intelligence activities will need to be developed to ensure a clear view of innovative developments and activities in the organization's supply markets, providing transparent and consistent information as well as a reduction in out-of-date information. The value added from this procurement-driven market intelligence will free up category managers to focus on core tasks and to develop relationships within the supply base.

- Reverse marketing and the achievement of preferred customer status are critical activities for the future procurement professional. By developing preferred customer status, the procurement function needs to fully embrace the notion of reverse marketing and it needs to become part of the DNA of category management. Recommendations regarding this activity include:

  - put your best and brightest people on to joint NPD activity;

  - customize your products to the customer's preference;

  - offer preferential treatment to the supplier if bottlenecks in pro-duction occur;

  - offer innovations first;

  - enter into exclusive agreements.

For those procurement organizations seen as the practice *leaders*:

- They will develop dedicated resources to uncover innovations and will better manage their supply markets worldwide. These highly specialized procurement professionals will work closely with other functions in the organization to ensure optimal relationships to drive the value-adding opportunities offered by the supply market.

- Buyer–supplier lines will blur – supply management professionals will look to extract more value from suppliers in coming years. But it won't always be about improving processes. Rather, it will be about leveraging supplier resources and integrating supplier functions one-to-one with your own.

Dedicated technologies such as smartphones, tablets, embedded chips and other not-yet imagined devices will create a massively mobile work environment for procurement professionals and suppliers alike. As procurement and supplier communities collaborate, buyers and sellers will increasingly rely upon digital trading networks and communities that allow them to quickly and easily discover each other, connect and collaborate.

Procurement has spent the last decade looking backward, at money spent last year, supplier performance in the past week, month or quarter. The coming decade will bring information and models that look forward as procurement intelligence moves into context, with full visibility regarding spend, risk and performance available by 2020. Ready access to accurate, timely, structured internal and external business intelligence will create unprecedented capability to synthesize information in support of decision making.

A global perspective on technological advances

The United States leads the way in the application of social media applications for business and this is radically changing the way that business is done. The application and leverage of these tools will open up the opportunity to maximize the benefits to be derived from open innovation. Driving open innovation in terms of creating a new enabler role for procurement – one that maximizes the leadership aspects of world class procurement teams – is an imperative:

- In Europe we are seeing the development of new technologies as possibly the most significant aspect of the trend; the threat of being surpassed by Eastern technologies is the stay-awake issue. Driving innovation via partnerships and collaboration will become the new normal.

- Goodbye products, hello solutions – suppliers in this decade will continue to take on bigger chunks of things they already do for their customers. Think of it as 'turbo-charged integrated supply', where suppliers step out of their comfort zones to drive customer performance.

- Finally, the timing of customer–supplier collaboration will shift; today, suppliers may be asked to contribute ideas to existing designs or to help fix existing processes. By 2024 they will be more consistently in on the ground floor.

In Asia-Pacific, and specifically China the goal seems to be emulation of the US system with similar levels of success. Efficiency gains are their major challenge in global terms – giving procurement a strategic goal brings added value in terms of market expertise and innovation through close proximity to the supply base; and yet there is a difficult balance here between effectiveness set against their desire for efficiency.

Game changer no. 3: globalization

Globalization has accelerated market interconnectedness, and fundamental market changes have spread between highly integrated markets as a result. Coping with international terrorism, tsunamis, sovereign-debt defaults, volatility of commodity prices and other crises are now a central feature of our increasingly complex business world. Risk management has become the recurrent theme of the decade; organizations need to react and adapt more quickly to developing market conditions and increase their ability to forecast changes. Changing supply market structures also need to be better understood and assimilated quickly.

Access to and availability of raw materials will become ever-more critical (see trend no. 1 above). Growing demand from markets with insatiable appetites for raw materials, such as China, are driving up prices, and since this is triggered (in China's case) by state-owned enterprises (SOEs) utilizing sovereign wealth funds, these activities are impacting global markets and prices – for example Chinalco's acquisition of the Toromocho mines in Peru in 2008. Governments will be pushed to the brink by deals like this, some to emulate them, others to cope with the fallout from them.

We are witnessing an evolution in the role that governments play in business, especially in the developing economies where they are prioritizing both national interests and local companies. But as protectionism is anticipated over the next several years in the light of this, in the longer term global free markets will rebalance, making the unrestricted circulation of goods and services a global reality. Derivatives too are creating an artificial scarcity – driven by speculation on the financial markets using raw materials as an alternative to financial investments – the volatility of commodity prices created by this activity and markets generally will increase as a consequence of the fact that demand is being artificially stimulated.

Then there is the ever-present spectre of peak oil, expected between now and 2050 to continue to impact markets and consequently prices.[7] Whilst there is no certainty regarding peak oil, or the consequences of it, this hypothetical event continues to send out ripples of uncertainty.

In the aftermath of the 2008 financial crisis and the uncertain economics of the eurozone today, it has become clear that the proximity of economies also quickens the pace of imbalances. Given the foregoing, we should be asking the following questions:

- Were the supply chain woes from the earthquake in Japan in 2011 predictable?
- Are we living beyond risk mitigation and living in a business world where risk must be weighed up on its probability and not our ability to avoid it?
- Given the misapplication of lean, do we need to think about risk and rational, regional, practical supply chains?

Furthermore, growing political activism has to be anticipated as times get tougher and competition accelerates. On the one hand, increasingly rare resources will be used as a political as well as an economic weapon; and on the other, in the race to make the most effective economic and technological advances market leaders will look for sovereign wealth funds to ensure their position. Protectionism seems the likely outcome of all this, but we are not seeing it. This kind of political activism leads to instability, primarily in non-democratic high-growth economies such as China where decisions can be taken instantly, leaving little reaction time for businesses caught up in it.

The challenge for procurement is quite clear. It must adapt to these changes through a solid risk-and-event-management approach, recognizing how changes in political and macroeconomic environments impact their ability to assure supply:

- Risk management needs to become more proactive, linking a deep understanding of the organization's value chain with its knowledge of its supply markets. Moreover, procurement needs to develop intelligence regarding alternatives in terms of suppliers, materials and geographical sources.

- Security of supply is and will remain the number one critical role for the procurement function. As raw material shortages grow, the strategic role of procurement professionals will come to the fore. These procurement people will need to be able to develop the right relationships with suppliers and understand how, for example, to use financial instruments to hedge risk. Understanding the political environments of their suppliers' countries will increase too, as conflicts of interest become an increasing barrier to trade.

- Finally, procurement professionals will have to manage reputational risk relating to the tiers of their supply chains. These risks, alluded to in trend no. 1 above in relation to CSR, have to be managed by the proximity of the buyer to the supplier through close relationships – it will depend too on the impact of procurement on policy making and setting and the development of mandated industry standards.

How is procurement responding to globalization?

For *achievers*:

- Risk management has to become far more focused than it is today, working more closely with the corporate risk unit and across other business units so as to understand all risks and adopting an holistic approach for assessing the impact of supply risks for the organization as a whole. Furthermore, the scope of analysed risk has to be extended to include not only financial and operational risk but also strategic and environmental ones.

- The mindset of procurement towards its role in managing risk should be one where everyone wakes up to increased supply risk. Converging trends will make supply relationships even riskier as the decade progresses and research recently commissioned by CIPS anticipates big increases in companies' awareness around supply risk and also an expansion in their perceptions of where risk lies.

- Risk information must improve dramatically, as the general awakening around supply-related risk demands a far sharper focus on it. We will see consensus develop around how to measure risk, as more standardized and readily available third-party information and networked communities develop, where people pool data for operational risk assessment.

- Risk mitigation has to be measured consistently by a set of appropriate KPIs that are integrated in the overall procurement approach to monitoring and managing risk. All these measures should result in a more consistent selection of suppliers and a redefinition of supply strategies with consideration given to a number of risk scenarios.

The procurement organizations that see themselves as *value-adders* are:

- Increasingly developing cross-functional risk assessment protocols and the production of meaningful corporately aligned management information, leveraged through knowledge management activity and tools that will deliver a comprehensive risk evaluation capability within the organization. Not just for procurement.

- Using scenario techniques and/or Monte Carlo simulations in critical categories that will begin to deliver strategic options and flexibility for the business.[8]

The *leaders* will:

- Develop close relationships with the politicos and other decision makers connected with the supply markets they operate in. This typically only applies to organizations that have an extended global footprint. In such circumstances the goal will be to be accepted as a 'local' brand. This strategy needs to be developed over a long period and requires consistent and reliable location policies, investment in 'in-country' operations with access to senior positions by local employees.

Observations on globalization

The United States it seems has taken to a policy of 'choose your friends carefully'. Government connections will be critical but also extremely sensitive. Rigorous risk management with an acute business perspective is fast becoming an imperative. Cross-functional and fully integrated risk management approaches via SRM are becoming critical for business in the United States.

In Europe, procurement becomes the lobbying arm of the organization in a battle to avoid the spectre of protectionism. Lobbying will become a critical part of any risk management strategy – with an eye to regulation and developing influence. Risk management must become an integrated function in all smart organizations.

In Asia-Pacific there is a move away from 'annularity' as one-year budget cycles become irrelevant. Scenario planning and contingency planning from one country (in the Asia-Pacific region) in the short term become a must. Procurement has to anticipate shifts in supply chain function and capability to ensure supply.

Game changer no. 4: demographic changes

As baby boomers head towards retirement, and birth rates decline globally, the available talent pool is shrinking; traditional barriers to employment such as age and gender are being reconsidered. Geographical disparities in fertility rates will create imbalances across countries in available labour, with India having the highest potential surplus in working-age population, as will Pakistan, Bangladesh, Indonesia, Mexico and Brazil. The United States and Europe (both with declining birth rates), and China (as a consequence of its one child policy), will suffer the greatest deficits.

Recruitment and talent management and retention are fast becoming the greatest challenges for Western businesses. All organizations now face increased competition for the best and the brightest people from businesses in the developing economies. Entry into and retention of women in the workplace is being seen as one of the immediate solutions to the talent issue.[9]

As the mobility of talent becomes ever more fluid, Western Europe will no longer attract the best and the brightest as it did for so long. Whilst it is still an attractive destination for workers from the United States, Australasia and Eastern Europe; it is Southeast Asia, Brazil and Africa that are snapping up knowledge workers from the developed economies.[10]

The availability and mobility of human resources will radically change by 2020. Whilst availability will move from the developed to the developing economies, overall mobility will decrease; young and skilled people will become less mobile, even in regional contexts, and people will be more likely to remain where their personal ties are strongest. That said, the unskilled will join an exodus to the Middle East or China, where the crane-dominated skylines are throwing up cities and skyscrapers while we stand and watch.

Availability of skilled talent is likely to come from India: with its over-capacity and the fact that it produces more university graduates than anywhere else in the world it could become the most attractive talent exporter on the face of the globe. It is the sheer size of India's surplus and the fact that they are English-speaking that is the non-negotiable competitive advantage for India's workforce. However, India and China will still lag in terms of average years of education in comparison to the global top three – Germany, the United States and Korea.[11] One final point, in the Middle East we are witnessing 'youth bulges' driving huge sociopolitical change – think the recent Arab Spring – and a very demanding new workforce looking for employment.

The single biggest issue is the demographic time bomb; whilst mobility will be enhanced by technological developments and we are seeing a softening of cultural differences, the increasing sedentary nature of society means that people will stay put, and this only lends itself to an upsurge in the war for talent. In effect, talented people will increasingly have their personal needs met by employers who fight to attract the best. This leaves behind the long tail of the less talented and less educated, who in turn will have to move further and further in search of better education and/or remuneration. Here we will see increasing flows of the workforce between the high-growth markets and the next emerging countries/economies. We are currently witnessing unprecedented migrations of workers between India and boom-time UAE, and between China and African countries.

For global organizations these evolving patterns of migration will pose real challenges. Attracting and retaining skilled workers will be more difficult than ever. In adapting to these changes organizations will have to develop new models allowing individual time planning and extended work–life balance in Western economies; whilst in Asia employers will be dealing with an expectation of regular promotion, salary increases and rapid personal growth through adapted or fragmented hierarchical structures.

At the same time, global corporates will have to find the right balance between local presence and international direction in order to remain attractive to a workforce that increasingly demands to be employed by a 'local' organization. As seniority with delegated responsibility moves to high-growth markets, confidence in and the loyalty of local management will be critical to success.

The consequence of this is that issues such as diversity and social and economic inclusion will gain in importance. The United States and Republic of South Africa (RSA) have long been aware of these issues – due to their respective legacies of segregation and apartheid. In Europe, and to a lesser extent Asia, these issues are becoming very high on both political and business agendas. As relationships play such a critical role in modern business, and especially in procurement, diversity is becoming an essential facet of the function.

The challenges outlined above regarding demographic change will have to be faced by all organizations over the next decade. More importantly, procurement professionals will be impacted more than any other business function. Whilst procurement professionals are dashing around the globe in search of the most reliable, cost-efficient, innovative and value-adding suppliers, they are often the first movers in markets where the organization is not equally active on the sales side. Having a global presence requires a deep understanding of local custom and practice – so the rapport between the buyer and the supplier is paramount. A diverse procurement team is a must.

With the shift in the economic centre of gravity from West to East, it follows that procurement organizations will move too. In the coming decades, the Asian consumer market will grow to become much larger than the combined consumer markets of the United States and Europe. The best-practice supply chain solutions of the West will be transferred to Asia, while new supply chain solutions unique to Asia will also be developed locally and successfully deployed.[12] Businesses will need to attract and retain a workforce despite not having the 'local' tag, and be able to demonstrate that there will be equal opportunities for their new recruits, allowing them to reach middle- and top-management positions.

Procurement's role is also likely to increase in complexity as the function evolves – procurement professionals will need to be technically savvy, internal networkers, supply-base developers and innovation magnates – the future procurement professional will need to be so much more than a buyer. Knowledge of the end-to-end supply chain, the ability to address internal customer needs and an authority on the intricacies of the supply market will become de rigueur.

Category management will also demand a new breed – an entrepreneurial approach with strong leadership skills will be the fundamentals. The sourcing-geek's days are numbered; whilst they may be highly valued in today's marketplace, people who excel at (sourcing) processes or at being big-time users of procurement and sourcing automation technologies – the 'doers' will find themselves working for third-party service providers, or not at all! The enablers – value-adders – will rule!

Procurement's strategy scope must widen. Much has been achieved in the past decade to transform procurement from tactical to strategic. But the idea of 'strategic' remains to some extent hemmed inside the function, the process or the spend category. With a cultured understanding of the (strategic) value-adding capability of procurement – the meaning of strategic is going to get much bigger. If procurement as a career is to become more attractive, it needs to both answer the challenges set by these global mega trends and those set by its evolution from 'doer' to 'enabler'.

Finally, procurement needs to attract the best from the millennials,[13] Generation Y and increasingly Generation Z, who as they scramble for money and status, and go in search of jobs, will bring a different set of priorities to the generation who went before them. They care less about salaries, and more about flexible working, time to travel and a better work–life balance. And employers will have to meet their demands. As well as working with and employing a different generational cohort, procurement will need to fundamentally change the way it works and is perceived. Be it through adapted job rotation schemes, where to some extent strategic business units (SBUs) absorb procurement or where the future brings a loose network rather than a tight function. A world of supplier-facing professionals needs to be embedded into strategic business lines, communities and processes wherever needed, constantly moving and reinventing their roles as needs shift.

How is procurement responding to these demographic shifts?

For the *achievers*:

- The procurement revolution has made it a much more attractive career of choice. Career paths can be developed around procurement and supply management (P&SM); the scope and complexity offered by the modern P&SM role demands a broader skill set and differentiated competencies ranging from technical, category specific, financial and legal to name but a few. On the 'soft (social) skills' side, procurement professionals need to be culturally aware, collaborative and innovative, with leadership skills and the ability to work across functional boundaries.

For the *value-adding* procurement professional:

- There is an immediate need to raise their internal profile and build credibility by promoting – but not selling – procurement. They need to become internal brokers of value, reflecting the scope and nature of the modern role they fulfil.

- Leadership programmes should be developed to meet the new skills requirements of these business-savvy procurement professionals: polished, intelligent, respected, influential, persuasive, visionary, strategic, sharp, global and collaborative executives.

- Job rotation is absolutely necessary to attract skilled individuals who will bring all the necessary language and capability to move across functional boundaries and be able to integrate with colleagues in other business units. Procurement should work closely with HR professionals to develop the best and brightest and place them on to high-potential career paths.

As for the *leaders*:

- A decreasing trend in mobility and the increasing need for specific skills will be supported by the advent of virtual offices. This in itself might well increase the attractiveness of non-traditional workplaces. Virtual offices are an excellent means of reflecting the bottom-line impact of an improvement in work–life balance.
- Due to the different challenges in attracting and retaining people, differentiated strategies for retention (eg awards/promotion) and recruitment have to be developed, based on defined career path prospects and personalized working-time models. Employees should have more flexibility and freedom of choice on how, when and from where they will be working. The organization has to give its employees time for their own ideas and for developing their own input into the organization's development.

New office concepts are redesigning the office space to create comfort zones to compensate for the stress, monotony and lack of options in day-to-day business. Avant-garde work spaces, bringing family life to the fore during evening hours and moving people into homeworking: the way we are working will continue to evolve around putting the employee at the centre of the equation.

A global perspective on demographic changes

In the United States, diversity and social and economic inclusion sit at the heart of HR and procurement people strategies. Talent shortages will rise by 2024. As diversity programmes develop, and procurement becomes ever more complex, skills and competency mixes will develop alongside them.

In both mainland Europe and the UK diversity and social and economic inclusion are growing issues, both in employment and the supply base. Procurement has to develop its reputation and strategic impact within the organization. Cross-functional working, supported by placements and rotation, will become the norm.

In China and Asia-Pacific, performance is king! Diversity is not explicitly on the agenda but social and economic inclusion is. As China builds internal consumption patterns, talent must 'stay at home' and talent retention will be critical to maintain performance. Corruption will remain a challenge. Career paths and the development of local leadership talent in procurement is critical – regular promotion amongst the best and brightest is also a critical component in this region.

Game changer no. 5: the shift in the global economic centre of gravity

Demand for the product of traditional industries is increasingly shifting to developing economies, while demand for new products adapted to service an ageing population is dramatically increasing in Western economies. The developing economies – the high-growth markets predominantly in the East – will continue to drive economic growth. Economic power and the centre of gravity is shifting away from the West and re-establishing itself in the Asia-Pacific rim. In addition to this shift in the centre of economic gravity, today's low-cost economies such as China will cease to have the now well-accepted advantage of low labour cost. Whilst Chinese labour costs are rising and will continue to rise, they are still some way behind those of the developed economies. In China the average annual salary is around £3,000 per annum and in the UK around £25,000. That said, Chinese labour costs will grow by 2020 and labour costs in other BRIC countries – particularly Brazil – are already on a par with Eastern Europe.[14] The question here is – considering globalization, increased logistics costs, increasing levels of risk and rising labour costs – whether now is the time for a serious reconsideration of the status quo.

Where should future global sourcing benefits come from given the foregoing? Will we soon be looking at something aligned to 'embedded procurement'? That is, establishing procurement teams locally, making them agile and in touch with what is happening in the particular region; and at the same time maintaining a focus on the limitations of global sourcing.

Europe, the United States and Japan will continue to have slow GDP growth and China is predicted to become the second biggest economy by 2020. India too will continue to experience high growth; Brazil will grow dynamically with a focus on its massive resource in raw materials, its engineering base and the potential for renewables such as biofuels; and Russia's growth will centre particularly on raw materials' export and energy.

The rapid growth too of middle-class consumers in the developing econo-mies, such as but not limited to the BRIC countries, will spawn a new gen-eration of globally competitive companies to cater for the needs of these consumers, and will be a critical measure for innovation and a launch pad for new consumer products. By 2034 the global middle class will expand by something in the region of three billion people, principally in develop-ing economies, and will be a springboard for growth for the next 30 or so years. This is because the emerging middle classes around the world will follow Western expenditure and consumption patterns, centring in the fast-developing urbanizations in India and China, with more than 50 per cent of the world's population living in these megacities.

Economic growth and opportunities will be concentrated in the urban areas and this will trigger increasing business opportunities arising from the development and growth of these megacities – principally involving building materials, sanitation, water treatment and green technologies. Leveraging this potential requires massive local investment, and doubtless global cor-porates will want to position themselves as part of this local growth if they want to be part of this unfolding market opportunity.

This shift in the economic centre of gravity will profoundly change the global business environment by 2020. Markets in the Asia-Pacific rim and South America are experiencing phenomenal growth and will continue to do so, following a similar trajectory to that experienced in recent years, buoyed by the anticipated exponential rise in consumption as millions join the middle classes in those economies.

Markets, described by Jim O'Neill as 'the Next 11' (N-11),[15] which are currently viewed as global 'extended workbenches',[16] will grow out of this role to become innovation sources in their own right and, as a consequence, the low-cost advantage once obtained through this trend will facilitate the move to still less developed economies. It is no secret that, in anticipa-tion of this, many global corporates and some of the businesses from the high-growth economies are already investing heavily in the N-11 coun-tries, anticipating the soon-to-be-gained advantages. China in particular is investing hugely in Africa. An adjunct to this change too is that European and US businesses will (as alluded to above) become increasingly depend-ent on growth outside of their national boundaries. This shift in the global centre of gravity will be the major challenge to business in the very near future.

The emerging middle classes in Asia and South America will have the aspiration for a 'Western' lifestyle but with their own very particular cul-tural and individual tastes. This will bring with it more complexity and a need for many businesses to re-evaluate and, in many cases, overhaul their product portfolios to service this new demand. One particularly interesting phenomenon is that of the increasing number of DINKs in China.[17] These households drive the dynamics of the market trends described above and are defining today what the standard in China is likely to be over the coming years.

To fully understand and be able to benefit from these trends and developing needs, a strong regional presence will become a must. Most global corporates will have to shift their mindset from the classic multinational corporate (MNC) mindset to a network mindset. Management will still be global, but regional activity and foci will be driven by their knowledge of contingent consumer markets.

Procurement has become one of the most important functions enabling cost-effective international growth for MNCs, as the markets they exploit are low-cost sources prior to their developments into sales markets – smart procurement professionals are active in these markets long before sales or marketing executives are even interested in them. Therefore, procurement will often hold deep business intelligence regarding them. As such, the challenge will be to couple the knowledge developed by P&SM with emerging consumer intelligence to develop a more complete vision of the needs of the market. The focus for procurement is to be seen as the enabler – the 'go-to' source – and to develop intelligence through cross-functional collaborative working.

It is well documented that supplier markets in high-growth economies are far more fractured and in many cases more dynamic than those in the West. As a consequence, procurement must closely monitor the supply market conditions in order to identify those suppliers that are willing to peruse 'downstream' integration strategies and potentially become competitors. The exchange of intelligence with these suppliers has to be carried out in such a fashion that intellectual property rights are not compromised.

There is absolutely no doubt that complexity in P&SM will increase as these supply markets grow and develop. It will be critical for P&SM to develop network approaches to their activities, fostering flexible management intelligence and decision-making regimens. To meet the needs of internal stakeholders a differentiated business model has to be adopted – so different approaches might be taken in-country to meet the needs of the local market as opposed to those applied to meet the needs of, for example, an export market, even if both business units ultimately deliver to the same SBU. In addition, P&SM's role will grow further as the need to be seen as a 'local' player becomes a prerequisite for collaboration with suppliers.

How is procurement responding to this shift in economic power?

For the *achiever* procurement organization, a 'local presence' is critical in high-growth markets and the development by the function of local procurement capability to meet this need is a given. The scope of local sourcing capability will depend on the perceived needs of the internal stakeholder and will be predicated on the demands of local customers. Probably the most effective way of meeting this need would be to establish an office with the capacity for expansion at a later date and to which decision-making authority can easily be delegated.

For the *value-adder*, local knowledge and intelligence capability is critical in high-growth markets – these functions need to be populated with teams with an explicit focus on the development of new business in the regions identified as ripe for exploitation. Here proximity to local suppliers, customers and decision makers is paramount.

Amongst the most forward-looking procurement organizations outsourcing will explode – many current procurement and sourcing activities, the ones that do not get redistributed to internal end users of goods and services, as mentioned above, will be outsourced by the end of the decade. And increasingly service providers will call the shots. With fast-growing demand for procurement outsourcing, both the quantity and quality of third-party procurement services will increase dramatically; their performance in many spend categories will surpass what can be achieved by an in-house equivalent.

The *leaders* are increasingly moving their procurement organizations into the growth markets, devolving into networks to bridge cultural gaps and develop competitive advantage through proximity to the supply base. This will require full integration with the internal organization of the business unit.

A global market intelligence capability within procurement to identify the hotspots will define investment decisions and focus new market development activity based on their prior knowledge of the supply market in the region.

A global perspective on the economic power shift

In the United States the shift in the economic centre of gravity to Asia has had a profound effect on its position in the world today. New organizational and business models, which can accommodate centralization set against the regional disparities, will be the major challenge. Procurement must establish itself centre stage as the monitor of shifting activity from home to offshore markets – only move if you absolutely have to.

Across Europe the maxim has become 'think global, act local'. What will be critical for success will be the ability of organizations to move from an 'HQ' mindset to a networked one – with the capability of developing a sustainable local brand in the high-growth markets. There are strong indications that to be successful procurement will have to decamp overseas to where the action is.

For the whole of the Asia-Pacific, market growth is set to continue. Close identification of the new market opportunities is critical as is, from the Asian perspective, developing knowledge of the complex legal requirements of export markets. Procurement has to vision where the emerging markets will develop next.

As organizations expand their global reach, more and more companies will need to consider how to engage suppliers and drive these types of relationships. One company that has learned quickly how to do so (as well as Honda) is Toyota. The case study that follows provides insights into how they structured supplier councils as a way to engage and work with suppliers not just in Japan, but all over the world, and harness their ideas and innovations.

CASE STUDY Tiered supplier partnership and supplier association models

The tiered supplier partnership (Kyoryoku Kai) model has become the current paradigm of best practice, even for firms in other industries. This model incorporates progressive steps in vendor certification, plus activities such as quality audits, supplier rationalization, joint problem solving, open-book negotiation, cost transparency and buyer–supplier collaboration in new product development (NPD).[18] Due to the positive publicity and generated results, various electronics firms (for example, Hitachi and Ricoh) and the aerospace industry have used tiered supplier partnerships. This approach is probably less relevant for high-tech industries whose products are evolving rapidly and for companies that make simple products or highly customized products in small batches.[19]

Firms in the automotive industry have reported startling results from seamlessly integrating suppliers into their operations, distribution and NPD. These successes have established targets for other companies to achieve world-class status by emulating best practices in the auto industry. The auto industry is highly concentrated, with high volumes, considerable component engineering input and limited product life. A firm trying to implement these approaches that does not have similar structural characteristics may risk failure or severely limit the true potential of their supply base.[20]

Tiered supplier partnerships link automotive firms to their key subsystem suppliers. The model recommends tiers of suppliers, with top-tier suppliers having increased roles as systems integrators. In the tiered approach, the auto assembler (the buying company) deals primarily with the top-tier suppliers, while those above them manage lower-tier suppliers in the pyramid. Establishing tiers of suppliers *according to their competence* permits auto assemblers to manage the NPD process more effectively by involving these primary suppliers in the design and development process of next-generation products. Using their expertise and knowledge can prevent problems at the critical design stage, develop the product faster and suggest alternative designs that help to meet target costs.

The tiered supplier partnership model incorporates progressive steps in vendor certification, plus activities such as quality audits, supplier rationalization, joint problem solving, open-book negotiation, cost transparency and buyer–supplier collaboration in NPD.

Supplier association

Supplier associations diffuse technological development back through the supply chain. Some final assemblers, such as Toyota, have added supplier associations to their arsenal to further improve supply chain management and effectiveness. Toyota, often viewed as the leader in the development of such supplier associations, has organized its top-tier suppliers into supplier associations in order to diffuse Toyota's best practices and support long-term development. These associations help to standardize quality control procedures, facilitate supplier interactions and provide a forum to build trust among member firms. The idea is that Toyota wants its key suppliers to form their own supplier associations for the pyramid's next tier, thereby cascading the concept down the entire supply network. By combining these two approaches (tiered partnership and supplier association), Toyota has gained a powerful advantage in its domestic market. An example of Toyota's supplier council structure is shown in Figure 4.1.

FIGURE 4.1 Supplier association

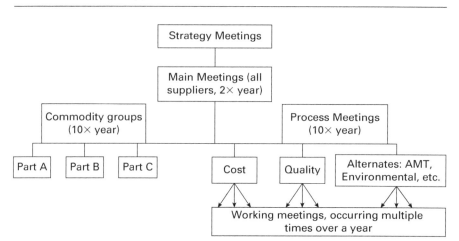

People who represent supplier companies in a council are typically executive level (CEO, CPO, VP and, sometimes, director level). Buying companies are represented by the executive office, VPs, directors and select managers.

A key to the success of these initiatives is to reserve different relationships for those suppliers with the potential to contribute to technological innovation and product design. ICL, a UK-based computer company uses the tiered supplier partnership model as part of their supplier rationalization process. It categorizes suppliers into four classes: member, preferred, partner and alliance, with only six firms receiving the alliance classification.[21]

There has been a widespread move towards the tiered approach, but supplier associations have not become as prevalent. Few companies have developed the first-tier suppliers as Toyota did when indoctrinating its key suppliers in the 1960s and 1970s. Typically, firms manage the first-tier suppliers independently of one another. Within Toyota, the supplier association concept has not been universally adopted.

Many firms have implemented the tiered supplier method even if their industries do not have the automotive supply chain's clear hierarchy. Some firms selected first-tier suppliers based on the following:

- Pareto analysis of dollar value.

- Non-substitutability of the supplied materiel.

- Unit volumes of purchases.

It is critical to select suppliers that can support product development and those suppliers that can effectively manage the next tier of the supply chain.

Weaknesses in the tiered model

First, without supplier associations, the model becomes a paired relationship, with independent relationships between the buyer and each of its preferred suppliers. This does not allow for cross-collaboration among suppliers during NPD (see Figure 4.2). If managers think in terms of paired relationships, they may not see the possibility of synergies. This approach fails to incorporate the supplier's needs for broader-based growth, reducing the potential for wider synergies and limiting the scope for innovation. A supplier in this kind of relationship is likely to focus on the important customer's specific needs and may ignore attractive markets and alternative technologies that might have broader application. Innovations derived from vertical collaborations (supplier partnerships) will be significantly less 'new' than if the partners are from different industries, if the sole rationale is technological innovation, or if the collaborators are aligned horizontally (for example, a research joint venture).[22]

The tiered supplier partnership model assumes that what is in the best interest of the buyer is in the best interest of the supplier, and that technological synergies are best achieved along the value-added chain. Relationships based on this model are likely to produce minor, incremental technological innovations. If a firm needs radical or business process re-engineering, the tiered approach may not be the best fit.

Second, the tiered model does not expect the supplier to contribute beyond the product or service or to undertake projects that do not support the buyer's specific objectives. The reported successes of the tiered model (for example, Toyota) have a common structural feature: industry commonality between the buyer and the supplier. The relationship is based on the product

FIGURE 4.2 Paired relationships between buyer–supplier in the tiered model

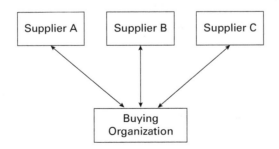

or services exchange and a supplier's willing involvement in a buyer's NPD is predicated on its follow-on role as the continuing provider. The tiered supplier model thrives in situations where a few large, powerful buyers influence the scope and direction of the supplier community's organizational learning and development.[23]

Third, the tiered supplier model clearly focuses on benefiting the buyer. Suppliers do gain from improved information flow, process improvements, increased leverage, reduced risk and growth, along with the buyer's success in increasing market share. Essentially in the tiered model, the direct benefits of marketplace success go to the buyer, whereas the supplier's rewards are mostly indirect or limited to market-share gains at the expense of the buyer's rival.

Toyota's emphasis on trust and collaborative supplier forums should 'not obscure the fact that the primary function of the supplier association for the assembler is to control suppliers and subcontractors'.[24] In many cases, relative power and supplier commitment may eventually determine a partnership's strength and longevity.

Leveraged learning network or supplier consortium

Rather than being a paired relationship structure, the supplier consortium is a series of small networks with common learning objectives. The networks have strong informal communication links, although in many cases, the firms have no business-to-business links. Because of overlapping interests, some firms span more than one network (see Figure 4.3).

The facilitator holds the entire group together through continuous information flows and acts as an information gatekeeper, providing promotional material, newsletters, weekly updates and book reviews. The facilitator integrates the consortium, ensuring that transferring it to the larger group leverages the learning and expertise developed within one smaller network.

The learning network emphasizes organizational learning within the supplier firm, instead of its superior performance yielding increased responsibility. In a learning network, performance becomes an outcome instead of a requirement for advancement to the top tier.

The leveraged learning network is an option in cases where the buyer needs to improve the performance of its supplier base but has neither the relative power nor the resources to induce the necessary improvements. For example, Toyota uses control through supplier associations; Allen Bradley (a much

FIGURE 4.3 Leveraged learning network

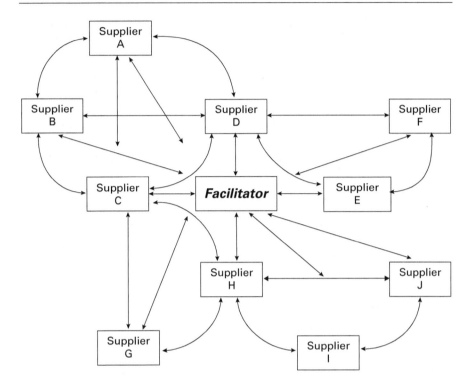

smaller electronics manufacturer) uses collaboration not a dictatorial model in implementing a supplier consortium.[25]

Limitations to the leveraged learning network

- Any advantages from the group's combined efforts can be undermined by perceived inequities in members' commitment and effort.

- Some of the more powerful members may exercise hidden or subordinated power.

- The buyer may gain considerable leverage for its efforts, but at the expense of control.

- It is unclear as to what environment is most conducive for a leveraged learning environment.

The effectiveness of a consortium relies on the facilitator, who must be able to assess needs and ensure that topics presented are relevant (see Table 4.1).

TABLE 4.1 Comparison of models

Relationship Form and Structure		
	Supplier Partnerships	**Toyota's Kyoryoku Kai**	**Leveraged Learning Network**
Participation Criteria	Proven performance yields increased responsibility	Performance and technical competence	Willingness to learn and teach others
Gainsharing Approach	Buyer-based objectives and buyer-dominated focus	Buyer-based objectives and equitable benefits	Collective advancement and benefits
Commonality	Product-specific focus	No difference	Holistic learning focus
Synergistic Emphasis	Synergy through paired cooperation	Synergy through paired and networked cooperation	Synergy through collective learning and wisdom
Dependency	Shared mutual destiny	No difference	Shared vision and leadership
Outcomes	Performance-based	No change	Organizational learning for improved performance
Trust and control	Explicit control. Competency trust	Implicit control. Habitualization trust	Inapplicable control/goodwill trust

NB Trust terms are based on B. Nooteboom *et al* (1997) 'Effects of trust and governance on relational risk'.

Critical success factors

Prioritize key initiatives:

- Divide and conquer tasks. Don't bite off more than you can chew, especially in the early stages of council implementation.

- Listen to suppliers even if it is not related to objectives.

- Have a good mix of people in the working groups, such as production and logistics, operations, sales, supply chain, etc – when appropriate.

- There must be cultural alignment between supplier and buyer.

- There must be commitment and follow-through by suppliers' top managements.

- Share risk and reward.

- There must be buy-in from supply chain management as well as internal customers. To accomplish this, it is critical for supply chain management senior executives to share their vision to their counterparts in other departments. There must be integration of goals (business level strategy) of different departments. This can be facilitated if supply chain management and its in-house customers report to the same senior VP.

- The council should be a non-threatening, non-competitive forum for exchange of ideas that benefit all parties. Incorporate inter-firm mechanisms as another tool to ensure council success.

- Understand supply chain power with network. This could significantly influence network relationships.

Some conclusions

In this chapter we have seen how procurement is increasingly gaining control over its main purpose – the procurement of goods and services for the organization. However, in this modern era, procurement professionals are facing a variety of broader challenges. All organizations are rapidly investing in new technologies to meet the challenges of procurement in the contemporary, global marketplace; however, procurement often lacks the skills required to take full advantage of these tools and circumstances.

As scrutiny of organizations' environmental and ethical practices increases, there is also a requirement for procurement to understand the implications of its corporate responsibility and sustainability within the supply chain. Efforts to make a bigger contribution to corporate strategy continue, but sometimes at the cost of misunderstandings between the profession and the rest of the business. And yet procurement has much expertise to offer, which can provide substantial financial benefits. Convincing colleagues across the business of this, and aligning not just goals but thinking about where the profession can – and cannot – add value, is potentially the biggest challenge in the years ahead.

That said, the only certain thing about the future is increased volatility and the consequential uncertainty it brings. But this is no reason for not trying to anticipate what may happen, or for not trying to shape developments for the better. It is true to say that the only way to predict the future is by helping to shape it.

Notes

1 Droege, P (2008) *Urban Energy Transition: From fossil fuels to renewable power*, Elsevier, Oxford.

2 Rogers, P, Jalal, K F and Boyd, J A (2008) *An Introduction to Sustainable Development*, Earthscan, London.

3 Fearne, A *et al* (2009) Sustainable value chain analysis: a case study of South Australian wine. A report prepared for the Government of South Australia, January.

4 Asia-Pacific is the part of the world in or near the Western Pacific Ocean. The region varies in size depending on context, but it typically includes much of East Asia, Southeast Asia and Oceania.

5 Christensen, C (1997) *The Innovator's Dilemma: When new technologies cause great firms to fail*, Harvard Business School Press, Boston.

6 Open innovation is a term promoted by Henry Chesbrough, in his book *Open Innovation*.

7 First created by M King Hubbert in 1956, peak oil is the point in time when the maximum rate of global petroleum extraction is reached, after which the rate of production enters terminal decline.

8 The Monte Carlo method (established in the 1940s by John von Neumann, Stanislaw Ulam and Nicholas Metropoli) are a class of computational algorithms that rely on repeated random sampling to compute their results.

9 McKinsey Quarterly (2011) How women can contribute more to the US economy, *McKinsey Quarterly*, April.

10 Knowledge workers in today's workforce are individuals who are valued for their ability to act and communicate with knowledge within a specific subject area. The phrase was first coined by Peter Drucker in 1966.

11 OECD, Deutsche Bank.

12 Paul W Bradley, Asian Supply Chain Manager of the Year, Lloyds FTB Publications in 2004.

13 Millennials (also known as the millennial generation or Generation Y) are the demographic cohort following Generation X. There are no precise dates when the generation starts and ends. Researchers and commentators use birth years ranging from the early 1980s to the early 2000s.

14 O'Neill, J (2001) Building better global economic BRICs, *Goldman Sachs Global Economics Paper*, No 153, 28 March 2007. BRIC, an acronym coined by Jim O'Neill, refers to Brazil, Russia, India and China, which are all deemed to be at a similar stage of newly advanced economic development.

15 O'Neill, J (2001) Building better global economic BRICs. The 'Next 11' – Bangladesh, Egypt, Indonesia, Iran, Mexico, Nigeria, Pakistan, Philippines, South Korea, Turkey and Vietnam – are described by Jim O'Neill to be the follow-on from the BRIC economies.

16 Maurer, J (2011) Relationships between foreign subsidiaries, DOI 10.1007/978–3–8349–6249–2_2, Gabler Verlag | Springer Fachmedien Wiesbaden GmbH. The term describes 'in-country' subsidiaries or local industry performing as extended workbenches to their corporate activities.

17 DINK is used to describe high-earning couples who do not have children and are therefore able to afford a more expensive consumer lifestyle than those with families.

18 Paul, D *et al* (1998) Case study: a leveraged learning network, *Sloan Management Review*, Summer.

19 Kamath, R and Liker, J (1994) A second look at Japanese product development, *Harvard Business Review*, November–December.

20 Paul, D *et al* (1998) Case study: a leveraged learning network.

21 Paul, D *et al* (1998) Case study: a leveraged learning network.

22 Kotabe, M and Swan, K (1995) The role of strategic alliance in high-technology new product development, *Strategic Management Journal*, November.

23 Miles, R and Snow, C (1992) Causes of failure in network organizations, *California Management Review*, Summer.

24 Paul, D *et al* (1998) Case study: a leveraged learning network.

25 Paul, D *et al* (1998) Case study: a leveraged learning network.

Taking a practical approach to improvement
Introducing the ACE model

05

I n the previous chapter we looked at the five game-changing trends that have necessitated organizations to re-evaluate how they operate and how they utilize the service functions within them to best meet new vision and capabilities needed to survive and thrive in the modern business world. Procurement must approach these issues in the knowledge that incremental changes will not do. In doing so, it must embrace a vision that goes far beyond the thinking of today, leveraging creativity and know-how to change not just the function from within, but the overall business value it delivers.

In developing and deploying procurement's true value proposition to the business, everything it has learned and practised from the past, and classic maturity model thinking, must be put in context. Modest changes in capability and thinking can help but will not bring the value that modern business demands.

In this chapter we offer some insights into how a procurement organization can interrogate the maturity model introduced in Chapter 2, and reflect too on the notion of the game-changing trends described in Chapter 4. From here, we look at ways in which we can practically develop capability and execution via procurement to deliver a greater contribution to strategy. We also look at ways in which the function can continue to remove the misunderstandings between itself and the rest of the business.

What do we aspire to be? Aligning procurement's value and capabilities

To realize the full potential of the procurement function, it is important to understand the alignment between its levels of capability and execution. In doing so we can uncover how value is delivered into the business in terms of the service mix, ie how procurement performs. Performance is measured in terms of capability levels – what level of capability do we have today or need to change? This is allied to the question of how well do we execute – how efficient and effective is procurement in the execution of its role?

Implementing the ACE model

Given the foregoing, it is critical to make sure that the capability levels we develop are aligned to some sort of demonstrable value proposition – via Aspiration, Capability and Execution. We introduce the notion of the ACE model (Figure 5.1 on p 116) to show how the function can enhance capability and execution and accelerate its transformation further by demonstrating the expertise it has to offer, which will bring substantial financial benefits to the organization. Let's begin by taking a look at the component parts of the model:

- *A: Aspiration.* Procurement leaders have to have a clearly defined procurement vision and supporting strategy, which must explicitly articulate how it ties to corporate strategy. Any misalignment will doom the function of aspiration to failure. Setting out on this journey may begin with a PR/communications programme. Raising awareness and finding new ways to build trust within the business procurement can extend an empathetic hand to work with spend owners to improve business outcomes. This might materialize in the form of a joint exploration of demand specifications, buying decisions and supplier engagement.

    Procurement must earn the trust of the business to fully succeed. It must embrace a vision that goes far beyond current practice, by leveraging creativity and know-how to change not just the function from within, but the understanding of procurement's potential to the business as a whole.

    Procurement leaders must therefore have a strategy, which articulates this and includes a list of transformation projects to achieve their aspirations. Key will be procurement's role and impact on financial performance, risk management, supplier relationships and its impact on customer satisfaction.

- *C: Capabilities*. There is a high degree of honesty required here. In examining capabilities CPOs and their teams need to be introspective when contemplating where they are today on the procurement maturity ladder (discussed in Chapter 2). This process is important because it is the first step on the journey of capability development; and if you don't believe your story regarding where you wish to see your procurement organization, how can you expect anyone else to believe you.

So once again alignment is critical because you do not want your plans to deviate from those of the wider business. CPOs must look at the capability of their procurement team and start to uncover the gaps between the 'as is' status and the 'to be'. Are your plans realistic? The CPO must sort out this aspect across all three elements of the ACE model described below as well as, from the outset, highlighting any alignment gaps between them.

There is absolutely no doubt that the number one issue in any discussion regarding procurement capability relates to skills and talent. An organization can have the best plan and technologies in the world but with the wrong people they are worthless.

Regarding these procurement capabilities, the modern procurement function needs to understand what enabling technologies are available to them and which they need. In particular, with the increasing impact of the 'internet of things', clarity is needed within organizations regarding how they accommodate such innovations. For example, can a degree of self-service be furnished? How will they tap into the expanding issue of master data management? And how can they introduce analytics into procurement?

Finally, procurement needs to develop its understanding of process sourcing, or put another way, the art and science of 'buying'. Procurement outsourcing is critical for non-value-adding transactional work that most procurement organizations do. For example, tasks such as supply data management (catalogue management), invoice processing, PO processing and PO communications to suppliers; business process outsourcing is emerging to manage these non-core processes and spend categories.

Removing these time-consuming and mundane tasks frees up procurement teams to carry out the increasingly important and value-adding work such as market intelligence gathering and full category management.

- *E: Execution.* The effectiveness of how businesses carry out procurement has significantly improved over time, as we saw in Chapter 1; however, the focus has quite definitely shifted. Today, speed of execution and the importance of outcomes have significantly increased.

  The demands of strategic alignment will help CPOs to determine the services needed for the business to maximize the benefits that procurement brings. The delivery and management model to support strategic objectives will be built around the CPO's knowledge of the corporation. Clearly the message is to simplify processes – to reduce complexity and implement good business and procurement practices across the organization. CPOs need to know where and what to automate – this will help to reduce manual effort and errors, especially in the least intellectually stimulating areas of process. Smart IT enablement for lowest service-delivery cost is imperative and the ability to deliver leveraged standard services through service excellence will also bring the vision into being.

FIGURE 5.1   ACE – the trinity of aspiration, capability and execution

The message that good procurement is not just about cost reduction, but productivity and speed in both transactions and purchasing has to be brought to life. Not only because our most traditional procurement value proposition has been challenged due to tight and volatile supply markets, but also due to the inalienable fact that maturing procurement execution has to be seen if we are to be believed. Whilst, for the most part, the investments that organizations make in procurement continue to pay off in a traditional sense, CPOs today have to bring the new value proposition to life.

The need to tread carefully

At the same time there is a very real need for procurement to tread carefully. It remains critically important to CPOs and their teams that they ensure alignment as part of their service delivery. Below are examples of what might happen if the three elements of ACE are misaligned:

- *Aspirational*: you have a set of performance targets that are not aligned to your capabilities, and your operating model does not allow you to effectively revise your targets.

- *Capability*: CPOs are not seen to be as capable as other CXOs. As a consequence the organization does not believe that procurement has the capability to add value at their level. Conversely, CPOs might be developing their strategic procurement capability in isolation, only to find out that the capability they eventually develop is neither valued nor sponsored by the rest of the business.

- *Execution*: CPOs busy themselves working on higher-value activities, but receive minimal or no credit for them. To make matters worse, they find that they are not being measured on these activities but are still held responsible for them. Many procurement organizations become aware that they are not measured on supply assurance, yet most would probably be blamed in the event of a stock-out or some other shortage. In developing the profile and delivery excellence of their procurement teams CPOs will need to ensure that procurement is given credit for profit impact from smart supply risk management activities employed by them.

While the discussion to date might make conceptual sense, to our knowledge there have actually never been any procurement studies that have isolated, quantified and compared the notion of procurement value to procurement performance and capabilities. The latter two are more easily understood in terms of how capabilities can enable performance. However, there is a caveat and it is smart at this juncture to ask: does a more evolved procurement value proposition really compare with improved performance or do companies talk a good game but fail to deliver (or vice versa)? This might mean in practice to shake off the taboos of the past, that procurement organizations need to perform well enough to earn the right to be taken seriously – and then use that performance to leverage cash to build the new capabilities to deliver the new sources of value on its own.

Re-evaluating the procurement function

In developing a better understanding of the procurement value proposition we need in some respects to re-evaluate procurement, its role and its worth. The journey since the mid-1980s, as described above, allied to the growing demands of globalized markets demand this. In fact we need to do this for two reasons: first to ensure that what procurement is doing is current; the second reason relates to procurement's brand, PR and visibility challenges.

So in 'redefining procurement' we need to develop an understanding of what the business needs from procurement and what it is capable of; and then apply what procurement means in the 21st century to this. These differences will, if nothing else, help procurement practitioners to accelerate change, continue in their traditional role of cost reduction and protect their brand and reputation.

As has already been alluded, procurement must understand its customers; set and deploy its strategic direction; and diagnose the problems in the three elements of ACE. The goal is to improve efficiency and effectiveness, transform the way procurement operates by collaborating across the business, and ensure that the changes made are effective and, more importantly, sustainable.

Whilst cost reduction remains the cornerstone of procurement, it is no longer at a cost to enterprise growth or product or service innovation; procurement's intense focus on costs is evidenced throughout the activities and programmes of any procurement function, by let's say improving productivity and efficiency. It is also the area where executives have realized that most past and future success will be about procurement's contribution to growth innovation and product development.

If we refer back to the procurement maturity ladder, we have already discussed the fact that procurement has to get the basics right – supply assurance and cost reduction – because procurement professionals have to earn their spurs first. And quite clearly mastery of the 'foundations' is critical.

The hard facts show that there are no 'silver bullets'; procurement has to find a way to press today's and tomorrow's 'hot buttons' for the CXOs across the business. Managing costs is about moving more quickly towards agile supply chains, which allow rapid response to changing market conditions and variable cost structures that ramp up and down with revenues. In fact, one might say that this flexibility in approach is the antidote for cost volatility.

The future of supply management will depend on bringing flexibility through interconnected networks of suppliers, manufacturers and service providers that can be tapped on demand as conditions change. To leverage resources optimally, supply managers will employ intelligent modelling capabilities; using these modelling techniques will allow them to see the cost, service level, time and quality impacts of the alternatives being considered.

That said, as the strategic impact of procurement really comes to the fore, how procurement as a discrete function will operate remains uncertain. Clearly businesses will still care about managing their spending – but deploying a large, enterprise-level function dedicated to doing it? Probably not.

A change of focus to a more entrepreneurial, brand-conscious group with expertise in both commercial and technical aspects of business will become the order of the day. Capability and execution will be paramount – a team of enablers, with increased business acumen; people who can make sound commercial decisions.

These will be the new breed of procurement professional – executive and business savvy; working in their elastic multifaceted strategic business mode they will communicate their value propositions to the organization via targeted marketing initiatives. Procurement has for a long time had a brand and PR challenge; and visibility continues to remain one of procurement's greatest professional challenges.

From zero to hero: procurement's PR challenge

Gaining the visibility and developing alliances internally does not appear to be attracting the attention it needs in terms of activities and programmes to achieve this. Whilst many CPOs say they are focused more on strategy alignment, continuous process improvement and cost reduction, to be taken seriously future leaders will have to decipher business objectives and communicate them regularly and effectively to their team and the rest of the business.

Procurement leaders must be purposeful and effective, and whilst there is an abundance of evidence regarding the power of good procurement, it would seem that it is largely ignored. Procurement remains in the eyes of many the Mr Bean of corporate functions. In the early days the function was seen as a 'blue collar' department commanding relatively little respect, and was generally regarded as a cost to the organization.

Yet in truth procurement's journey from afterthought to core capability parallels the way in which the business landscape has changed since the 1980s and 1990s. As Mark Twain once wrote, 'the very ink with which all history is written is merely fluid prejudice' – and whilst others continue to pick at procurement's growing contribution and recognition, it often comes across as an obdurate form of status anxiety.

While some might view procurement's role as somewhat like that of Sisyphus, condemned to repeat for ever the same meaningless task of pushing a boulder up a mountain, others are seeing its role as having meaning and, more importantly, value. As for the cynics out there, now might be the time to imagine Sisyphus happy.

So, for procurement, the time has come to focus on ever-closer inner and outer synchronization: to build bridges across the top team and the operations of the organization and tighten its links between the supply base and out to the customer base. Aligning with inner and outer contexts is key for procurement. CPOs must think and talk strategy, culture, stakeholders and competitors.

Visibility, influence and focus are vital; contemporary supply managers have to be able to decipher business objectives and communicate them regularly and effectively to their team, the rest of the business and its stakeholders. Effective supply managers will garner the interest of the 'right' people about the important issues. The more the business appreciates their role, the more likely they are to include it in their determination of what strategic changes the organization needs to make. CPOs and their teams must aim to be 'go to' people in their organizations.

Application of the ACE model: a tool kit for business leaders to implement change

Ensuring clarity of direction and purpose will without doubt improve the competitive advantage of a business. Use of the ACE model will help business and procurement leaders to test that their strategy is clear, understood and fit for purpose. This relatively simple strategy deployment model can help you avoid costly strategic mistakes and ensure that resources are aligned and incentivized around a common vision.

By utilizing a methodical tool you can also build trust. You can promote the procurement brand across the business by having a clear and shared strategy to help present a single consistent face to your stakeholders, which is a key element in engendering trust.

Diagnose the problems in your procurement function

Conducting a rapid and objective diagnosis of how your procurement function is established and performing will drive action that will impact on how you are seen in your business. Proximity to the problems and a desire to realize your true potential are at the very heart of successfully bringing about change. It is critical, therefore, that you understand and address the real causes of problems.

Addressing the real problems will ensure that your action plan is focusing on the right improvement actions. It will help you to avoid the cost of failure by understanding where the issues are and the true problem at the root of those issues. All too often businesses become embroiled in perceived problems, spending large amounts of money on change processes that turn out to be wholly inappropriate.

The anatomy of successful change

Most people will agree that change is hard. Machiavelli in his famous (business) book *The Prince* talks about change makers at length, observing that it is a very dangerous role to be leading or conducting. He puts it thus: 'For he who innovates will have for his enemies all those who are well off under the existing order of things, and only the lukewarm supporters in those who might be better off under the new.'[1] Lukewarm support from those who will be better off! Lukewarm for the simple reason that they will never admit the merit of anything new, as Machiavelli writes, 'until they have seen it proved by the event'.

That said, change is necessary and when implementing change there are three golden rules to follow:

1 Take time to ensure readiness before launching into implementation.

2 Gain the appropriate support from senior management and, better still, the board – and install appropriate leadership.

3 Be resilient. There is absolutely no doubt that you will meet resistance to the change project, programme, journey or whatever else you choose to call it. Reflect on the above and stay true to your goal.

Transform the way you do business: develop a customer mindset

Transforming your business will enable you to achieve your vision and deliver value to your stakeholders. Achieve a step change in business performance by using techniques such as 'assumption busting', which aims to identify and challenge the rules that dictate the way you do things. Find new ways of working, by employing strategic planning with innovation processes and creative thinking exercises with both your team and those you will work with across the business.

Aligning with the corporate strategy will mean that procurement must understand and align with customer demand. This is amongst the highest challenges to supply management today. There is a real need for procurement to have a customer-centric mindset and to become integrated with customer demand to deliver business value.

As a result, the role of procurement should be re-emphasized and customers must now be viewed almost as an extension of the business in order to help achieve corporate objectives. Customer input must add tangible value to your supply chain – and organizations do excel at meeting customer needs once they are known: it is the 'knowing' part that is difficult. Some supply chains connect with customers primarily to provide timely, accurate delivery.

However, despite the obvious need for customer interaction, many procurement organizations are pushed to focus more on their suppliers than their customers. Even in supply chain planning, with all the demand-driven hype, customer input is frequently overlooked. And yet, because customer interaction seems costly and time-consuming, it seems that many businesses feel that the cost can outweigh the benefits. But as the pressure grows to be more profitable, businesses will not be able to afford the excess inventory, lost sales and missed innovation opportunities caused by inadequate customer collaboration.

Essentially, managing value can help to deliver profitable growth; for example, innovation is focused on products and services that provide value to your customer. Procurement is expected to deliver innovation often from the supply base and this is reflected in the end product or service. Any innovation that does not provide additional value relative to the best alternatives is in essence money wasted.

Businesses need to get smarter and interact with customers throughout the product life cycle. In effect, any interaction with customers should become an opportunity for inherent customer collaboration. Smart procurement professionals should use their judgement and business intelligence to rise above and beyond the noise.

For the visionary organizations out there, many of which have embraced change and have already developed and continue to develop smart integrated procurement functions, there are clear financial as well as culturally tangible benefits to be enjoyed. Let's now consider what benefits top-performing procurement organizations deliver to the business.

The smart things that top-performing procurement organizations do

In a superb study, published in 2010, the US consultancy the Hackett Group identified a list of 10 things done well by world-class procurement organizations.[2] Doubtless some of these things will have changed, hence our comment above that the visionaries continue to change, but as a basis on what 'good' looks like they are a useful starting point. We have adapted them somewhat for the purposes of this book but they are useful in that they reflect the art of the possible, in practice:

1 They leverage the full capability of their supply markets. The procurement team helps the organization to harness safely the power of supply markets in order to glean additional value from external spending. They shift their posture and become gate-opener as well as gate-keeper. For these procurement teams, value can mean spending less; but also it means getting more utility from spend – so procurement influences the business strategy rather than just supporting it.

2 They have flexible rather than rigid operating models. This helps them to adapt their service delivery and transformation models to a diverse set of budget holders – who they see as functional partners – in the value chain rather than fixating on how to organize and control an n-step procurement process. They create clear value propositions that are understood and valued by stakeholders: they create a very clear value proposition and procurement 'brand' that can be understood, articulated and championed by the spend owners themselves.

3　They execute 'customer management' processes, which ensure that they are getting most value both from the suppliers, as well as procurement. They engage in business spend planning, not 'spent analysis'. By working with the business on 'spend planning' as part of the financial and operations planning and budgeting team, they gain the earliest influence possible. This enables them to provide forward-looking economic spend and supply information rather than forensic of the typical 'spent analysis' activity or the 'post-mortem' strategizing of traditional procurement organizations.

4　They explicitly align to the business through a project portfolio plan. In essence they 'join the dots' in tying metrics, processes and capabilities to their value proposition. Traditionally, procurement organizations would work on them individually and in most organizations there exist many disjointed activities across the business's procurement project portfolio.

5　They protect the business from supply risk and from itself. By combining risk management and market intelligence techniques they provide the business with visibility into risk, as well as providing a governance structure and process to gain consensus with the Finance department and the wider business on which risks to treat, and how best to treat them systematically – often with constrained or limited funds.

6　They understand how to shift the game from talent to knowledge. In these days of talent scarcity, or as is more common talent retention, these procurement organizations have moved from a purely talent management model – 'throw the best people at it' – to a knowledge management model. They do this by shifting from current full-time equivalent (FTE) staffing models to more flexible or agile resourcing models. Second, they invest in the provision of better IT support for better capture and reuse of knowledge and business intelligence.

7　They dedicate time and resource to turn data into information, intelligence, knowledge and insight. Essentially, they use information management as a weapon to transcend basic ERP/e-sourcing to a more thoughtful information architecture that helps to manage extended supply chains and external intelligence.

8　They measure suppliers, but also tap their hearts, minds and budgets. They work collaboratively with suppliers to reduce total supply costs, not just supplier margins, and create innovations that will deliver economic value. Today businesses are directing more and more of their budgets towards a complex web of global specialist providers and suppliers in order to help deliver on their core strategies.

9 These procurement organizations treat their suppliers as if they are an extension of the business. As they would their internal workforce, they incentivize, coach, endorse and reward them in order to help achieve corporate objectives. They are around not just when you most need them, but also when they most need you.

10 Finally, they understand how to use P2P transactional processes as an asset and not a liability. They establish not just 'hands free' processes to make life easier for procurement, but rather a fail-safe 'guided buying' experience to channel employees to preferred buy–pay channels. This implies integration between P2P and procurement as well as a deliberate 'P2P transactional channel optimization' methodology – a bit like applying lean processes to the P2P 'transaction factory'.

The following case study provides insights into a CPO in a large global financial services company who is challenged to make headway, against a strong headwind of resistance to change. In this environment, one has to recognize that it may take years to change the culture – but change occurs one person at a time.

CASE STUDY Becoming a trusted adviser – procurement transformation at a global insurance provider

This case develops some strong themes in the following areas:

- internal transformation of procurement;

- building internal relationships;

- challenges of implementation in non-traditional industries where there is low procurement maturity;

- building a foundation for growth.

This case study examines the approach to transformation being adopted at a large global insurance company. The CPO in this case came in and quickly built a team of people around several key categories, aligning several key players:

- Category Manager 1: has been in procurement for 10 years, and leads Professional Services and Marketing category.

- Category Manager 2: oversees the Claims category and is leading a new offshore strategy, as well as leading work around supplier innovation and strategic alliances around innovation specifically.

- Category Manager 3: newly arrived, but has 20 years of procurement experience. Responsible for sourcing, procurement, supplier relationship performance and management of technology, and 20 years of procurement experience.

The new CPO of Sourcing and Procurement Solutions (which was recently rebranded internally as Procurement Governance) arrived only two years ago, but has over 25 years of experience in in-house procurement as well as outsourced procurement functions. She has a strong presence when she enters a room, and people always listen when she speaks. The following two sections of this case study are described in the CPO's own words. She first discusses the many challenges that existed when she arrived at the company.

Moving from generalist to SME

We started in 2011 when the organization – the Executive Leadership Team – recognized a need to build procurement. Previously we were structured into Sourcing and Supplier Management. Sourcing handled all upfront sourcing work and SM handled everything post sourcing event – even if it was a renegotiation or an addition to an existing statement of work. This was very much of a generalist model, in which work was allocated on a first in, first out basis, and directed to three sources based on availability. The perception was that we were working from a procurement 'generalist' model, as opposed to any specific category subject matter expertise that was available in the organization.

   The first thing I did with my team was reach out and collect feedback from internal customers and suppliers, and incorporated the feedback around adding value, mitigating more risk, and then defined how to be structured going forward. From these discussions we moved to a category-based model. We didn't have people post for their jobs but we did sit down and ask them to assess their skills, attributes and strengths, as well as the things they didn't want to do. We aligned people by categories:

- Professional Services and Marketing;

- IT;

- Travel;

- Enterprise – Facilities, Print;

- Claims;

- Innovation and Offshoring.

Those buckets of alignment combined with a new group called Procurement and Operations. We defined the initial structure, and we are defining the scope of that group, or a third party to do it for us in a lower-cost location – and that forms our procurement capability.

Becoming a trusted adviser

One of the things we are doing in a pronounced way is to focus on our position as a *trusted adviser*. Year one was just getting us ready for the journey – and ensuring we had the tools and processes and policies, and where we had gaps we had to proactively hire people with skills. For example, in IT we didn't have leadership, and weren't connected to the tech strategy and hired Category Manager 3 in December 2011, and brought him on board to build out the IT capability. Similarly we didn't have a focus around travel and recognized that to develop great travel deals we needed in-depth skills, and hired an individual who is now going out assessing process, tools and skills on this team to ensure we can make the leap on the journey.

We are focused on ROI on our operating budget, and supporting our chairman and board of directors on taking operating cost out of the enterprise. We have more people pulling at the beginning of the process, as opposed to our prior perception as just being the people to sign the contract. We now are involved to facilitate the entire contracting and sourcing process. We are also focused on managing our suppliers. We have somewhere between US $6–7 billion in sourceable spend, and 18,000 suppliers, with 20 per cent accounting for 80 per cent of spend. But we know we have to do a better job in getting suppliers to build a better yield for the enterprise, through innovation and more thought leadership. The fact is – it is a daily grind. We can write soap opera material with the dramas that we face day in and day out on this task!

Speaking the same language as stakeholders

Category Manager 1 (Marketing): to me it is the blend of people in the right procurement category teams. The procurement solutions team works optimally when we have those with good procurement experience and good functional experience. So for our marketing category, we hired advertising agency people and taught them procurement. That has its challenges, but the benefit we got from that ability to build a *trusted adviser* function was invaluable. We are doing passive recruiting for more marketing people on our team because we feel we have solid procurement experience but need the marketing experience.

We are also using this same approach in other categories. When you think about the field make-up of the claims and IT team – we have a solid blend of people with procurement expertise, and people who have worked in the functional areas, as well as those from the claims organizations who know what is important in how to settle a claim and focus on the customer experience. But we also need everyone on the category teams to have communication skills that align with our stakeholders. A set of cohorts are on all of our teams who come from finance, who all have previous treasury and finance experience. The insurance industry most readily aligns to financial services and the company has hired people with deep finance acumen, so even in the functional areas, most people speak the language of the industry, which is finance. So we need the right blend of people who can speak the same language as our stakeholders.

And how do we leverage those skills to deliver more value to the company? As an example, Category Manager 2 is helping us to build an offshore presence. This is a path that wasn't aligned to the procurement function in the past, involving global staffing and site selection. But because of a broad range of experience in offshoring, risk in working offshore, and other skills in the organization, we are bringing in people on to the team who can help support the strategic plans that are at the board level, and do so in a way that will deliver more value than the team can do alone. Procurement people have to be comfortable in dealing with ambiguity and expanding their role as business needs present themselves. We aren't able to do it now, but if we are able we need to be able to exploit the opportunities to deliver the strategic outcomes.

Category Manager 3: I'm facing all of the same challenges along those lines. One of the challenges we have, the 8,000 pound gorilla, is the lack of spend visibility across the source continuum as a way to track exactly what we keep driving towards. In my experience it is extremely critical to have source-to-pay visibility moving into 2015. But a lack of visibility can also be used to drive opportunity when you know what to do in the situation! For example, one data point is having a look at our lease portfolio, which is US $2 billion in technology, and to lower funding costs associated with those lease portfolios. There are opportunities to buy out technology, and continuing to use product beyond the life of the lease and saving millions of dollars. We are employing subject matter experts to drive fact-based models around these scenarios to help us deliver measurable results as a result of that effort. But we have to ensure we are getting the full ROI from hiring those 'category' SME's because others (elsewhere) are not.

Balancing the tension between internal and external knowledge expertise

Category Manager 3: We are always seeking balance between sourcing expertise and business knowledge. Prior to our new CPO arriving, we were more focused on business knowledge, and less on sourcing expertise. With our new CPO arriving came the recognition that the use of life-cycle planning and the importance of being on the front end of the discussion become critical, and in some cases having people with the insurance knowledge is good. But having the sourcing and procurement knowledge that goes with that is more important. We have lots of insurance people sitting in our sourcing organization who have the full grasp of what is going on, and we are now starting to get more opportunities to take on a far more important role on the front end of contracting conversations. It was okay to push it to be a SME versus a generalist so long as you had insurance people in sourcing roles. But bringing in new people from outside the insurance industry will sometimes rock the boat.

Category Manager 1: The historical view shows us the evolution of how we can expand our influence. Prior to the changes here we were very dedicated to the procurement role in this process, with a focus on supplier relationships, which sometimes teetered into partnerships. But we weren't engaged in discussions that allowed us to drive innovation and do new things. With this transformation and the mission to be trusted advisers and do things that are not traditionally in procurement's role, it has elevated the performance of procurement and it has been recognized.

Three keys to transformation: metrics, people, culture

Category Manager 1: Prior to our transformation the *only* metric by which our performance was measured is *how much money we saved* for the organization. People are compensated only on some of the money they save – and it drives some interesting behaviours, and we took a step back to take a more balanced view of our performance. We had higher attrition, mixed customer satisfaction feedback and hitting home runs on savings while increasing our output. But we had no focus on developing our people. We took best-in-class balanced scorecard research and recognized we need to measure against a myriad of attributes, including operational processes and efficiencies, and began implementing some source-to-pay technology, and investing in our people and change in our curriculum. We developed consistent surveys of our customers and financial metrics on performance.

We are on a four-year journey and we need to be able to recruit the *right people* and the right skills. We have a lot of open roles and everybody is facing that. There are a lot of procurement people on the market – but they are there for a reason, and we need to be diligent and prudent. The right skills are not just about being able to do a sourcing event, but having the right person who can live within our mantra of becoming a trusted adviser. This means being able to establish and maintain partner relationships in the enterprise. A lot of the opportunities we get today are not because people are told they have to use procurement, it is because we have demonstrated value – but we are in a relationship-driven organization and we have proactively gone out and built relationships. People want us to be successful in our journey – so they engage us.

Third is *corporate culture*. This is a discussion we have spent a lot of time on. We can have people with the best strategies and solutions around delivering value to support X business needs – a renegotiation, a supplier elimination, etc – but, in the end, culture eats strategy for breakfast every day. So part of this has to be top-down and bottom-up support for what we are doing, and timing is absolutely essential. It feels like the stars are aligning – we have bright people with solid skills – and we have internal customers who have a need to deliver value and become more cost-effective. But we are always faced with whether we can deliver on this quest in the current corporate culture. Insurance is a very stodgy old culture, which has always made high profits in the past, and is not very open to major changes. We fight that every day.

As a result, we know we can't move too quickly. Unless something blows up, we let it ride and have taken a different role towards creating a significant change that impacts the enterprise. All we have described here is a change in business acumen that this company has not been accustomed to. But it is a change that is anchored in source-to-pay. We are a multi-billion-dollar entity on an annualized basis with millions of transactions on a monthly basis. A small percentage goes through POs, so the visibility isn't there. We are in an environment where there is a lot of buying and no central procurement entity to govern those purchases. So without even considering the mechanics moving towards source-to-pay is quite a change. I underestimated this, coming into this company from another industry, and it was a shock. I show up at meetings at very senior levels on budget planning and technology planning, and people at the meeting ask me – 'Where did you come from?' 'How do you provide services?' 'How do we work together?' 'And what will the outcome be?'

It is like building an organization from scratch, and the new capabilities we have developed are coming together. The exciting part is driving the culture of change and business acumen around expense management, procurement sourcing, and the way we acquire assets and build. A lot of times we are not doing anything wrong. Sometimes I feel (like when internal audit comes into our space) like making it as simple as possible. I am your *trusted adviser*! I'm here to help and I want to enable you! You aren't doing anything wrong. I am a professional, and we have done this in various environments, and I have a point of view that will help you become more efficient and more cost effective. And even better – I live with you and I am assigned to you! One of the things we want to ensure is not just to be aligned by category. We have people who sit in various areas and are seen as an additional team member. And we want to be where the action is, and ready to serve.

Some conclusions

In closing, and with a view to how purchasing organizations gear up to tackling the demands they face in the modern business world, we need to understand that the nature of what a 'company' is has changed dramatically. Moreover, the labour cost of 30 years ago is today a supplier invoice – in that their job has now been outsourced. As a consequence, rather than condemn Sisyphus to repeat for ever the same meaningless task of pushing a boulder up a mountain, business leaders should reassess and clearly define the role of procurement in the company philosophy. Is it a process-oriented, savings-obsessed function? Or does it focus on customer service and helping the business to achieve its strategy?

Additionally, procurement should be gauged on its connection to the objectives of the budget holders it is there to serve. It must be fully aligned to what the business is trying to achieve and design metrics around areas such as innovation, stakeholder experience, risk mitigation, improved ways of working, and spending effectively rather than less.

All of the above will necessitate a new curriculum for procurement executives. Today's procurement professionals require a set of skills and abilities that stretch across a very broad range. Skills such as relationship development and influencing with suppliers and stakeholders are seen in a completely different hue. They also need to be analysts, process mappers, researchers, negotiators, change managers, contract managers, project managers – in essence, students of their industry – bimodal in that these people will be commercial managers and analysts.

So, how well have your actions made the procurement organization and the broader enterprise stronger, more agile and better able to weather future challenges? In Chapter 11, there is some guidance on how to use this alignment framework to ask some hard questions about your current level of alignment across these three foundational aspects to running your procurement processes.

In the next chapter we explore where we find the right people, how we develop them and how we keep them.

Notes

1 *The Prince* is a 16th-century political treatise by the Italian diplomat and political theorist Niccolò Machiavelli.

2 Hackett Group (2010) 'An Evolution of Value and Capability', conference presentation.

It's all about people
Talent acquisition and retention

06

In Chapter 5 we looked at how and why the game plan for most businesses remains fairly conservative in spite of the seismic shifts we have seen. Many are revising their perspective on the rapidly changing business world to cultivate their understanding of the emerging issues and are developing strategies to take account of the inescapable changes that every business services function will have to make.

Central to this is the focus on the knowledge needs and priorities for those working in the procurement function. Consequently, the pressure on procurement to perform is increasing. As businesses turn their attention from compliance to growth and innovation, businesses must focus too on developing their strategy to enhance the commercial acumen and professional capability of their procurement people, beyond the skill sets traditionally required in their roles (as discussed in Chapter 5).

Modern business is being defined by 'ideas'-based companies and 'knowledge intensive' businesses with their significance determined by innovation and agility. In order for us to identify and recommend good practice for procurement teams, we need to know what happens in business, why it happens and what works in these commercial environments.

The key issues

From a business perspective procurement's evolution has increased its importance enormously. Consequently, to meet the new demands of business – be it as an embedded procurement function or, more importantly, a fully 'commercial' arm of the businesses – several key issues have surfaced, as set out below.

Skills and abilities

Perhaps the chief concern of business and procurement leaders today relates to the scarcity of talented people in the field. Real or imagined, the perceived lack of knowledge and understanding here relates to general business acumen as well as knowledge of specific markets and sectors:

- There is a particular focus on the need to develop the *'social' (soft) skills* required in business and particularly those associated with relationship management, such as communication, collaboration, co-dependence and influencing. So strong is this message that it warrants the top spot on the bill.

- There are *specific skill requirements* highlighted too, such as risk 'gurus'. There is also a great deal of debate regarding the shape of or the profile of the modern skill set – typically about depth and breadth of knowledge. Commercial skills feature highly, as do a need for people to be more visionary, flexible, agile and resilient.

- Finally there is a heavy emphasis on a need for procurement people to have more *'scientific' skills* sets. There is a real and immediate need for people with the ability to handle and analyse data. These people have strong quantitative fluency and are competent in developing and deriving solutions from data sets.

Modern procurement professionals today need to be expert, with a deep knowledge of their industry, sector, the geographies they operate in as well as the products and services they are dealing with.

Organizational change

This need stems from the considerable change that business has gone through and the development of new business models and formats. Some businesses still need to be convinced of the worth of a total value outlook, as opposed to one centred on cost. The total value concept is a more holistic approach; people development within organizations is clearly an ongoing process and necessary for all, from the most senior of senior management to front-line staff. The organizational changes that business requires will only come about through (professional) lifelong learning.

Some of the evolution in procurement is a consequence of the increased use of technology and, as has already been alluded, how the more tactical aspects of procurement operations are increasingly outsourced to third-party providers. Many businesses are now focusing on exactly what can and cannot be outsourced in the future and how this will affect their operations and their staffing needs. Increasingly businesses will need to address the question of what an 'appropriate' procurement organization looks like. Will it be an in-house service, a loose network or a tight function within the business? In addressing this, businesses will need to decide whether the procurement and supply management function will be embedded in other parts of the business as a fully integrated part of them, or remain stand-alone.

Increasingly we are seeing procurement teams that are smaller, value-adding and with a broader remit. They deal with 'externalities' – relationships; with many different sources and work to the boundaries of their territory. They do this by being fully integrated inside the organization, with cross-functional accountability and governance for supply chain management, but jointly owned with other business functions. They will have the capability to manage relationships with increasingly dominant outsourced providers. Finally they will need agility, resilience and vision, which will be the prerequisites for the modern/future professional procurement team. These will be solutions that are driven, versatile and with a broad knowledge base.

Relationships

Supplier relationship management (SRM) is a perennial issue for procurement – and rightly so. Supply assurance has always been the most critical role it plays. So to operate in this space procurement people must master collaboration, co-dependence, interdependence and the changes in the balance of power, be it between the buyer and the supplier or other third-party organizations. Relationships are key and form a large part of what the value procurement delivers.

Collaboration is the new way. The old adversarial posture of procurement is as outmoded as it is inappropriate. There is a new challenge for procurement – to become an intelligent customer, the buyer of choice.

Risk

Awareness of risk and 'whole supply chain insight' are or should be the bread-and-butter of procurement. The notion of risk managers with 'guruesque' insight to the supply network with a well-developed understanding of both the opportunity and threat presented by risk scenarios must become de rigeur.

Commercial focus

There is no doubt that the level of sophistication in procurement has developed since the mid 1980s. Nowhere is this more apparent than the strong commercial focus anticipated by all organizations from their procurement and supply management professionals.

As the strategic scope of procurement broadens and its capabilities are increasingly recognized within organizations it will have an increasingly financial (commercial) focus. The management of the legal/contracting base to affect consortia and greater interdependencies will demand a commercial mindset and mastery of acquisition as well as procurement know-how.

Evidence of this change

There are a plethora of reports by major consultancies, which bolster the requirements set out above. Some of the most recent reports and studies reflect the burgeoning demand for a new breed of procurement professional. These people will be '*bimodal*': business savvy as well as tech savvy, they will have a well-developed commercial acumen as well as deep analytical competence.

Recognizing that procurement is not the career backwater it was once considered to be, and capturing the significant strategic and financial value embedded in this function, are two different things. Indeed, to profit from an elevated respect for procurement, businesses may well have to undo decades of bad habits in the recruitment, training and development of their procurement professionals. No longer can businesses afford to place competent but unimaginative people in these jobs. Nor can they afford to ignore their current procurement people by offering them few chances of advancement and neglecting their skills.

Merely hiring good people is not enough if businesses want to build a world-class procurement function. Rather they must make 'all-star' appointments – filling their senior procurement jobs with people who can become tomorrow's business leaders. Managerial talent of this calibre does not develop by accident. Businesses must hone executive abilities by identifying and encouraging promising individuals and providing them with the right opportunities over years, even decades.

The industry recognizes that inevitably programmes will be needed to develop top procurement executives and must be implemented as more and more procurement managers themselves evince a budding sense of optimism about their prospects. In a recent Booz & Company survey of 100 CPOs and supply chain management leaders, 66 per cent of respondents said that the CPO will play a larger role in setting business strategy in the next 5–10 years, and 44 per cent of respondents said that activities in the procurement department will be a top priority.[1] The general conviction in the executive suite seems to be that procurement needs to be more strategic – closer to the leadership agenda.

This suggests that although it will continue to be important for the procurement professional to have functional expertise enabling them to get the best deal on what they are buying (as well as to leverage more value from the entire supply base), strategic capabilities, political know-how and leadership talent are increasingly important priorities and fundamental skills for procurement people.

In fact, in the same Booz & Company study, 46 per cent of senior procurement executives believe that strategic understanding and overall business sense will be the most important traits for procurement managers in the future. Meanwhile, two traditional measures of procurement professionals' functional expertise – their ability to manage supplier networks and their understanding of the products or services they are buying – were not rated as the top priority by even 5 per cent of the respondents.

It would seem that the challenge for tomorrow's procurement officers will be setting the strategic agenda through growth and innovation. Those businesses that are determined to develop a new generation of corporate procurement leaders – while maintaining a competitive supply chain – will be the winners. The report suggested that smart businesses do a number of things:

- recruit from top universities, but also from other functions;
- revise and expand training;
- create career paths for your talent.

These are discussed in more detail below.

Recruit from top universities, but also recruit from other functions

The bad news is that, by and large, organizations have not bothered to seek out the best and the brightest for purchasing; most recruiting has historically been internal. The result, of course, is a self-fulfilling prophecy – second-tier candidates could not raise procurement to a strategic competence, and their underperformance seemed to justify the function's relegation to a supporting role. If procurement is to achieve its promise, companies must seek out top performers to fill these jobs.

The good news is that the level and quality of procurement talent is rising. Responding to the new demand, some top business and industrial management schools have added Procurement and Supply Management to their curriculum.

The need to be able to build strong managers who possess not only strong analytical skills, but also the 'soft' skills, is deemed fundamental to the evolution of procurement. In our research for this book, every executive we interviewed mentioned talent as a shortfall facing their organization. Every procurement leader is focused on prioritizing and assessing the skills within their procurement organization on a worldwide basis, to ensure that:

- people are right-fit for their roles;
- that there is a plan to up-skill the entire organization;
- to enable procurement to move from an enabler of cost savings to a strategic partner to the business.

Proactive organizations are taking deliberate steps to upgrade talent, and are spending less time talking about it than taking action. There is also recognition that procurement must first begin by recruiting people who have a strong understanding of business-line context first, and who are then brought into procurement roles fully cognizant of stakeholder challenges. Development paths typically involve several approaches, as noted below:

- 'We are leading our organization through a general and individualized self-assessment, and moving towards a model that provides more consultancy types of skills. We are emphasizing a higher level of accountability as we work that into a fabric of consistency and cross-pollination around the business. This is also being emphasized through comprehensiveness in decision processes. When we approach the market or any internal stakeholder, there needs to be a consistent and methodical experience. To ensure this we engage in sourcing review committees, and any project goes before that committee at least twice before it goes before our stakeholders.'
- 'Category management breeds an arrogance that allows others to take advantage of it. I prefer generalists who can look at business issues and solve them and move on. Procurement can become bound

by its ignorance of business issues. With the right calibre of individual who is more eclectic, procurement should be a shared service of people who move in and move out. But to develop this talent, we need to apprentice smart people, as it is completely dependent on the type of people who move into these roles. I prefer those who are hungry, smart and humble, who are willing to move around.'

- 'In the end, procurement success will be defined by the people who can apply a level of proficiency to derive value for the business. The greatest successes I've witnessed in our business is where you have people who are embedded in the business and become effectively an integrated consultant to help shape the business strategy from the outset, and not just support it once it has already been solidified. We achieved this by embedding procurement capabilities into the lines of business at every level. Wherever we had the right capability and skill set, there was exponential change and integration with the business. This takes coaching and leadership – and most important of all, forcing people to be accountable for results. Otherwise, they will continue to do what they have always been doing.'

In establishing the type of individual who can operate within procurement, organizations may need to reach out to non-traditional sources of talent to recruit the right people. What worked for 'red-meat-eating hard-ball negotiators' 10 years ago may not be the right fit for today's more consultative form of engagement with internal stakeholders.

An interesting proposition that is evolving is that procurement executives may be pulled from multiple other areas in the organization, based on where they are needed. One area of potential recruitment is from the marketing and business development area. In effect, the same set of skills is prevalent, albeit from a different perspective. In most of the organizations we interviewed, the level of collaboration between procurement and sales is minimal, but represents a huge opportunity. In fact, we propose that both marketing and procurement talent pools can learn skills from one another that are valuable for application in each of their respective areas. The merging of buy-side and sell-side capabilities is one that was adopted by the International Association of Commercial and Contract Management (IACCM), and provides a natural basis for integration.

To some extent, the merging of sales and purchasing roles is a call to prior times, during the growth of the textile industry in North America. During the period, responsibility for the output, quality and style of the cloth produced by the mills was usually the duty of the selling agent. The selling agent was also responsible for all purchasing decisions, since the grade of cotton purchased was a factor in determining the quality of cloth produced. These selling agents represented a simple and direct interface between market demand and production scheduling. Customer orders were directly transformed into purchase orders for cotton and subsequently into planned production. The types of cloth produced were somewhat limited, however, by the processes available to manufacture them. This degree of standardization within the domestic and international market made the job of the selling agent much easier, as the majority of cloth could be produced on a 'make-to-stock' basis.[2]

Revise and expand training

The training required to function effectively as a purchasing officer is much more complex than it was just a few years ago, because it must include both traditional purchasing expertise and broader financial and managerial skills.

Procurement professionals still need such core skills as negotiation techniques, supplier market analysis and cost modelling, but training pro- grammes involving these once-basic skills often require revision as the field of purchasing becomes more advanced and challenging. For example, tradi- tional cost modelling involved little more than short-term analysis of com- modities markets to lock in prices over perhaps a three- to 12-month period. But today that is only the beginning. CPOs now must be adept at macroeco- nomics and have wider corporate finance skills to manage futures, puts and calls, fixed contracts, and other strategies and instruments that are designed to cover purchases over many years. CPOs increasingly need the financial acuity to accurately forecast supplier prices 24 months out or more, so that they can make better decisions about long-term contracts for oil and other commodities, or the raw materials that should be used in their company's manufacturing processes and products.

In some industries, such as the airline industry, the last few years have demonstrated that the cost management of a key commodity such as fuel can sometimes be the key not just to profitability but also to corporate sur- vival. For example, with long-term hedging of more than 80 per cent of its energy costs, Southwest Airlines avoided the turbulence that many airlines suffered when jet fuel prices nearly tripled between 2002 and 2005.

To help develop the broad areas of expertise that procurement profes- sionals will need to thrive in the new era, businesses should turn to the top business schools to develop and train their managers.

Create career paths for your talent

Ironically, capabilities training carries a greater risk to the team because these bright young things will be equipped with a wide array of skills and more expertise than other purchasing professionals – and so will find it easier than ever to leave for better opportunities.

To prevent such a brain drain and ensure that businesses can capture the full potential of their purchasing talent, it is essential that they offer concrete and compelling career paths for these people. To determine which procurement executives deserve special treatment, HR departments should build into performance appraisals measurements to take account of the new set of skills needed by purchasing managers – this higher degree of financial acumen and finely honed strategic thinking – and procurement people who meet their cost and delivery targets should be rewarded with greater compensation. The greatest accolade would be when the business sees procurement as a training ground for senior positions in the 'corporation'.

Sceptics will doubtless argue that thinking of well-trained and innovative purchasing managers as indispensable talent assets is a short-term trend, generating at best a modicum of real change before it disappears. However, the rising need and desire for highly skilled purchasing professionals is a somewhat lagging indicator in the long-term trend of the supply side evolution. Since the mid-1980s businesses have become increasingly aware of the pivotal role that supply management plays in corporate success. And yet even as they understood the profound impact of supply management, executives and purchasing professionals alike remain oblivious to procurement's unequivocal contribution to the efficiency of the business.

In another recent study carried out by Deloitte, published in late 2013, they argue that by 2020 current operating models will be defunct and they suggest that a 'new procurement' requires a near revolution to operate in the modern business world. They feel that many of today's fundamentals will stand in the decades to come, such as category sourcing, baseline procurement systems, human resources management, purchasing performance and knowledge management. But the purchasing organization of the future will need far more.

Procurement, Deloitte says, requires a finance-centric orientation if it wishes to engage other business owners, ranging from those responsible for P&Ls to functional roles including legal, IT, HR, marketing, design and manufacturing. The key capability developments for businesses to survive and thrive include core talent. Procurement capability and talent transformation are seen as paramount in preparing for any procurement transformation journey that will be successful.

It goes without saying that top talent requires leadership and enthusiastic stakeholder engagement, and it is these two capabilities that will enable procurement to operate as a peer. Having an honest reckoning over talent is essential. Clearly, one size does not fit all team members, and one of the most important roles for procurement leaders is to embrace diverse skills, capabilities and background – and deploying these people to the appropriate positions.

Today, a good procurement team must be able to engage and interact with constituents across the business. One way to think about procurement skills and expertise is that the type of talent that resides in the highest-end chief financial officer (CFO) and finance organizations today is similar to that which will be required of procurement in the future. Analytical skills and a data-driven orientation will be the table stakes, but will not stand alone in assembling the right team members. Overall, how organizations conceive of talent will transcend just identifying 'A-players' at all ranks and levels:

- Emphasis will shift to the assembly of talent teams; HR and procurement will need their fingers on the pulse of talent in both labour and supply markets. Talent will be looked at individually and globally. Criteria will include not just listed skill sets and capabilities, but past performance, demographic/cultural nuances and preferences. For example, a system may flag a particular candidate for a role not based on a past similar rotation, but a collection of indicators in a profile that suggests success in the desired new role. Leading companies will likely be able to do this externally too – mining candidates from social networks, jobs boards and curriculum vitae items across public sites.

- CPOs will use multi-tier succession planning as a necessary requirement to create lasting impact past their tenure and that of their reports, especially as they move into more advanced positions running the corporation. In their report Deloitte argue that proactive talent and skills-level strategy and programmes matter at all levels, not just the top. Talent management and skills development require the thoughtful blend of outside talent (ie recruiting) coupled with skills development and procurement rotations internally.

- HR will collaborate with procurement to jointly assemble their required team; operating as human capital integrators, leveraging both internal and external sources for specific needs, by deploying a proactive, aligned mindset. For procurement's overall talent picture, businesses will need to strike a balance of smart, youthful and malleable talent with seasoned and empathetic management. Ultimately, this type of effort requires a fundamental reset of HR's role in procurement, not in terms of just recruiting talent, but nurturing and growing it as well – and helping to strike a balance of roles and the right expertise at all levels of the procurement function.

Nick Gunn from Hewlett-Packard noted that most people don't start a 40-year-career thinking they will be working in procurement, but that over the course of a career many, many things can change. How HP engages stakeholders is a critical talent, since procurement at HP is a shared service, and as such their stakeholders are literally their customers in every sense of the word, except that they don't have a choice to go elsewhere if they don't like what HP procurement does for them. Procurement sits down with their senior executives to understand their business, and plans accordingly on how they will deliver value. He also talked about the fact that people in procurement need to stay relevant and abreast of current issues, just like doctors who keep up on their journals. He says that 20 years ago HP was hiring 'red-meat-eating negotiating professionals', but while cost savings are still important, it is a softer set of skills that underlie the ability to create better relationships with customers.

In a report by KPMG the need to develop capable managers who possess both strong analytical and soft skills is mooted from the outset. The main thrust of their argument is that the development and deployment of 'soft' skills is fundamental to the evolution of procurement. Talent is a major issue facing organizations, so much so that every CPO should focus on prioritiz-ing and assessing the skills within their departments globally, evaluating people to role fits, and ensuring that there is a plan to build talent within the function. This is seen by many in the industry as critical to procurement's ability to move from being an enabler of cost savings to becoming a strategic partner to the business.

It was noted by KPMG that proactive organizations are already taking deliberate steps to upgrade talent, and are increasingly recognizing that the most effective procurement managers first gain strong understanding of business-line context and then bring knowledge of the stakeholders' chal-lenges into their procurement roles. Moreover, KPMG say that given today's need for a more consultative form of engagement with internal stakehold-ers, an increasing number of procurement organizations are reaching out to non-traditional sources of talent to recruit the right people for them.

By way of a contrast, in a report by the Chartered Institute of Purchasing and Supply (CIPS), 80:20 Vision (published in 2012 to coincide with its 80th anniversary), it was argued that professional skill sets for procurement people need to change. This need to change was heralded by 30 years of change to business models and the business landscape. Globalization coupled with rapid developments in new technologies has meant that the need for the proper management of the supply chain in its entirety is fundamental for all organizations to remain sustainable.

Procurement professionals, CIPS argued, must become experts: respected; influential; persuasive; visionary; strategic; sharp; global; collaborative; executive and commercially focused. Procurement needs to develop a new definition of 'expert', where the new supply professionals will know everything about their sphere of interest – the science, economics, law and politics of their supply markets on a global scale.

CIPS also reinforce that the competition for talent will heat up, and while there is considerable opinion regarding the talent pipeline, one thing is sure – there will be intense competition to attract the best and the brightest into the profession and this will increasingly be on their own terms.

CASE STUDY   Value orientation through supply entrepreneurship and integrated business processes

In 2011 a global industrial chemicals company was looking to up its game through developing its procurement capability. They wanted to enhance a well-positioned global procurement set-up and its processes; they had a clear vision of what they wanted and this was to be supported by the management of risks and sustainability.

Key to realizing their aspirations was active talent management. This was to be achieved via an intervention designed specifically to shape their procurement team and develop practice excellence within. Their ultimate goal was to become a value-oriented and lean procurement organization. They were cognizant of the need for a clear and aligned strategic focus, making a significant contribution to profitability, developing competitive advantage and providing a clear career path to their employees. To achieve these audacious goals they introduced a staged process:

- *Stage 1.* Examine their core competences and needs. These included: creativity, specializations, reliability and self-renewal. By pulling these issues to the fore their immediate goal was to achieve sourcing excellence, hitting their savings targets and setting procurement's posture throughout the business. They introduced the planned intervention at an internal company-wide procurement conference that would take in their global teams to avail them of what the business and procurement was embarking on.

- *Stage 2.* This saw procurement alignment with the corporate values and, in particular, having the courage to innovate, taking responsibility for their actions and total commitment to the initiative. They explicitly defined their actions as being: value orientation, a strategic focus, the development of efficient process and, most important of all, an active talent management programme. This was supported by an employee survey to develop an understanding of commitment, needs and ideas/knowledge development from within.

- *Stage 3.* The programme was deployed and was to establish three levels: foundation, advanced and leadership. They would also introduce a 'train the trainer' programme to strengthen the impact of locally delivered training and development programmes.

They supported the programme with solid research carried out by McKinsey & Co, which reflected what is to be gained by a capability development programme. In essence, that procurement pays because high-performing procurement organizations support business success significantly. Also, that capability and culture are key to procurement success.

The capability development programme was comprised of several elements, as mentioned above. These were tailored to specific needs of participants, with learning programmes comprised of such things as:

- specific procurement assignment;

- tailored training modules;

- coaching sessions;

- practice knowledge exchange;

- structured feedback sessions;

- developing internal training capability.

The training sessions were delivered on a 'just in time' basis covering off activities over time and were designed around supplier and stakeholder engagement, ie they were live and therefore had a real impact on the business.

They quickly realized that organizational capability development would make the business and procurement's role sustainable. Capability development was to be based on knowledge development with capability building focused on 'block' development with initial external support (see Figure 6.1).

FIGURE 6.1 Capability development over time

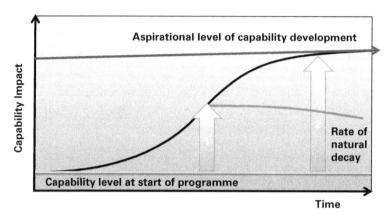

Step 1:
Project-centred capability development
- Immediate enabler for sustainable, cross-functional step-change.
- As 'block' development.

Step 2:
Role-based capability development
- Investment in capabilities along clear career path or specific role.
- As 'sequential' enablement/development.

FIGURE 6.2 Capability development-stage process

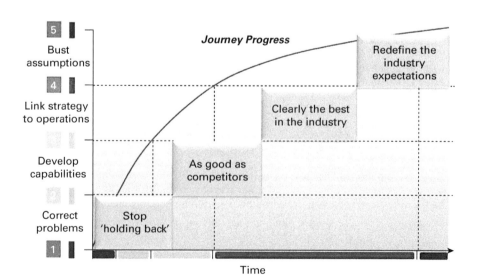

Selected participants then took on trainer roles in subsequent rounds of the advanced programme and finally the programme consisted of multiple interactions over time. These capability activities can be seen from a macro perspective in Figure 6.2.

What is clear from what this organization did is that it recognized that this investment in its procurement organization will make the function look and operate in a very different way and within a very short period of time. They knew too that it would alter existing assumptions and introduce emerging hazards. It required additional skills, knowledge and tools development to address entirely new challenges while solving current ones more creatively. And it will likely change the very core of how their company viewed procurement as an organizational function and its impact on overall company competence. The investment they made was about sustainability – sustaining the enterprise!

This organization experienced the first steps on this journey in 2011 and 2012, but in the decade ahead there will likely be a dramatic shift that will require further capability and competence development; and they are likely to be mandatory. Any businesses that fail to embrace new procurement models may fall further and further behind the competition, jeopardizing overall competitiveness and even their viability.

Different types of talent are needed for different roles

As noted in the study conducted by Handfield in 2013, there are different types of future procurement capabilities that align with different abilities in the individuals that take on these roles. The key roles identified in this report are shown below and some of them are detailed further in Table 6.1:

- *Internal consultant*: ability to connect, listen and deliver business value to internal stakeholders. Building a strong P2P system to drive improved procurement transaction excellence, and driving results that matter to the business.

- *Market intelligence and cost-modelling analytics*: deployment of total-cost analytic modelling and cost to serve capabilities, application of analytical cost-modelling approaches for decision support, and building supply market intelligence-data gathering and knowledge dissemination capabilities. Deep knowledge and understanding of macroeconomic forces and ability to relate them to future market movements and forecasts.

- *Financial acumen*: knowledge of currency, capital markets and contribution of procurement to P&L and balance sheet. Ability to contribute to CFO and other financial leadership discussions and debates. Ability to build logistics cost models, understand contribution of supply management to capitalization, facility productivity and other key metrics.

- *Risk mitigation*: knowledge of different sources of risk, ability to build risk profiles, link recognition of risks to risk mitigation and scenario planning, and understanding how to manage disasters when they occur. Building a business case for risk mitigation planning.

- *Supplier coach*: ability to deploy supplier development to drive improvement in high-need categories or regions, especially in emerging countries where local content is required. Becoming a customer of choice, and driving improvement in supplier capabilities. Harnessing supplier innovation and developing solutions to stakeholder requirements.

- *Relationship broker*: managing teams in multicultural environments, managing virtual teams, and understanding pros and cons of different organizational models (centralization versus decentralization). Working with global engineering teams and understanding of technical knowledge. Managing outsourced relationships and services. Driving supplier innovation and linking to internal teams.

- *Legal expertise*: building relational contracts, understanding legal contractual language, terms and conditions, legal clauses and vernacular. Building good price- and cost-modelling indices for contracting, and managing risks and rewards through improved contract structure. Best practices in ongoing contract management. Managing conflicts that emerge post-contract signing. Dealing with intellectual property (IP) issues when working with suppliers.

- *Talent management*: building a pipeline of leadership and supply management expertise, mentoring and leadership development.

TABLE 6.1 Future roles of procurement

Role	1 Ad Hoc	2 Defined	3 Managed	4 Leveraged	5 Optimized
Internal consultant	Small team handles ad hoc requests for transactional work	Quarterly reports generated and reviewed with stakeholders and follow-up	Global team coordinates with stakeholders via defined statements of work (SOWs) and designed templates	Global team and site representation provides local insight and engagement	Global team and co-located teams participate in meetings and are able to anticipate requirements
Market intelligence and cost modelling	Low level of common tools, processes and methodology	Cost models apply publicly traded financial information to create high-level product models	Dedicated cost model and supplier intelligence databases established with management information (MI) portals, feeds and updates	Dedicated cost modelling, MI analyst and ground-level roles established. All major categories have updated MI feeds	Cost models, MI and global event management is leveraged across the business for application in design, production and marketing decisions

(Continued)

TABLE 6.1 (*Continued*)

Role	1 Ad Hoc	2 Defined	3 Managed	4 Leveraged	5 Optimized
Financial expertise	Secondary data dumps pulled into ppt and shipped to users	Secondary data complements internal SME interviews on as-required basis	Multiple insights pulled using triangulated results, SME insights, ongoing database updates and market indicator reports	Co-located teams collect local supplier insights and complement global team updates and reporting on real-time basis	Co-located teams plus networks of SMEs located within the supply base and other outsourced service providers update market conditions and deep future state insights
Risk mitigator	Financial health measured annually using Dun & Bradstreet sources	Multiple indicators of financial health and operational risk established quarterly	Risk profiles include multiple measures of primary/ secondary operational and financial health check	Risk profiles include primary and secondary measures of tier 1 and 2 supplier risk	Global risk event triggers are monitored in real-time with impacts and mitigation plans in place

In terms of the road map to building these capabilities, our research also suggests that an evolution may require stages of maturity evolution, which may change over time. There is a need to be able to execute on what is needed *today*, even while a vision is kept in mind for building capabilities in the future. Today, procurement is inundated by requests from multiple stakeholders and, in some cases, may be pulled in different directions in the value chain. The roles that procurement is being asked to do may also present competing priorities for attention:

- *traditional role*: right part/right place/right time; not historically strategic or career oriented;
- *emerging role*: supplier risk management, integration within supply chain;
- *future role*: relationship manager, innovator.

As the evolution to the future state unfolds, there is no doubt that the structure of procurement organizations will change in response to broader business imperatives that are shaking organizations globally. For example, one executive noted that procurement may look more like an R&D organization, where there is a separation between a limited number of resources working on the programme side, and supporting business leaders on turning concepts into innovation plans and research. The procurement organization will lead certain commodities and skills into an R&D organization. We may also see procurement move entirely away from the P2P space, which becomes highly automated in an 'Amazon-like' interface, and become primarily focused on relationship management, and analytical insight and support. This may evolve into a project-based structure, where programme managers work directly with the business on different product/service cycles, and become integrated team members dedicated to the product.

At any rate, we expect to see a significant evolution occur for procurement by 2024. These insights are intended as a focal point for managers to begin thinking through these ideas and developing them.

Conclusions

To conclude, it is clear that no single blueprint exists for talent acquisition, development and retention. And yet many people have identified the need to find, train and commit to bringing on a new breed of procurement professionals. In this regard Optimum Procurement Group's recent white paper offered some observations, developed from a round table event where CPOs came together to debate what procurement's future role might present, and their thinking on some important new directions that will require investments in talent management and the subsequent development of this talent.[3] According to this white paper, becoming a procurement leader of tomorrow requires focus: a focus on the discernible and tangible benefit that they as procurement leaders will bring to their organization. The outcomes echo much of what is generally being aired by other professional observers and a summation of the next section, regarding what will be required.

Align, execute and deliver

As C-level executives chart the future course of their businesses, they will have several simultaneous objectives:

- Aligning their strategies with rapidly changing business contexts.
- Execute those strategies, to ensure their supply chains are sustainable, flexible and responsive through their networks, collaboration and focus.
- Delivery of procurement's new value proposition must be seamless, without operational interruptions or performance slips.

It will be a strategic balancing act and one that requires a strong leadership crossing all lines of business and reporting to the board.

Actively deploy new skill sets – bimodal procurement executives

There is now a universal acceptance of the pivotal role that supply management executives play in the success of businesses. But as business models evolve what does that imply for the executives who manage them? What kind of skill sets and capabilities will be required?

The traditional transactional skills of procurement on which the function was built will change, with increasing importance on people who are culturally aware. They will be collaborative and innovative diligent optimizers with strong leadership skills. Future supply professionals will offer decision makers more choices and alternatives, higher-precision controls and levers to achieve desired outcomes. They will be capable of optimizing global networks of assets and talent – not only their own but also those of partners and customers.

Understand the full extent of sustainability – social, economic and environmental

These responsibilities also extend to environmental stewardship. Perhaps more than any other role, top supply management executives must have an end-to-end understanding of the business, a broad view of external risks and the ability to manage holistically.

Businesses will need people focused on a career in procurement, attracting top graduates away from investment banks, consultancies and law firms by raising the profile of supply management beyond these traditional corporate 'staples'.

With the benefits of globalization has come increasing supply chain interdependence and a heightened level of volatility and vulnerability that is unlikely to subside. With such a clear mandate for change, supply management executives have an opportunity to re-evaluate current strategies and initiatives and set them in a context that will make talent attraction part of their strategic direction.

Create peace of mind for the board

With the massive global economic shifts we have recently encountered, 'change or perish' pronouncements pile up. Supply management has at its disposal the necessary ingredients to make supply chains substantially better connected and more important to current strategic enablers. The CEO's growing understanding of how critical the function is to the company's success establishes the challenge and the opportunity to create change and peace of mind from the supply side. To do this they will need to be innovative, focused and collaborative. These skills and abilities need to be transferred through systematic and ongoing training and development programmes, as well as talent-focused recruitment programmes.

In previous chapters we looked at how the changing world order has impacted everything from demographics and consumption levels to a shift in the economic centre of gravity. We have also contemplated how procurement has changed and the different levels of procurement maturity that exist today.

In this chapter we have begun to look at where we can find the people with the qualities required to work in the contemporary business world and why these skills are becoming even more important in the age of technology. In the next chapter we contemplate the people aspects of this change via an examination of issues such as talent and creativity.

Notes

1 Booz & Co (2014) [accessed 11 August 2014] The New CPO, white paper http://www.strategyand.pwc.com/media/file/New_CPO.pdf

2 Chandler Jr, A D (1977) *The Visible Hand: The managerial revolution in American business*, Harvard University Press, Cambridge, MA, p58.

3 Chick, G and Rushton, P (2013) Procurement's New Value Proposition to Business, Optimum Procurement Group.

Cometh the hour cometh the man

Realizing procurement's potential by building winning teams

In previous chapters we have contemplated how procurement has changed and the different levels of procurement maturity that exist today. We have looked too at how the changing world order has impacted everything from demographics and consumption levels to a shift in the economic centre of gravity and the game-changing impacts of globalization. It is becoming obvious too that people, talent and creativity are key.

All too often we hear that there aren't the people 'out there'. But clearly these people are available. How is it that other parts of business such as finance, HR or marketing can find people with the qualities and skills required to work in the contemporary business world?

Procurement's journey to core business capability truly began when it became apparent that they could win market share by making products that buyers yearn for, and delivering them consistently at the right time, in the right quantity and at the right location. In doing so procurement recognized that this would be key in gaining the dominant market position they yearned for.

A quick refresh

Let's begin by reminding ourselves of the new practice developments since the mid-1980s and the major issues that have brought the need for professional procurement to the fore. The emergence of just-in-time and make-to-order business models brought higher levels of efficiency to businesses – models that require extremely efficient supply chains in order to be effective:

- *Globalization.* As enterprises expanded internationally they came to realize that profiting from global growth is not possible without supporting supply chains. Buzz terms such as offshoring and, latterly, near-shoring, became part of the business lexicon.

- *Changing world order.* The rise of economic powerhouses such as China and India has underscored procurement's role in facilitating global trade. Within these regions companies have to learn how to create supply chains that deliver goods worldwide, while Western companies must adapt their supply management know-how to unfamiliar markets in these culturally diverse developing economies.

- *Market volatility.* The financial meltdown that rocked Western economies continues to reverberate through markets. As a buffer between companies and their customers, supply management plays a critical role in helping enterprises to face the volatility that has become the normality in the business world.

- *Technology.* The explosive growth of online commerce has further enhanced procurement's position within businesses. The sheer pace of change in the markets requires enterprises to be very responsive to shifts in demand. Moreover, online consumers have a low tolerance for mistakes or delays, and can injure a brand by communicating their displeasure far and wide via social media sites. The bottom line is that businesses that do not have efficient supply managers supporting their online operations will almost certainly stumble.

- *The growing awareness around sustainability.* Procurement is one of the primary players in the global movement to develop sustainable businesses.

- *Risk management.* As businesses adopted many of the practices outlined above, and their operations began to span the globe, they became exposed to a wider range of risks. Moreover, the procurement push to drive cost out or down has led to a situation where they have managed risk in. Whether it is the discovery of lead paint on toys, deplorable factory conditions, the devastating impacts of the weather, or terrorism, the disruptions created by unanticipated outcomes can and does lead to extensive operational and reputational damage.

This rise in the role of procurement has also brought a major challenge: how to ensure that there is enough talent to meet the profession's needs now and in the future. In addition to increasing the demand for talent, procurement's elevated role requires a mix of skills that is very different from what was needed in the early 2000s.

As already discussed, for some time professional bodies and academic institutions have been playing their part to build a better talent pipeline. Meanwhile, the big question is how do we get the best and brightest talent to realize that designing, deploying and managing the sustainable flow of goods, information and finance across the globe is one of the most exciting and fulfilling careers imaginable today. High finance is alluring, and the law offers some attractive challenges, but procurement offers much more. Procurement leadership as a profession now provides a route to the C-suite.

It is easy to spend a lot of one's professional life looking at what the future might bring. Of particular interest right now is the debate about the rise and impact of big data and the power of the cloud. Maybe it is this introduction of a more scientific procurement that will bring the smart people into the field. The perennial discussion regarding just how big a change this might be, reminds me of something Peter Thiel said: 'We wanted flying cars, and they gave us 140 characters.'[1] So maybe we should watch this particular space with a degree of suspicion.

Peter Thiel notwithstanding, it is increasingly apparent that the most debatable issue is that no matter how much procurement tries and succeeds there are still those who treat it with disdain; George Bernard Shaw wrote that, 'the difference between a lady and a flower girl is not how she behaves, but how she is treated'; so what procurement professionals need to do right now is to persuade the rest of the organization that they are what and who they say they are.

Deep 'smarts' are key

In Chapter 4 we suggested that one of the key game changes (no. 2) related to technological advances. Technological innovation has placed the availability of an unprecedented volume of information at one's fingertips. Add to this the availability of tools and techniques available to business today to make sense of this mass of data, in the hands of the right people with the right skills mix – and a picture begins to unfold regarding the potential of the modern procurement team. Put simply, being a smart procurement organization is the differentiator: knowledge and a talented team are key – and they need to develop new concepts on old themes.

Procurement leaders need to deliver 'a different mindset', a whole different approach to convey the value of procurement practices to the whole organization and, in particular, to the CEO. To do this CPOs need to develop ideas about the highest leverage changes that have the highest probability of succeeding.

Despite a plethora of readily available and high-quality commentary about contemporary procurement practice – which is frequently backed by solid experience and empirical data – many remain loath to move beyond the most basic levels of professional procurement practice. The progress of real change in supply management has been slow. It is now well documented that few if any companies can allow procurement to be managed in isolation from overall business systems. Bath School of Management have produced evidence that suggests supply management requires greater integration, stronger cross-functional relationships and more senior management involvement. Identified too was that the days of the sourcing 'nerd' are numbered. The era of 'scrape out the barrel', where people squeezed suppliers for every last drop, is going or has already gone. With it, the hard-nosed beat-'em-up attitude of 'the barrel ain't scraped until there are splinters in your tongue' is fast disappearing too.

This viewpoint has been echoed by many of the senior procurement professionals we have worked with, who agree that a new modus is what is needed in order to get some traction in their businesses. It is incredible to think that it is 30 years since Peter Kraljic published his seminal paper – *Purchasing must become supply management* – in *Harvard Business Review*. Today this serves to underscore the issue of change inertia in procurement.

And yet one still hears voices in procurement calling for the so-called 'silver bullet' – that one thing to get them a seat at the 'top table'. Frequently their calls are answered with responses framed in a procurement-only context. But in contemporary businesses we are seeing the shrinking of silos, and an evolution in professional procurement. Organizations are moving away from large, discrete, enterprise-level organizations dedicated to *doing* procurement to a more *aligned and agile* procurement with a firm focus on profits rather than simply cost-savings.

We have seen too the growing trend in loose networks rather than the tight functions mentioned above – networks of supplier-facing procurement people embedded into strategic business units. Procurement is becoming increasingly linked to financial supply chains, with the role of optimizing cash flow and working capital and implementing dynamic discounting and supply-chain financing. Finally, with the growing trend in procurement out-sourcing, supply management practitioners are increasingly faced with the curious paradox of buying 'buying'.

Brave new world

A cursory glance at the foregoing gives us a flavour of not only the changes in business models and operations but also that skill sets need to change to meet the new challenges.

Procurement professionals must become experts in multiple fields:

- respected;
- influential;
- persuasive;
- visionary;
- strategic;
- sharp;
- global;
- collaborative;
- executive;
- business savvy;
- and, above all, focused.

As a profession, procurement needs to develop a new definition of what 'expert' means in supply management today. Contemporary supply professionals must be or soon become students of their own industry. They must develop their skills in and knowledge of the sectors, categories and geographies they work in as well as the practical aspects of securing supply into, as well as from, those markets. They must also offer expertise and cultural awareness to sales-focused areas of business.

This may look something of a tall order, but competent people, the best and the brightest, will meet the challenge and excel. As the shift in procurement from 'doer' to 'enabler' continues, those who remain will be consummate professionals who will drive forward supply management and business. Many of these competent, confident, high-achievers are already in the profession – some are waiting to be recruited. Above all, these professionals need to be nurtured and directed by competent leaders in the field.

In supply management, competence must be based on an understanding of appropriateness – knowing what to do to deliver strategic goals operationally within specific supply chain and market circumstances. Supply management professionals in the future will be people with a well-developed professional knowledge of the procurement tools and techniques at their disposal, supported by well-developed commercial acumen. Key will be their ability to discern, in detail, the range of contingent supply chain market circumstances facing them and know what needs to be done. In essence, they will know how to use the right tools in precise circumstances to deliver corporate goals operationally.

If we pause to reflect on the supply chain complexity we are faced with today, the need for these 'special' people becomes quite clear. Factory collapses in Bangladesh, Somali pirates, counterfeiting, conflict minerals, the Bribery Act, batteries catching fire in aircraft, obsolescence, cultural boundaries and child labour: contemporary procurement requires people to be entrepreneurial, brand-conscious, skilled analysts with a bimodal capability:

- Commercial prudence is a prerequisite in the contemporary supply management professional.
- Competent and confident, they will be able to work with both risk and reward in contracts, and to accept and manage greater risk in relationships.
- They will be the 'intelligent client' able to motivate suppliers.
- Technology too has created challenges – smartphones, tablets and embedded chips have all initiated a mobile work environment in which the modern supply professional must feel comfortable.
- In the era of 'big data' they have to be adept at handling and analysing data while being able to see major trends and important takeaways at a glance.

As has already been mentioned, special skills need special people. So who will they be and where will we find them? Possibly the most immediate and impactful thing that organizations can do is to develop a 'talent mindset'. Organizations must believe that talent is essential to success now and for the future: talent breeds competitive advantage. Supply management leaders should recognize the broad set of capabilities outlined above and understand that this requires eclecticism. The diversity of skills and experience required will take time to find or develop in people.

Committing time to building the next generation of leaders also requires a degree of introspection. You must be an innovator and spend a lot of time looking for and developing your eventual replacements. Many of those filling these roles will be 'millennials'. The term millennials generally refers to the generation of people born between the early 1980s and the early 2000s. Perhaps the most commonly used birth range for this group is 1982–2000. The millennial generation is also known as Generation Y, because it comes after Generation X – those people born between the early 1960s and the 1980s. But are Generation Y people all that different from the rest of us? According to a study commissioned by the Institute of Leadership in Management (ILM) they most certainly are.[2] According to the ILM study, Generation Y tend to have (among other traits) high self-esteem, don't trust the system, are idealistic and extremely tech-savvy. They are the 'digital natives' – as opposed to earlier generations who are the 'digital immigrants'. They also find different approaches easy to tolerate and are naturally collaborative. When it comes to their expectations, they respect people who are organized, open-minded and expert in their field. They look for mentors who are respectful of their generation and have an understanding of their need for a work–life balance.

As we enter this new era, where business models are increasingly agile, we must play our part in leading and inspiring people who think differently and faster, and who are looking for continuous challenge. To lead talented people and make the most of their talent we need to learn quickly how to spot and respond to talent, how to develop it and understand what role they play in the organization's success. Most important of all, as their leader you must be credible and respected and be the person that a talented individual is happy to be led by.

Two big questions

There is clearly a need, then, to explore two big questions: first, whether an alternative procurement mindset is starting to emerge; one that recognizes the enduring need for functional legitimacy and authenticity (ie there is no substitute for having deep procurement skills) together with a sense of ambition, accountability and self-responsibility – accepting that senior roles sometimes trade responsibility for influence. This more collaborative and inclusive personal credo must be aligned with specific organizational goals but, more significantly, should be actively aware of strategic issues and longer-term horizons. The second question is the need to ask in what ways this new attitude can be nurtured and how individuals can themselves make the transition.

Coming together is a beginning; keeping together is progress; working together is success

Regarding the first question, in today's complex world there is a clear need for a new business mindset and procurement is at the heart of establishing this. Listed below are some specific elements to be considered when trying to understand how to put together a winning procurement organization. Procurement clearly needs to develop sophistication in thought and deed. Moreover, reflecting on the five game changers discussed in Chapter 5 we can highlight a list of attributes that are demanded of procurement today:

- *Effective execution*: delivering against your remit.
- *Perfect alignment*: systems, procedures, people and leaders all aligned.
- *Agility*: adaptation is necessary for external as well as internal changes.
- *Clear and 'fuzzy' strategy*: this will allow you to adapt to change and put right mistakes.
- *Leadership*: being able to lead and develop a 'following' is critical.
- *Focus*: your focus must be both internal to deliver results to your stakeholders and external to be aware of markets and customer needs.
- *The right people*: it is important to get the right people. Teams work in harmony and team players, the right people, are not prima donnas and are not into self-aggrandizement.
- *Manage the downside*: evaluate risk well and plan for risk rather than attempting to become risk-free – it will never happen.
- *Balance everything*: combine the above.

If procurement is to deliver its value proposition it has to be united. Not just within the function but also across the business, it must focus on synchronicity. The supply chain and its internal and external relationships is the glue that holds the business together. Ever-closer synchronization is key. Tighten links between suppliers, operations and your customers. Procurement should be central to the building of information bridges to suppliers and stakeholders. Through the establishment of a flow of information amongst and between stakeholders, suppliers and customers, procurement can build a common bond of trust.

One of the most important elements for procurement professionals to focus on is the development of sustainable enduring relationships.

A re-examination of existing relationships to determine whether they are effective will deliver clear value to the business. It is ridiculous to imagine that the establishment of a partnership with every supplier is possible or even pertinent. Consequently, procurement leaders need to ascertain which of them are likely to be sustainable. Establish the strategic changes to make; and then make time to tightly focus on the supply chain. These considerations are a joint exercise and must take into account other parts of the business in order to clarify the optimal relationships portfolio – so some hard and careful thinking needs to be done.

By doing this procurement brings this collaborative mindset to life. In developing an understanding of the need for connectivity they make the value chain everyone's business. The more people think about their individual impact in the business, the better they will do their jobs. In promoting greater coordination at all levels between procurement and the other service functions across the business there is a greater chance of stimulating innovation through this united approach.

A winning team is as strong as the relationships within it; its driving force, the creation and maintenance of excellent relationships adding robustness to the team's dynamic. Focus on gratitude and vitality to strengthen and deepen the relationships within.

We have already discussed the recognition of the value of the broad set of capabilities and an understanding of the diversity of skills and experience required, and the fact that it will take time to find or develop the right people. Committing time to building the next generation of leaders also requires a degree of introspection. You must be an innovator and spend a lot of time looking for and developing your eventual replacements.

Where to look for the right people is often the stumbling block, and in that search there are a number of underlying traits to look for:

- Seek out people with intensity, with extra energy and enthusiasm.

- Look for people with sensitivity, reactivity; those who will readily offer discretionary effort. These people thrive on ambiguity; they thrive on 'impossible' problems and change. They will give their wholehearted effort and tend to be sensitive to the concerns and feelings of others. These people are eager to learn, understand and improve.

- Also look for people with a certain complexity, with extraordinary perception, vision and the capacity for original, multilevel thinking. These people are very fast learners and they learn more effectively than others. They are creative, visionary, quickly grasping complex ideas and problems and will readily offer unique perspectives and solutions. You need independent thinkers.

- Finally, look for people with drive and who are clearly engaged in what they are doing. These people will be self-directing, dedicated, often exceeding expectations of them. They are intent on excellence and can develop or will already have multiple areas of expertise. They are natural leaders and influencers both within the team and outside.

The future of you

In addressing the second part of the question posed above – how this new attitude can be developed and how one can make the transition – we need to hold up a mirror to ourselves and ask: is this the future of me? Globalization and technological changes are reshaping the nature of work. Having a great job does not guarantee personal success: your competence no longer depends on what you know, and being an affluent consumer matters less than becoming a sought-after product. Welcome to a new era of work, where your future depends on being a signal in the noisy universe of human capital. In order to achieve this, you need to master three things: self-branding, entrepreneurship and hyper-connectivity.

Self-branding is the signal you give off amongst the din of business activity. The stronger your brand, the stronger that signal. In today's world, self-branding matters more than any other form of talent, not least because the mass market is unable (or unwilling) to distinguish between branding and talent. Being or becoming a brand means showcasing that which makes you special, in a way that is distinctive, predictable and meaningful, it allows others to understand what you do and why. As Antoine de Saint-Exupéry put it, 'perfection is achieved, not when there is nothing more to add, but when there is nothing left to take away'.

Entrepreneurship is about adding value to your organization by disrupting it and improving the order of things. It is by creating a better future. We are all busy, but the only activity that really matters is enterprising activity. Entrepreneurship is the difference between being busy and being a business, and the reason why some are able to stay in business while others get outsourced. Every transaction between people is a business transaction.

The most important commodity in human capital today is people who can grow a business. Be that person. In today's battle for talent the big issue is identifying, developing and retaining true change agents. Change agents are hard to find, hard to manage and hard to retain. Entrepreneurship is about being a change agent; change agents are signals, everyone else is noise. If you are not bringing growth, you are replaceable and recyclable.

Your future depends on your ability to offer something new: new solutions for existing problems; new services and products; new ideas. Everything that isn't new is old, and if you are doing old you are stuck in the past. Today it is important to develop a 'self-brand'. By this we mean that your personal brand development will get you noticed and create value for you and your employer. Your value depends on your knowledge reputation and ability to see and do things differently. As computer scientist Alan Kay pointed out, 'a change in perspective is worth 80 IQ points'.

Hyper-connectivity is about being a signal in the ocean of data and making some waves. Everyone and everything is increasingly online, but what matters is being relevant. Hyper-connectivity is not about being online 24/7; it is about optimizing the online experience for others. Unless you are a hyper-connector, only your friends care about what you had for lunch and whom it was with – but when you are a hyper-connector, thousands of people will be shaped by your views. In the era of information overload, being a trustworthy source of information is a rare commodity – it is the digital equivalent of being an intellectual and the latest state in the evolution of marketing. The most important form of knowledge today is knowing where to find things: answers, ideas and points of view. In fact, the ability to find things is becoming as important as the ability to create things.

In short, the future of you depends on your ability to be a brand, a change agent, and a link to useful information. Paying attention to your personality and managing how others see you will turn you into a successful brand; paying attention to your ideas and defying the status quo will help you to become a change agent; and bridging the gap between useful knowledge and collective interests will turn you into a hyper-connector.

Building a winning procurement team

Only a few smart companies today know how to develop a winning procurement team: a team that is essential to maximizing efficiency, buys the best products and profits from new ideas in the marketplace. But many more are becoming aware of the inalienable fact that procurement is an area where businesses can reap major benefits.

This is because procurement impacts the whole organization, and in order for a business to preserve its reputation, the goods or services it provides to the market must be appropriate and fit for purpose, they must be the right quality and arrive on time. This is where customer value is gained.

Putting in place the right skills is arguably the most important foundation for maximizing the procurement function's success. A procurement operation must ensure it has the skills needed to deliver results in areas such as cost, innovation, resilience, quality and flexibility. Employing and nurturing the right talent, while fostering good communication throughout the company and with suppliers, is important – given that procurement in most organizations spends in excess of 50 per cent of business revenues.

Assembling a strong procurement team is difficult because the function is perceived to be less alluring than, say, marketing or finance. For some reason, it doesn't have the same reputation as these other service functions. In addition, because people are becoming aware of the need for smart people in procurement there is strong competition from other companies for talented staff.

The issue has become the number one challenge for CPOs and there is currently a threat of a procurement 'brain drain' as organizations scramble to find good people to fill their knowledge and skills gaps. In addressing the staffing problem many CXOs as well as CPOs say that the growing 'science of procurement' is attracting smart people to look at the area. These new and interesting aspects of procurement, such as the use of analytics development of collaborative relationships, the search for innovation and sustainability, are becoming much better understood by potential employees, who are being drawn to procurement by the prospect of working in a multifaceted, value-driven environment.

In recent years a number of specialist undergraduate as well as postgraduate degrees in supply chain management are on offer, and organizations such as CIPS offers its own globally recognized professional diploma. Increasingly, too, the people or 'soft' skills have taken a prominent position in the mix. Clearly these are limited to supply management and the need is perhaps heralded by the increased use of technology. As e-solutions take over the mundane tactical aspects of procurement, those working in the field are moving to the more sophisticated aspects. Whereas more traditional procurement teams did deals and managed contracts, contemporary procurement needs people who can influence, lead and invoke change.

This sophistication and new-found acceptance also facilitates a deeper integration between departments and thus creates opportunities for procurement staff to gain deeper insight. It is this kind of movement within an organization that enables a broader skills base to exist in procurement.

A procurement organization that serves the whole business and is aligned with the whole organization is the holy grail of procurement. Moreover, business needs to ensure that the board as well as the chief executive support procurement – and an increasing number of CXOs recognize the importance of having their head of procurement sit on the board. For this alignment to occur more widely, businesses need to rid themselves of 'corporate ignorance' of procurement's value to the organization.

Other service functions approach procurement in the wrong sequence, usually starting with cost. Instead, when they understand the function, they can begin with value creation – how they can optimize the supply chain, work well with suppliers and make use of suppliers' capabilities. Procurement teams must create a welcoming atmosphere for suppliers. If procurement is allowed to operate effectively, suppliers should be treated as a driving force for innovation and viewed as critical partners in the company's success.

When procurement deploys people with the right skills, encourages and facilitates communication and works efficiently with suppliers, a real strategic gain is achieved. Modern business will demand that these factors are put in place – it will want a winning procurement team. The case study below shows how such a winning team can make a big difference – especially during a major crisis.

CASE STUDY The Thailand issue

Many of the companies that make hard disk drives (HDDs) are located in Thailand and production is there. In October 2011, the unthinkable happened. A major flood hit Bangkok, and the major supply impacts hit in the middle of November for all of the major PC manufacturers. As a result, computer manufacturers witnessed massive shortages of HDDs: Apple, IBM, Lenovo, HP, Dell – and others. Everyone uses HDDs; they are in every computer and in every DVR and computer electronics. The only substitute technology is solid state drives, but they have not come into play as much to be an alternative. HDDs are a valuable piece of every computer.

The two biggest HDD suppliers – Western Digital and Seagate – both have their major final assembly as well as supply operations in Thailand. Both have essentially been shut down because of the floods that occurred in October 2011.

Western Digital had a lot of downstream components that resulted in worldwide shortage of HDDs, which will have multi-quarter impacts on *all* upstream customers who had disk drives in their equipment. All of these companies in November 2011 were facing massive component shortages and massive cost increases in order to get out of the mess.

The business management system

This large global computer manufacturer (called 'COMP' in this study) has a business management system that emphasizes monthly progress to key stakeholders, but during the Thailand event the company delivered daily progress reports. The thinking here is that because COMP's supply chain is embedded and critical for execution, it is critical that daily communications occur with customers, investor relations and, of course, suppliers.

After the crisis, there was a lot of internal discussion around how to allocate product mix and profitability: product mix drives financials and, in normal conditions, allocation is not an issue. But there are questions that have had to be addressed.

Thailand has been the biggest test of COMP's senior executives' business management system for communications. The reason is that, first, it had a major impact on a specific piece of the business – hard disk drives – which are in *every* machine! This impacts on every one of COMP's products and those of its competitors: 50 per cent of the world's supply of hard disk drives are in a flood zone.

One of COMP's senior executives noted that:

> We first had to work through the realization of the impact – not a lot of press about this – and had to convince customers and ourselves that it was a major issue. As you go to mobilize quickly we had to first of all convince ourselves and then convince others that this situation was worse than the Japanese tsunami in terms of impact to our business. People challenged us – how could it be worse? Floods happen all the time! We got through Japan so well – we can do the same here. . .
>
> The realization that it was worse than the tsunami in Japan required us to mobilize and assess and get on the ground and send people there. We shifted immediately to a crisis management role – and key supplier relationships and leadership were key. We had to go in and establish knowledge, and gain the communication with suppliers to truly understand the impact, bring it to credibility, and describe to the business and to customers. This played out in weeks – getting a handle on what is happening – and suppliers were also trying to figure out how to answer our questions and competitors' questions! Getting a handle on the facts and getting the business reset was the second phase – and once you understand supply impact, cost impact, and competitive response

we had to figure out the overall impact – and that is still in process for us. The driver for all of this was focused on our key supplier relationships, which we have cultivated through our actions. We communicated with them to really, really understand what was truly happening, what we could count on – what we could look forward to. We had to manage the cost impact – and also had to deal with competitive response. First, Seagate said they would raise prices – and then Dell informed the market there would be a huge impact – and this caused complexity for us. Next – once we understood this – we created a plan: optimizing the business was the key.

The first thing we did was to allocate parts to build, and allocate product to customers. And we did seek balancing objectives in alignment with upper management priorities; the agility driver was business alignment. Typically we work monthly communications but we were doing it weekly and daily. We had to decide which customers we would satisfy – and do we optimize growth or profit? Do we maintain our momentum with dealers, or back off – and make sure end customers get the product? Those were the issues we had to decide on.

From an agility driver perspective, the BMS communications are central to this and executing the plan is key. It is one thing to communicate – but another to drive major alterations and do it daily. We found an alternative supplier for hard drives, but the supplier we thought we had might not have the quality we needed – so we dispatched engineers to test and qualify that – and if not, we had to lose that supplier and reset that plan. We have an ability to reset and unify decisions based on this plan and a good example of the real major crisis that has tested our agility and done so formally and visibly, but the jury is still out on this. We are hopeful we will land competitively – we are all struggling with this.

Last year we also came close to a flood in Thailand during the rainy season, and the water receded. If we had looked at that and made changes to our supply base, maybe we could have been okay. But finding other sources of supply in this space is costly! But after this issue, the industry will reset! There is 50 per cent of supply that is all in the same area of the floods – and this is the first time it has happened! We will definitely change our approach – and there will be lessons learned on how we managed through it – and we will do things differently. . .

As a result of the event in Thailand, all PC companies definitely experienced volume and market share loss. But COMP has got great investor attention with their growth (reaching number three worldwide in global volume and sales), and view this disruption as another opportunity to prove to investors that they can manage through a crisis – through procurement agility and risk management.

Some conclusions

Sporting metaphors are plentiful in business – we 'play to win'; executives 'coach' their teams; you need to have the 'best players' to compete. But quite often people in business work against each other or against colleagues from other parts of the business. This misalignment is as ridiculous as it is common.

Even when you strip away the analogy and look solely at how top sports organizations actually develop on-the-field talent you begin to get some idea of how rigorous, demanding and comprehensive the focus needs to be. In businesses, on the other hand, the focus on tangible assets, capability and products frequently obscure the most important asset – talent. In sport, there is no such white noise. Continued success is achieved solely through people and their relentless focus on performance.

If procurement is to be the star player, determining what makes a winning team and where procurement fits in is difficult. And yet cutting through the noise is essential if we are to get anywhere near to understanding what 'winning' behaviour is and how it creates value for the business.

Winning is about having a clear and aligned strategy. It is about being realistic but ambitious. There is no place for the eponymous BHAG (big hairy audacious goals).[3] Not unless you are a base jumper or some other kind of adrenaline junkie. It certainly isn't about one big initiative. Winning is the outcome of a lot of decisions and activities, not one and not luck. In business, winners are a group of people, coupled with systems and processes, which make up the winning team.

Structures in winning businesses are constantly evolving in order to cope with new projects starting and old ones finishing. Promotions, external challenges, innovation and new organizational themes demand structural change. Just as in sport: a captain or coach will restructure the side as things change, or build teams that can operate out of position in order to cope with the unexpected.

Another misnomer is that success is only about profitability. Profitability is one measure of organizational success; doing well on the financials is important, but winning businesses also excel at understanding customer needs, efficiency, development, employees and key stakeholders – in essence, all-round long-term performance, a sustainable organization.

In this chapter we looked again at the impacts of the five game changers and how traditional procurement simply does not cut it in the new business world. We also looked at how procurement can realize its potential by purposefully building winning teams. In the next chapter we begin our examination of what the future might hold for procurement and supply chain management.

Notes

1 Peter Andreas Thiel is an American entrepreneur, venture capitalist and hedge fund manager. Thiel co-founded PayPal with Max Levchin and served as its CEO.

2 The ILM Index of Leadership Trust, 2009.

3 A big hairy audacious goal (BHAG) is a strategic business statement similar to a vision statement that is created to focus an organization on a single medium- to long-term organization-wide goal that is audacious, likely to be externally questionable, but not internally regarded as impossible. The term was proposed by James Collins and Jerry Porras in their 1994 book entitled *Built to Last: Successful habits of visionary companies*.

The dawn of procurement's new value proposition

Innovation, collaboration and focus

08

Uncertainty is perhaps the word to describe the feeling in today's global marketplace. Increased exposure to shocks and disruption is an outcome of economies, financial markets and supply chains growing into global interconnected webs. Complexity exacerbates the problem; today even minor mishaps and miscalculations can have major consequences as their impacts have something approaching epidemic proportions throughout complex supply networks.

In this chapter we begin to investigate what the future might hold for procurement and supply chain management: by absorbing what we have introduced through the book so far as well as contemplating how those who are likely to be making decisions now might prepare for what comes next.

We have spent considerable time looking at the three most significant aspects of capability development: people, processes and technology. This trinity is unequivocally the power behind procurement capability. Moreover, it is incumbent on procurement and business leaders to avail themselves and the organizations they run of this fact. However, in doing so they must scale a problem that burdens so many leaders and their managers – and that is answering the question 'what is best practice?'.

The question of 'best' practice

There is no such thing as 'best' practice. Best must be judged in context; it is relative to needs and circumstances. Another way of looking at it is to ask: what is right for this organization? What is right for your own needs and, crucially, for your own needs at a particular point in time and in particular market circumstances? Needs vary and they vary by organization, location, culture, geography, industry sector, capability, maturity, philosophy, personality and over time.

The broadening range of the procurement profession's contributions to organizations has made this concept even more significant over time. Reducing cost is clearly important to all organizations, but organizations also have other decision drivers, which demand the derivation of greater value. Examples of these value drivers include security of supply, speed to market, service levels, quality standards, and social and environmental responsibility. So it should be patently obvious that one organization's 'best' practice might not be 'best' practice for another organization.

Needless to say, there is still 'good' practice and we have suggested an idea of what 'world-class' practices might look like. Much of the writing on procurement in the last 30 years or so has focused on and provided a wealth of research, data and experience that indicates the characteristics of both good and bad practice, but so far no one has found that single, superlative, best practice.

The characteristics of what good practice is can be reasonably well defined. They can even be graded and quantified to show a linear progression across a broad range of criteria (as was highlighted in Chapter 2). They can also be used as part of a process to define progress and set goals (as was discussed in Chapter 4). But, such characteristics are outcomes really. They are the benefits to be gained from sustained effort and continued investment in good procurement practice. However, if these characteristics are to be developed and built into the organization's processes and mindset then much hard work and serious influencing has to be brought to bear. As Dan Milman (1980) wrote in his book *Way of the Peaceful Warrior*: 'to rid yourself of old patterns, focus all your energy not on struggling with the old, but on building the new'.

Issues in the management of modern procurement

A great deal of focus and writing on procurement has been on the relatively simple context of a large and powerful buying organization, procuring an uncomplicated product or service from an acquiescent supplier.

However, in reality things are not as simple as that and real-life procurement is a far more complex issue. Procurement managers have to manage for innovation, manage often well-established markets and be able to do this in the increasing complexity of our globalized business world.

In today's business-to-business environment the complexity of the procurements made are reflected in the complexity of the business-to-business relationships required to support the procurement activity they are engaged in. Today, with the multi-organizational alliances often created to develop strategic leverage, procurement and supply management crosses many organizational boundaries and especially that of operations.

The contemporary procurement professional is engaged in optimizing the balances of risk and cost in the context of the increasingly complex procurements they are making. Issues such as the adequacy of contractual arrangements, which as we are aware can never hope to cover all eventualities and circumstances and, as a consequence, impinge on both governance and relationships. Both of these issues – risk and cost – are business critical and procurement must play its part in the emerging debate on risk and cost management by means of the implementation of relational mechanisms, which will operate alongside traditional contractual mechanisms to support them.

Procurement: why traditional approaches no longer fit

A focus rounding on uncertainty and risk are central in establishing the rationale of any contemporary procurement strategy. Today the very core of the discipline centres around a tool developed in 1983 by German consultant Peter Kraljic. He devised the 2 × 2 matrix that maps profit impact against supply risk. Most procurement people use Kraljic's tool to analyse their purchasing portfolio and to divide how procurement resources should be allocated. However, while this approach was fine in the context of procurement in the 1980s – where there was a greater degree of certainty in markets, and the impacts of offshoring and a globalized market were much less impactful – the commodity-led approach that this tool drives does not address some of today's big issues. For example, the political dimensions of contemporary procurement, where powerful interest groups will pressure for things that are not aligned to the economic efficiency of the commodity model – CSR being possibly the most obvious. This results in a complexity in the 'procurement' of both investment and coordination across multiple stakeholders. This in turn leads to fragmented decision making and an increase and decrease of focus on who is important – customer or the project depending on the external environment, typically in the form of media scare-mongering or the career path or even the recruitment of specific individuals.

Many contemporary procurements are bespoke, especially those in sectors such as construction or the manufacture of civil or military aviation. Here, different skills and competencies are required as are different relationships between the customer and the procurer. Today many contractual and other relationships, especially those with strategic suppliers, need to be dynamic and in some cases iterative. Procurement professionals need to be able to align outputs and requirements rather than provide compliance. This demands a performance mindset, which looks to spread risk and reward sharing across the entire supply network.

Traditional procurement has brought little if anything in terms of new practice. Kraljic's Matrix was developed in the 1980s, before the shift in the global centre of economic gravity from West to East. The five 'game changers' discussed in Chapter 4 signal that the demand for products, services and utilities will increase and there will need to be a corresponding increase in the agility of supply chains/networks as well as procurement competence and skill sets to meet these new demands.

FIGURE 8.1   Procurement's triple focus

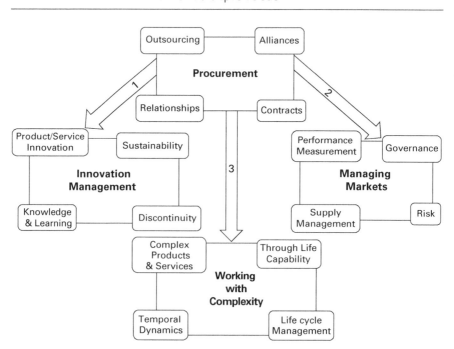

Global procurement practice in the 21st century goes far beyond the mere compliance of the late 20th century; it must move towards the imperatives associated with long-term growth innovation and a closer and more strategic proximity to the supply base.

Today a difference is emerging in procurement distinguishing the 'old' from the 'new'. Contemporary procurement demands that procurement activity is freer, less proscriptive and restricted, more interactive and certainly much more about the long-term. It is clear that a new set of challenges are facing procurement leaders today. They need to be able to forge and maintain relationships with suppliers with the capability to innovate and supply match the long-term requirements of the buying organization (see Figure 8.1). These areas include:

- the management and co-creation of innovation;
- the management and understanding of markets;
- the ability to operate in complexity.

Managing for innovation

Today it is no longer enough to build a supply management capability that is efficient, demand-driven or even transparent. Procurement must offer the organization something that is value adding; procurement needs to deliver innovation through its collaborations and longer-term focus.

Terms such as state-of-the-art have a much shorter shelf-life as the pace of technological advances quickens across the world. Suppliers invest heavily in research and development – it is not uncommon for this to be as much as 10 per cent of their annual revenues. It is important to have supplier relationships in place that allow this innovation to flow into the business – and equally for the suppliers to understand the business needs in order to guide and tailor innovation.

There is also a greater need for clarity over intellectual property (IP). Through the necessity in modern business to outsource, much IP has shifted out of the company and into the supplier base. This creates what is termed a shallow depth of manufacture. As supply management professionals look to extract more value from their supplier relationships it stands to reason that, in time, leveraging supplier resources and integrating supplier functions one-to-one with their own will become a reality. Much in business is about timing; the unreachable becomes reachable, the unavailable become available, the unattainable becomes attainable. Customer–supplier collaboration will shift, and whilst today suppliers may be asked to contribute ideas to existing designs or to help fix existing processes soon they will be frequently in from the beginning.

For some time manufacturing has been led by the 'make versus buy' paradigm,[1] and whilst the manufacturers intend to stay there, services organizations will join the outsourcing melee too. The expanding trend to extended enterprises promises interesting times for supply professionals in the very near future.

To take advantage of IP in the future, it is imperative for businesses to understand what IP is being generated through their activities – whether that is formal IP assets or simply organizational knowledge – where it sits, and who owns it.

Managing markets

Procurement will remain core in that businesses need to have the right procurement strategies; but it is not core to the extent that today's outsourced procurement service providers can better leverage markets. Many of these organizations have developed exponentially better capabilities than businesses have in particular commodities or spend categories, because they source them on a more regular and broader basis than we will ever do internally.

This situation has been developing for a number of years as service providers honed their offerings – building their business models, tying in the technology, and so forth. Today, we see service providers getting to the point where they do things better than many seasoned procurement organizations.

The role of procurement leaders will be to leverage the expertise and excellence and then to developing relationships with the service providers that put them completely into synch with their own business models. This will enable CPOs to extract more and more value from outsourced relationships.

Another factor relates to high-performance enterprise procurement organizations – those that began their strategic transformations in the early 2000s and have attained high levels of spend management maturity. These organizations will continue to spin out discrete business units that offer procurement and sourcing services often geared to specialized segments of industry. This is already happening in sectors such as health care, hospitality and food services.

A significant characteristic of the new procurement professional will be the extent of their expertise. Whilst procurement has spent the last 30 years looking backward at money spent last year, supplier performance in the past week, month or quarter – contemporary procurement professionals will be forward-looking deal shapers. These people will need to be both analysts and commercially proficient, guiding the business in its strategic planning.

We have lots of data at our fingertips in procurement, but it is data that tells us what has already happened, how many defects we had in the last month, how many shipments were late, and how much savings we achieved (or not). To operate in today's volatile global markets procurement will focus more on forward-looking, predictive analysis:

- Procurement will use models to project where supplier defects are most likely to occur, and have KPIs for suppliers that measure the discrete pieces of their processes that are most likely to affect our end customers. We will be able to prioritize supplier processes according to our customer requirements and measure them.

- While the ability to execute predictive performance management is elusive today, procurement needs to push in this direction if it wants to become more deeply ingrained in such functions as business strategy development and new product design, development and launch. Procurement needs to be able to predict how a product or service will perform from both quality and total cost perspectives. Businesses need to know when changes in data predict problems in the future.

- Supporting and reinforcing predictability will be business communities trading information in real-time in much the same way that communities such as LinkedIn enable one to obtain predictive information about how a person is likely to perform on the job, eBay gives one information about how a particular buyer/seller is likely to behave, and Amazon can suggest books that one is likely to enjoy by comparing searches and purchases among people with similar habits.

  Depth and value of predictive information being exchanged among trading partners will grow as participation in networked business communities expands exponentially and procurement professionals will be capable of analysing and understanding the worldwide dynamics of markets on a variety of fronts. By way of example, it may be prudent in some countries to pay people to witness your containers being loaded on to ships, while in other countries you do not need to make that investment. Procurement professionals of the future will have that kind of deep, detailed insight into the markets that matter most to their enterprises.

● No company can afford to be surprised by one supplier leapfrogging past another. Procurement professionals will need to be like investment analysts, possessing both deep and broad knowledge in and around their supply markets and industries.

Procurement's role is increasingly to maintain a constant understanding of the marketplace and those working in it are going to spend much more time understanding markets from longer-term perspectives rather than always looking through the lenses of sourcing events or transactions.

What is more, their understanding will extend down into the lowest tiers of the supply chain, to understand how to build a product or service as effectively as possible by taking knowledge that is inside the supply chain and bringing it forward to the designers within their own companies.

With technology innovating at such a rapid rate, supply management will be expert enough to understand if a supplier is staying current, innovative and creative in its marketplace or if there are new players coming along to unseat them.

Working with complexity

Over the last 120 years two paradigms have dominated management thinking and both naturally have a value centricity. The first of these was Taylor's *Principles of Scientific Management* (1911), which focused on 'performance' with a command and control approach to the structure of work.[2] The second, which emerged in the 1990s, was business process re-engineering (BPR), which encourages revisiting your business objectives and defining the outcomes and goals.[3] You then establish the values and/or behaviours you want your staff to adopt.

In parallel, and increasingly since the 1990s, we have seen the emergence of a third paradigm, one that is people-focused, exploits mass collaboration and universal social computing, and relies on shared understanding. We live and work in a globally interconnected world and this is where complexity stems from.

In a nutshell, complexity is a function of the structure and uncertainty we have created in the business world. Outsourcing, offshoring and the universal use of information and communications technology (ICT) have made our supply chains and markets increasingly sophisticated and chaotic in equal measure. In the past we dealt with systems that were complicated, but very low in complexity. Complication and complexity are very different. If something is complicated (like a watch) you can disassemble it and then reassemble it and it will still work (if you have the right knowledge). If something is complex (like the weather or the global markets) it has the power to shock. For example, the 2008 financial crash or unanticipated storms. We know they can happen but we often get little or no warning. Complexity differs from the notion of complicated (systems) because, as highlighted above, something complicated – like a wiring diagram – can be looked over and understood, even memorized and it will do what you expect it to do. A complex system has so many variables that you cannot take account of them all and thus it has the capacity to surprise.

Value creation in business remains the order of the day but where value creation in the past was a function of economies of (industrial) scale – mass production, efficiency in repeatable tasks – now it is achieved by delivering innovation into the business to impact profitability and customer satisfaction.

We have in essence moved from economies of scale to economies from creativity – mass customization, new products or service improvement to market – where knowledge workers rather than manual workers are deployed to find a solution to perplexing business/customer problems.

So how do we do this? How can CPOs and CXOs adapt to this, the third paradigm? We can start by seeing modern business as three system or network models:

- Ordered systems where the actions of the people working in it are limited by the system; making their behaviour predictable. For example, where standard operating procedures are applied or best practice – there is no room for change or innovation.

- Complicated systems where people are unconstrained and independent of each other. This is the world of subject experts and the province of statistical analysis and probability. For example, the aerospace industry or law or medicine.

- Complex systems where people working there are lightly constrained by the system, and have mutual interactions with each other and with the system environment. The people working there also modify the system. As a result, the system and the people in it 'co-evolve'. For example stock markets, and modern supply chains.

Since the global economic downturn in 2008, we have entered a new turbulent economic era where complexity is the predominant domain for procurement. The key to managing complexity is to attune yourself and your organization to emerging trends as early as you can. Here are some ideas you may want to contemplate to encourage this:

1 Develop a mindset of 'theory-informed practice' by analysing data from your organization and your networks and using analytics and 'big data' for innovation, competitive advantage and productivity. Best-practice databases tend to lead you to rely on what you 'learned' in the past.

2 Set aside time to carry out analysis based on surveys or focus groups, which capture and display evidence-based findings, rather than measuring performance against targets. Measuring the impacts of activities allows for emergence and adjustment.

3 Instead of using centralized scenario planning why not set up approaches that allow for scenarios to be generated by your team. Take people out of their boxes. See your procurement team as part of a dynamic, boundary-spanning group on watch to spot trends. Also, working across boundaries develops your knowledge collectively and shares intelligence across functions, rather than in silos.

4 Deliberately build an eclectic team and commit significant time to building the next generation of the new procurement professionals.

5 Finally, act with demonstrable integrity and the highest professional ethics. Had this principle been applied in banking and accounting, would we be in the mess we're in now?

From our perspective, as professional procurement practitioners, our job today is to decipher business objectives and communicate them regularly and effectively to the team and the rest of the business and its stakeholders. Focus on ever-closer inner and outer synchronization, from building bridges across the top team and the operations of the organization to tightening the links between the supply base and out to the customer base. Crucially, it is also about being part of the solution and not only running a function.

As stated above, it was in the early 1990s that the idea of applying complexity science to management was first being discussed. People were developing management models based on systems thinking. Managers' eyes were opening to the reality that organizations are not just complicated but complex. And yet this interest and work in complexity did not lead to imme-diate changes in management practices. This is unsurprising given the way that business reacts to changes of any sort.

Complexity simply wasn't a convenient reality, given managers' desire for certainty and control. They were not prepared to change even though they knew that the 'lessons' of the past were no longer a guide for future action. The old methods would not furnish managers with the agility and intelli-gence to respond to emergent threats and opportunities. Consequently, the potential of applying complexity science to business has undoubtedly been held up by managers' reluctance to see the world as it is.

Where complexity exists, managers have a predilection to create mod-els that simply wish it away. It is much easier to make decisions around a straightforward understanding of cause-and-effect. A good example is Milton Friedman's shareholder value philosophy, which determines so much of how today's corporations operate. Annularity becomes the norm; because placing a rigid priority on maximizing shareholder return makes things clear for decision makers and relieves them of having to consider any alternatives.

Counter-intuitive management decisions, such as constantly cutting costs to boost short-term margins, damage the long-term health of the business – but they still do it. Fortunately some people do realize that a complexity approach keeps in view competing values and priorities and the effects of decisions on them – and not just for businesses, but equally for investors, analysts and the regulators.

Added to this, technology back in the 1990s was not powerful enough to capture much or make sense of complexity. However, the proliferation in computing power and the progress in statistics have propelled us into the era of 'big data' and analytics. With our ability to draw on databases and map networks at scales that were unthinkable even in the mid-2000s, we can understand the various flows across large supply and/or value chains, and the impact of disruptions on these flows.

Finally, for many managers the prospect of non-human decision mak-ing is unnerving. The surge of computer processing power has developed another nagging concern in managers' minds. Does the fact that massive computing power is required for systems-level comprehension mean that the interpretation of information, sense making and learning will become 'extra-human' activities? Will we reach a point where brainpower is obso-lete? Well, frankly no. How often have models designed to predict the future state of complex systems, on their own, fallen short on accuracy? There is no substitute for the brain!

In fact, the overeagerness of futurists who advocate machines taking over evaluation of situations and decision making has created this myth, because sense making is always informed by values. The idea that we might look for value judgements from systems is daft. Fortunately, there is a growing recognition that, while computers can provide us with enormous extensions in storage and processing capacity, they will only ever be inputs to human brains, where the ultimate evaluation and deliberation must continue to take place.

Our awareness of complexity and the acknowledgement that simplistic thinking and linear approaches are no longer sufficient are the first steps in embracing complexity. Managers must now get ready to face the full complexity of their organizations and the prevailing economic environment and, if not control them, learn how to intervene with deliberate, positive effect.

We need to take a more nuanced view of complexity. When organizations simply take it as something to be overcome, they are missing a trick. If complexity in all its aspects is seen as a challenge – as something that needs to be managed and potentially exploited rather than something that needs to be eradicated – it can be used to generate additional sources of profit and competitive advantage. Managed deftly, complexity can increase an organization's resilience by enhancing its ability to adapt to a changing world.

Complexity is a feature of modern society, whether apparent to consumers or not. It is characteristic in the variety of processes and outcomes linked to consumer choice and stoked by increasing customer expectation regarding the range of options available today.

The six signposts to procurement's future value

The procurement function, as we have already discussed, is expected to address an increasingly sophisticated agenda in meeting the needs and demands of modern business. As set out in earlier chapters, our long-held view is that competency in procurement and supply chain management is a prerequisite skill set that must be fully embedded inside organizations. Only then can procurement truly satisfy the strategic imperative of consistently delivering incremental value that offers tangible competitive advantage to the businesses it serves.

Procurement's new value proposition is multifaceted requiring a focus on cost management, supply risk and sustainability. Unfortunately, the skills gap to deliver all of these elements remains an ongoing challenge for procurement leaders. However, there is growing evidence that overall delivery capability is being enhanced by CPOs more readily utilizing third-party specialists and, where appropriate, outsourcers to bridge knowledge and technology shortfalls and to enable hard-pressed procurement teams to focus on strategic issues.

Some businesses have already secured incremental investment for their CPOs and their teams, providing enabling technology and putting forward a compelling business case to their organization that clearly shows how their new value proposition will deliver a significant return on investment within a short time frame. Other procurement leaders, one can only hope, will soon be able to follow suit by digesting the issues in this book. The ways in which we do business are ripe for transformation. Building on the typologies developed in earlier chapters it is possible to distinguish six activities that address the changes discussed and act as signposts to procurement sustaining its future value to business.

Intelligent cost-reduction strategies

New commercially focused demands are rocking this traditional area of procurement strength. Globalization has proven to be more about revenue growth than cost savings. Spend management is shrinking and the focus is on profits. Today CEOs might well ask the question: 'how much might that price cost the business?' Procurement leaders will have to be able to answer it.

That said, and whichever way you view it, cost reduction remains procurement's number one responsibility to the business – ahead of enterprise growth and product or service innovation. This intense focus on costs is evidenced throughout procurement activities and programmes, for example, by improving productivity and efficiency. It is also the area where executives have realized the most past success. Undoubtedly CPOs and their teams must continue to get the basics right now and in the future; earning their spurs via attention to the 'foundations' remains essential.

Shifts in costs and other operational fundamentals can happen so quickly that conventional strategies are becoming obsolete. And yet there is no panacea. Today flexibility and agility are the watch words. CPOs must use their experience and adaptability because when it comes to managing costs they must be agile; flexibility is the antidote to cost volatility and helps to improve the organization's cost structure and growth.

If this is to be the case then the elastic procurement organization will be composed of an interconnected network of suppliers, manufacturers and service providers that can be tapped on demand as conditions change. To leverage resources optimally, supply managers in the future will employ intelligent modelling capabilities; using these modelling techniques will allow them to see the cost, service level, time and quality impacts of the alternatives being considered.

A holistic focus around risk

CFOs are not the only senior executives urgently concerned about risk today. Risk and the management of it rank remarkably high on the procurement department and supply management's agenda too. Risk management in the form of mounting supply chain risk, more so than increasing customer demands and higher costs, is becoming the 'stay-awake' issue. The current economic environment, although it may be exacerbating concerns, is not the impetus for this response to risk. It is stimulated by and from a deepening realization that globalization and greater supply chain interdependence have not only elevated risk, but also made it more difficult to manage.

Alongside a general awakening around supply-related risk comes more agreement regarding how we should measure it. We need more standardized, readily available third-party information shared amongst networked communities where people can pool data for operational assessment. Whilst many businesses have programmes in place to monitor compliance it would seem that there is a clear need to take risk management a step further – incorporating it into business plans and using IT to monitor and act on disruptive events.

Risk comes in many forms. The last 10 years has been peppered with wake-up calls: tainted food and toys, acts of terrorism, oil spills and counterfeiting. As supply chains become more complex and interdependent, risk management must become more comprehensive, extending far beyond what any one enterprise can control.

Risk management has to become everyone's business as capacity and demand soar and complexity dominates our thinking. The process of selecting suppliers will carry more risk, more complexity and become increasingly fluid. As converging trends make supply relationships even riskier as this decade progresses, innovative cross-organization solutions will need to be developed as contexts and challenges change. Supply management will need to anticipate scenarios and increase awareness around supply risk, plus an expansion in its perception of where risk lies.

Customer-centricity

Demand-driven mantras require procurement to be involved in determining what the customer wants and what the organization needs from suppliers to deliver business value. Aligning with customer demand ranks pretty high as a supply management challenge, and there is a real need for procurement to have a customer-centric mindset. There is also an increased importance of integrating procurement choices with customer demand to deliver business value.

Procurement must become more involved in determining what the customer wants and what the organization needs from suppliers in order to deliver it. Direct engagement with large business-to-business customers must become a key part of procurement's role. However, despite the obvious need for customer interaction, procurement continues to be pushed to focus more on their suppliers than their customers. Even in supply chain planning, with all the demand-driven hype, not everyone includes customer input.

And yet, because customer interaction seems costly and time-consuming, many businesses it seems feel that the cost can outweigh the benefits. But as the pressure to be more profitable grows, businesses won't be able to afford the excess inventory, lost sales and missed innovation opportunities caused by inadequate customer collaboration.

Essentially, managing value can help to deliver profitable growth; for example, innovation is focused on products and services that provide value to your customer. Procurement is expected to deliver innovation often from the supply base and this is reflected in the end product or service. Any innovation that does not provide additional value relative to the best alternatives is in essence money wasted. Customer input must add tangible value to your supply chain.

Most organizations excel at meeting customer needs once they are known. As has already been stated, it is the 'knowing' part that is difficult. Some supply chains connect with customers primarily to provide timely, accurate delivery. Yet organizations should get smart and interact with customers throughout the product life cycle.

In effect, any interaction with your customers should become an opportunity for inherent customer collaboration. Smart procurement professionals should use their judgement and business intelligence to rise above and beyond the noise. Through advanced analytics, they can identify ever-finer customer segments and support the organization to tailor their offerings accordingly. Products and services become a function of knowledge.

Sustainability and diversity challenges

In today's business world we face an array of difficulties whose scope and complexity can make them intractable. Sustainability, once considered the preserve of the impassioned few, has become a burning issue to all in business. And yet if we think carefully through the trends affecting procurement and supply chain management today, and focus on using resources productively, sustainability needn't be one of these intractable difficulties.

A key sustainability theme today is supplier diversity. Suppliers have an impact on the price and quality of an organization's products and services. They affect efficiency and ultimately they can affect the performance of an organization, including its relationships with key stakeholders. It is becoming clear too that supplier diversity programmes can benefit businesses in a number of ways. For example, engaging with suppliers who are more efficient, flexible and innovative, adding value to your supply chain as well as providing you with access to new markets. They can also help businesses to meet corporate social responsibility (CSR) objectives, improving sustainability and reducing risk.

Many organizations feel that they must think about quality, cost and equality to ensure the company's reputation and reduce risk and this is one route to meet these needs. It is apparent too that the next generation of procurement professionals will understand the benefits of having a diverse supply chain because it will reflect the world they live in; and, increasingly, multinational companies will be asked about their supplier diversity programmes in bids for contracts.

As was emphasized in Chapter 5, there is a strong sense that ensuring that small and medium enterprises (SMEs) are given equal opportunity to bid for contracts will put them way ahead of the game; by guaranteeing that their supply base is innovative, flexible and that it represents the changing face of the company's customers.

Supply management must establish itself as the 'differentiator' in all matters relating to sustainability by working with the business to define tomorrow's standards. By leading on issues such as sustainability and supplier diversity, supply management will drive innovation for smart organizations through engaging small businesses or 'green' applications and in doing so bring competitive advantage to the business.

Supplier diversity has long been neglected as part of a source of innovation, and a specific aspect of procurement's role. Social and economic inclusion has to have equal weighting to environmental considerations. Supplier diversity is not about quotas, it is about widening the applicant pool to secure the best suppliers. The supply base and value chain must be re-evaluated and aligned to seize competitive advantage opportunities emerging from developing supply markets.

Embracing change

Flooded with more information than ever, supply managers need to be able to discern and act on the right intelligence. They also need to think about their visibility and impact within the business. This refers to both the impact that the organization's own purchasing choices has on its brand, as well as a need for procurement to build its own internal reputation within the organization.

As we have already seen, procurement has a brand and PR challenge. Although information is freely available it would seem that less is being effectively captured, managed, analysed and made available to the people who need it. Procurement leaders must be purposeful and effective. Gaining the visibility and developing alliances internally does not appear to be attracting the attention it needs in terms of activities and programmes to achieve this. Whilst it may be argued that more focus has to go to the issues around strategy alignment, continuous process improvement and cost reduction, if procurement as a service is to be taken seriously then future leaders will have to decipher business objectives and communicate them regularly and effectively to their team and the rest of the business.

The development of ever-closer inner and outer synchronization is paramount, from building bridges across the top team and the operations of the organization to tightening the links between the supply base and out to the customer base. Aligning with inner and outer contexts is a key part of the procurement leader's task.

Contemporary supply managers have to be able to decipher business objectives and communicate them regularly and effectively to their team, the rest of the business and its stakeholders. Effective supply managers get the attention of the right people about the important issues. The more people appreciate their role then the more likely they are to include it in their determination of what strategic changes the organization needs to make. Procurement's aim must be to become the 'go to' people in the businesses they serve.

Procurement's bright future

Much of the foregoing suggests that procurement's bright future may actually be a change of modus. One where the incumbents are more entrepreneurial, brand-conscious, skilled analysts with a bimodal capability; a team of enablers, operating under a name that is as yet to be determined. But it will come. And with it the need for essential up-skilling to deliver a new value proposition; armed with increased business acumen and working in 'elastic' multifaceted strategic business mode they will communicate their value propositions to the organization via targeted market-led initiatives.

To take advantage of some or all of these opportunities, knowledge and intelligence development are key to gaining competitive advantage and developing capability in our rapidly changing world. Procurement professionals must become focused and respected across the business, collaborative, influential, persuasive and visionary. With access to knowledge and market intelligence, the function will progress from providing decision support to a predictive capability.

These factors suggest that modern procurement professionals are under considerable pressure, with the weight of expectation on them to deliver value-adding business performance. As supply networks have become more complex, costly and vulnerable, those leading procurement are finding it increasingly difficult not to move away from conventional purchasing and supply management strategies and seek out something new. It is no longer enough to build a supply management capability that is efficient, demand-driven or even transparent. Procurement must offer the organization something that is value adding; a new era of supply management where the strategic scope of procurement adds tangible value. In essence, procurement's new value proposition will be delivered via innovation, collaboration and focus.

CASE STUDY   Harnessing the power of supplier innovation

At a large farm equipment manufacturer, there is an increasing recognition that innovation will need to come from outside the organization. As this company expanded its agriculture and turf care division, an increasing number of product lines have portions of their portfolio that have been outsourced for production, through a focused process assessing the cost/practicality of internal design/build versus external development and production by third parties. Examples of products in this category include blowers, brooms, tillers, blades, backhoes, commercial mowers, golf and turf equipment such as aerators, as well as cabs and enclosures.

As the portfolio of products in this category of outsourced design and production has grown into a major category, questions have arisen regarding the right approach for establishing and maintaining relationships with this category of third-party suppliers. On the one hand, the traditional sourcing process entails a rigorous process involving supplier qualification, part qualification, quality audits, process audits, etc. The opportunity cost (the loss of other alternatives when one alternative is chosen) relates to the time lost in putting all the innovative suppliers through the process, which can take as long as six months. However, the process ensures that suppliers are fully integrated into the extended enterprise family.

The converse of this is more of an 'arm's length' transaction relationship where less emphasis is placed on supplier integration. Such approaches are quicker to execute, but in cases where a supplier's product is complex there is a risk that, by not fully vetting the supplier, the supplier may 'compromise the brand' through a performance deviation. (It should be noted that the actual product attributes associated with the brand have not been fully defined here in terms of product reliability, durability, quality, etc.)

In the context of this situation, defining the role of an integrated partner for targeted innovation has become an important question for the team. An initial view of how to deploy the partnering process focused on alignment of key processes, including deal development, programme management, supply chain integration and quality/manufacturing. The team is facing more conservative R&D budgets, yet is being asked to drive towards 2018 growth plans. To date, purchased goods have had good revenue growth, but have not been as profitable as ideally needed. The supply base consists of about 80–90 suppliers, but only the top 10 or 12 are significant in terms of spend and scope.

The portfolio projects team has a somewhat different approach to managing integrated partners that tend to be a bit more 'hands off'. There is recognition that some level of governance and process standardization is needed between the two extremes, and the development of a common approach to managing partners.

The opportunity

The team set out to establish requirements for an integrated partner programme:

- Establish an approach to manage risks associated with purchased complete goods.

- Establish approaches, tools and methods to build trust in and leverage capabilities of partners that ensure:

    - differentiating speed;
    - lean cost structure;
    - capable processes;
    - end customer focus;
    - flexible supply.

- Ensure partners are able to efficiently launch and manage new products.

- Ensure consistent application of partnering process across suppliers and across both programmes.

- Ensure an optimized approach for calibrating level of process effort based on different types of solutions required.

A number of questions exist relative to this situation

- What is the 'right' level of management attention that is required to optimize the transaction and relational costs with suppliers in this category?

- What is the 'right' supplier integration process to ensure that reliability, warranty coverage, quality and costs associated with customer expectations are assured?

- What are the opportunities to encourage suppliers to drive new products that can create possible revenue growth opportunities?

- How should the organization be optimally structured to align with internal stakeholder needs for new product solutions globally? Should it be supply-oriented or platform-oriented?

- What are the roles and responsibilities associated with a partnering organization that will minimize risk and maximize product innovation and growth?

- What are the appropriate set of audits and assessments required to conduct due diligence prior to contracting with a new supplier?

- What are the characteristics required to make a supplier a good partner supplier, and how should the relationship be managed over the life of the relationship?

- How should supplier growth aspirations be managed relative to a supplier's core capabilities over time, while potentially leveraging those capabilities across product platforms?

FIGURE 8.2 Assessing the innovative supplier relationship

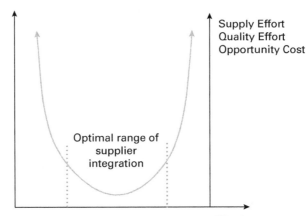

Cost of poor
perfomance
Risk to brand
Customer
reputation

Supply Effort
Quality Effort
Opportunity Cost

Optimal range of
supplier
integration

Increasing levels of supplier audits and qualification

The challenge associated with this problem is shown in Figure 8.2. The issue ultimately comes down to the right level of effort to be expended for different types of supplier situations that will yield the optimal efficiency and costs, considering both the opportunity cost of expending effort on qualification and assessment versus the risks of supplier non-performance and compromising the brand.

These questions raise the need to study the partnership attributes more closely to carry out a third-party assessment, conduct internal stakeholder mapping and explore insights from external companies in this area. The team is working to build a systematic decision-making process for creating partnerships with new or existing suppliers. Such an approach would integrate various decision filters to establish a fact-based business process to establish and manage relationships with current suppliers, and provide a foundation for rationalizing the introduction of new products and parts into the portfolio.

These approaches would enable the company to reduce manpower costs associated with supplier assessments, bring additional insight and clarity to the commercial team, and potentially drive increased revenue to the business. The approach should be based on existing governance mechanisms encouraging collaboration between commercial and supply chain groups. Parameters that may be included in the process include product development resource allocation, fully burdened overhead rates, supplier qualification testing costs, and potential commercial revenue lift created by adding a new supplier.

Such a decision filter should also recognize the full set of risks that are impacted by different types of portfolio decisions. The potential impact of the risks associated with the approach needs to be factored into the decision-making process, including risk of supplier default, supply disruption, product quality performance, cost increases and other factors.

Finally, there is also a role for the supplier to interact more with the customer to understand needs. As one supplier noted:

> One area we'd like to be more involved in is to provide training on our products and to be involved with the sales team. We'd like to get more feedback about what can be changed – what do you like, or not like. Right now we only talk to product engineers, scheduling, purchasing and warranty, and it is a big funnel, because the quantity of feedback we get on our products from dealers who deal with customers is nothing. We'd like to be involved higher up in the funnel to get interaction on our products with end-customers. Can we be invited to the dealer meeting, to represent our products at that dealer training? As customer needs change, maybe we need to adapt our products.

These and other opportunities lie ahead as companies seek to exploit more of their supplies' ideas.

Some conclusions

Reflecting on the future of purchasing and supply demonstrates that the future of purchasing and supply management is an important concern and that it is possible to identify some key, common themes regarding predicted future developments in purchasing and supply as a profession, function and process.

The key factors such as globalization, technology and greater need for the integration of business processes are influencing the development of purchasing and supply. There is a need to understand better the changing identity, structure and processes of purchasing and supply within organizations, from a broad business perspective. There is a need to better understand the role and process of strategic purchasing in corporate success, and the link between purchasing performance measurement and corporate performance.

More focus is required around risk and sustainable procurement, and other issues such as the increasingly complex contextual issues in procurement, and how patterns of change vary across different sectors, including SMEs.

Whilst we have a reasonably good understanding of the key factors that need to be taken into account when considering the future of purchasing and supply there are a lot of important innovations in sourcing, which have been initiated outside the purchasing function, raising important issues too. One immediate question is whether, for example, there has to be a much greater cognizance of the need for interdisciplinary cooperation in thinking and service provision in the field of purchasing and supply at the highest strategic levels.

It seems that there is the possibility of a convergence of several disciplinary groups all attempting to develop their strategic contribution by moving into one 'domain', supply chain management/supplier management. To understand the future role and contribution of procurement in dynamic business environments, it is essential that procurement leaders consider the views of specialists from other functions and senior managers, not just those within professional procurement.

To deliver its value proposition and meet the needs of the business today implies a different role and set of responsibilities for the procurement and supply profession. At their disposal will be smarter systems increasing responsiveness and limiting but not excluding the need for human intervention. These strategic thinkers, collaborators and orchestrators who optimize complex networks of global capabilities will have the mandate (and the enablers) to deliver to the business.

Procurement's future role presents some important new directions that will require investments in talent management and then the development of this talent. Becoming a procurement leader of tomorrow requires you to emphasize your focus on the discernible and tangible benefit that these developments will bring to the organization.

Notes

1 A paradigm is a typical example or pattern of something; a pattern or model. The historian of science Thomas Kuhn gave it its contemporary meaning when he adopted the word to refer to the set of practices that define a (scientific) discipline at any particular period of time, in his 1962 book *The Structure of Scientific Revolutions*.

2 Frederick Winslow Taylor was an American mechanical engineer and is regarded as the father of scientific management. Taylor summed up his efficiency techniques in his book *The Principles of Scientific Management* (1911).

3 Business process re-engineering (BPR) is the practice of rethinking and redesigning the way work is done to better support an organization's mission and reduce costs.

The future
From strategic procurement to value procurement

09

Much of the writing on procurement since the mid-1980s has focused on the operational mechanisms that are used, in what are termed dyadic relationships. Put simply, a dyadic relationship is between two people both of whom have the ability to influence the other. This can provide set roles that in turn creates the glue for the relationship to stick. The stronger the connection, the bigger impact they have on each other. Essentially it is an understanding that requires both to cooperate with each other for the benefit of both. These relationships – in our procurement world – create, develop and sustain exchange transactions between buyers and suppliers.

Much of this literature owes its genesis to three philosophies. The first is transaction cost economics, then there is the 'interactions' approach and, third, the much broader and growing 'relational' approach associated with lean and agile principles of production and supply management thinking.[1]

However, few of these approaches focus explicitly on the interests or the value that buyers and suppliers receive from transactions. Despite this, most writers assume that some element of mutuality (value as defined by the interests of both parties in the exchange) must occur for transactions to exist.

This implicit view of value does not allow practitioners to fully understand which elements of value must be achieved to sustain relationships for buyers or for suppliers, or the complex commercial and operational tensions over interests that exist in transactional exchange, whether in dyadic or the more realistic network relationship. Furthermore, one might argue that much of the current thinking tends to overemphasize operational and underplay the commercial interests that exist in business relationships.

The mutuality alluded to above needs to be contemplated, as in the majority of buyer–supplier relationships the buyer would benefit from an enhanced understanding of the supplier's needs and wants. An understanding of the sources of supplier value could help buyers to manage a whole range of buyer–supplier interactions and develop them to gain strategic competitive advantage.

In the majority of buyer–supplier relationships the buyers often assume that they are in positions of dominance where they can simply instruct or command suppliers. However, the opposite is far more likely and buyers need to persuade suppliers to perform in their desired manner.

To be persuasive in the absence of significant levels of power, and without incurring significant on-costs, it is necessary for the buyer to understand what it is that suppliers want from buyers other than more revenue. Some suppliers, for example, might want stability and be prepared to improve their performance in return for simple, low-cost changes in ordering practices.

The rise of strategic procurement

Since the global economic downturn in 2008 suppliers became far less dominated by their customers, in fact we began to see increasing numbers of 'buyer' specific investments. These include tangible investments in buildings, tooling and equipment dedicated to the supplier, or in products and processes customized to the components procured from the supplier.

What is particularly interesting here is that one of the biggest adaptations in procurement has been that of category management from the marketing field. Businesses, particularly those in consumer markets, quickly realized that success could be enhanced enormously by focusing on the customers' needs rather than their own. If procurement as a function is to help improve the performance of the business, there is a need for a mirror image of the 'marketing revolution'. So armed with insights into supplier preferences, and seeking to maximize their contribution to organizational strategic advantage through enhanced supplier performance, procurement could employ its knowledge of sources of supplier value to make themselves more attractive to the supplier markets.

Category management in procurement terms is essentially a structured process to realize and maximize value across an organization's categories of third-party expenditure. Since the mid-1990s, many organizations in both the private and public sectors worldwide have adopted the practice of category management. While much progress has been made on many fronts, however, there are still significant advances yet to be made.

Category management: the heartland of modern professional procurement

The objectives of category management are strategic in nature, but many procurement organizations never get beyond the 'procurement push', cost-reduction mindset. Consequently they don't maximize the value generated throughout the entire life cycle of the category they manage.

This is often because the needs of a particular category are developed through a process inside the business with a view to maximizing profitability from a category. When it is funnelled through the procurement process to the suppliers, the goal of the procurement team becomes disjointed and they are looking to find the lowest price supplier, often at the behest of the leadership of the business. So whilst the business is measured on overall profit – the procurement team is being measured on cost savings.

In the middle are the suppliers, constantly being asked to engage in tighter integration of the supply chain, supplier investments in ground-breaking initiatives using 'big data' and analytics so that they can do a better job of matching demand and supply, tracking the effectiveness of promotions, understanding consumer behaviour better and so on. Yet their interface with the business via procurement is typically geared towards reducing cost, managing TCO and lowering inventory levels. It could be argued that the goal of these activities is to enhance the profitability of the category by reducing price – but it does so at the cost of sub-optimizing the overall profitability of the category.

The supplier is being set up to fail, because their decisions and behaviours are being influenced far more by the traditional procurement mindset of 'drive cost out' than they are by a mindset looking to maximize profitability and create value. Thus we see these somewhat competing processes with somewhat misaligned goals trying to influence the decisions and behaviours of the suppliers – this tension between the desire to implement category management and the traditional procurement mindset needs to be acknowledged and recognized so that it can be resolved and aligned.

If this is done then all stakeholders will benefit tremendously because everyone's decisions and behaviours will be driven by the goals of the business. If not, then the suppliers will quite naturally utilize any misalignment to their advantage and work to gain from the situation. The ultimate goal for business therefore should be to get rid of any misalignment and develop congruency.

Procurement professionals are increasingly being seen as the 'glue' that holds the business together. They play liaison to internal business partners, suppliers and customers. When procurement works, everyone up and down the supply chain is happy. The key is operational excellence having the right combination of adoptable processes, technology, and skilled people with a strong customer focus, unerring attention to detail and the ability to lead change.

Category management has to begin and end with stakeholders

As we have alluded already this is not always the case, but the value to be gained by companies when they use category teams to develop supply management strategies is unequivocal. Moreover category strategies, by definition, need to include stakeholders as part of the team. For instance, if the procurement team is procuring engines, then it makes a lot of sense to include people from operations as well as engineering and marketing. By working across boundaries this team can provide forecasts, establish guidelines for selecting suppliers, bring greater understanding of new product introduction requirements, and so forth. This is where the notion of procurement being the 'glue' is most obvious.

We can deduce from this that as the 'customer' impact of the category increases, it becomes more important to involve key cross-functional team members. These individuals may be part of an 'extended category team', in that they come together on a periodic basis at key points in the decision process, when much of the data is collected and consolidated for them to review. Together, the category team will develop a commodity strategy that provides the specific details and outlines the actions to follow in managing the category. A general guideline to follow is that category strategies derive their direction from business unit and corporate level objectives for success: ie they are aligned.

Before initiating any category strategy, there must be buy-in from the key stakeholders, especially at the senior leadership level. Without executive commitment, strategic sourcing results are unlikely to be successful. To ensure buy-in of the corporate team, supply management must clearly define the 'prize' or goal in order to obtain the go-ahead to pursue the strategy. To enable an effective category strategy, the team must:

1 Allocate resources initially, including assessment of current spend, data collection, market research, training and people.

2 Validate the savings or contribution to other company objectives achieved by supply management and drive them to the bottom line.

3 Sustain the initiative through presentations to senior executives who support the move towards an integrated supply management function with other functional groups in the supply chain, including marketing, research and development, and finance.

To be perfectly clear, it is imperative that category team leaders establish their direction for building strategies directly based on business unit requirements. Supply management, in general, needs to build strategies that enable businesses to be more successful in developing new solutions that provide the best value to customers, and meet corporate objectives for cost savings, revenue and shareholder value. When in doubt, view every decision from the point of view of the customer (stakeholder).

By applying this rule of thumb, you will find that it is much easier to consider and evaluate issues that arise as you work through your category plan. By no means is this an easy undertaking. You will struggle with data collection, project scope creep, and uncertainty in decision making. However, by applying your best judgement to these situations, you are more likely to develop a plan that will not only meet stakeholder requirements, but will exceed their expectations and have them coming back for more!

Influence is critical

The importance of working with stakeholders in category management is clear and obvious. Ironically, most procurement skills – beyond, say, the MCIPS designation awarded by the CIPS – relate to people skills. The ability to build relationships and understand that value relates to levels of satisfaction points to how important it is to identify stakeholder (customer) feedback on procurement. The awareness of and ability to use methods such as face-to-face discussions, surveys and cross-functional comparison can help the category leader to ensure that the voice of the stakeholder is heard.

Procurement doesn't own internal stakeholders' budgets. What procurement does in actual fact is provide a professional service. Procurement's customers, in this case the stakeholders/budget holders should be provided with fact-based proposals on how to better manage their spend based on reality, their professional expertise and good procurement practice. To reflect how important influence, brand and reputation are for procurement, picture this scenario: a new CPO had just joined your business, and invites the entire team together to make sure they are absolutely clear on what is expected of them. However, rather than express these expectations directly to them, the CPO brings in the CXOs from Finance, Marketing, R&D and Manufacturing to come and tell the procurement team exactly what kind of a job that, from their perspective, they are doing.

How would you react? Would they give you a rough time with or without justification? Would you recognize the shortcomings and/or good performance being highlighted by them? The thing is: whether they criticize you or not is not the point. They need to know you and they need to know exactly what you can and can't do for them. Procurement people need to 'get out more': they need to express the value they can contribute and then deliver it.

Value: is it time to reveal procurement's latest game changer?

Cost reduction will never disappear from procurement's agenda: after all, it is the cornerstone of good procurement practice. The ways in which cost savings are made, however, are high on every CPO's agenda. There are indications that procurement is entering a further period of flux that will bring about further change as the function matures, which looks similar in its order of magnitude to the comprehensive introduction of category management. It could be that this change is no less than the demise of category management.

Organizations that embraced category management at the beginning of the 2000s have gone through their spend portfolios for as many as three or possibly even four iterations. Each category and subcategory has been standardized, rationalized and commoditized. If the big windfalls have not manifested themselves yet, it is possible that they will remain elusive. The savings were eked via price leverage; but the big gains came from the challenges set by demand management and total cost of ownership. Category management had a big impact but what, if anything, will be its legacy?

As has been alluded to above, in many organizations there exists a misalignment between procurement and other business functions. In fact, a poor understanding of strategic procurement/category management can lead to disastrous outcomes and a further diminution of procurement's name and the consequential questioning of the value to be derived from it.

For those organizations that have embraced strategic procurement and made category management work for them, there is no denying that it raised the profile of procurement. It got it engaged at a more senior level and secured an ongoing interest with the leadership of the business. Procurement began to call these people internal 'clients'. It also began to contemplate stakeholder partnerships and corporate alignment. It bashed down the boardroom door. But the hubris created by this activity ignored a unique aspect of procurement practice, creating a fundamental flaw in the notions of partnership and alignment – procurement's business 'clients' do not have cost reduction as their primary aim. However, procurement does!

Why value procurement differs from value-based procurement

Many of today's procurement systems are largely built on purchaser/vendor mistrust, the lack of rigorous purchasing procedures and a lack of tools that can be used to compare bids and assess value. Going for the cheapest option and pushing the risk on to the supplier looks attractive in the short term, but is actually ridiculous in the long term.

Value-based procurement requires you to buy the goods or services that produce the best overall value. For example, if company A offers to build a software system that costs £5 million and later yields £10 million in added revenue, then company A's bid has a net value of £5 million. In contrast, if the system offered by company B costs £10 million but returns more than £40 million in added revenue, then company B's bid has a net value of more than £30 million.

Under a traditional procurement approach, company A's bid (the low-cost solution) would win the contract. Under value-based purchasing, company B wins, paying more up-front but receiving much more in return over the long term.

Value-based procurement can take many forms. The benefit may be measured, for example, in an expanded set of services provided by one supplier's solution over another. In other cases, gaining benefit may involve procuring a system with higher initial costs but lower life-cycle expenses and easier updating capabilities. Procurement's problem is how to judge the value of competing proposals; a task that isn't easy when dealing with large or complex bids.

Value-based procurement is about developing solution-oriented bids, where the bid articulates the problem to be solved and requires the supplier to use their expertise to propose a solution. Or perhaps evaluating suppliers on factors such as total cost of ownership; the technical merit of the vendor's proposal; the vendor's past performance; and the probability of meeting your current and future business objectives rather than just cost.

A closer proximity to your supply base and involving the suppliers in a risk/reward structure incentivizes supplier flexibility and performance. Finally, by looking at the delivery promised by your supplier set against projected performance rather than past failures is another way of tightening the relationship and incentivizing the organizations you work with.

Defining value procurement

Value procurement is the realization of all of the benefits to be gained by the implementation of good procurement practice (as described in the model in Chapter 2). Everything from the foundations, the application of procurement's 'five rights' through to the reduction of unneeded demand activity, complexity, immediacy and variability; ultimately stimulating good demand and increasing business value derived from spend (and supply markets) rather than simply reducing spend magnitude.

This demands full alignment with the corporate strategy, and integration internally with stakeholders and externally with the supply base. Procurement must be as mindful of delivering customer satisfaction as any other business unit in the organization.

Value procurement has to begin and end with customers

The big question with the shifts in the ways that business is done is: are we witnessing the dawn of a big shift in the way strategic procurement is done? Category management has been the only credible procurement strategy since the late 1990s and that may be about to change. The techniques devised in category management strategies to choose suppliers and build strategic partnerships are due for an overhaul.

Today procurement professionals are under considerable pressure to deliver value-adding business performance; and it is no longer enough to build a supply management capability that is efficient, demand-driven or even transparent. Procurement must offer the organization something that is value adding; a new supply management where the strategic scope of procurement's value is delivered via innovation, a networked function and focus.

Procurement must be the function that is continually challenging ways of working. It must look to ensure that it helps its internal business stakeholders to achieve their goals and targets whilst, at the same time, taking the opportunity to challenge total cost, and facilitate customer of choice benefits such as access to innovation and, of course, the management of risk. Most critical of all is that procurement must be aligned to the corporate focus addressing the key question for any business: 'what is value to the customer?'

The customer never buys a product. By definition the customer buys the satisfaction of a want, which in economics is defined as value. In essence, value is utility: ie the total satisfaction derived from a good or service. As we know, the utility that one derives from a good or service is difficult to measure, but we can determine it indirectly with customer behaviour theories, which assume that consumers will always strive to maximize their utility.

Caveat emptor

Many CEOs may not understand or even care why procurement wants to align with budget owners at all. Procurement's job, as CEOs often see it, again as alluded to above, is to be in conflict with them. The CEO as well as the CFO might well feel that it is they, not the budget owners, who are the only real clients of procurement. Moreover, as far as they are concerned, procurement's job is to deliver cost reductions, and certainly not to get involved with issues outside their traditional remit.

And yet, as business functions become aware of what procurement has always asserted, that the proficient management of supply markets is a critical capability, they are developing their *own* resources to take it back. Today it is the 'other' functions, for example IT, which are increasingly being outsourced and the responsibility for managing their 'own' suppliers is being taken back from procurement. HR too in many organizations is heavily outsourced and getting equally concerned about their responsibility for their own service supply chains; but have no doubt at all that this burgeoning development of shared service centres for all support functions will continue.

What is becoming increasingly apparent is that many businesses have already made a move into what one might term *value procurement*. Moreover, those that have are increasingly relegating straightforward cost savings to a lesser significance in the procurement operation. These early movers are focusing on intelligent cost reduction; a holistic approach, which looks to activity in the supply market where they expend their efforts on vendor management, not the zero sum game of incremental savings.

The drivers of this change relate directly to the way business itself is evolving. The proportion of spend that is accounted for by business and professional services has risen. Organizations now understand that their resource pool extends beyond the boundaries of the organization; and competitive advantage today is as much about the construction of supplier relationships as commoditization and competitive tendering has been to category management.

Taking the view from business to market

It is ironic how often the term *value* is bandied about, especially as it is so difficult to define what value actually is; moreover, its loose and frequent use across a number of contexts makes it difficult to anchor its meaning in supply management.

We can, however, reasonably attach various connotations to value:

- Value is relative to an alternative – value cannot be judged in isolation.
- Value is composite and decomposable – value can be analysed into a set of value drivers: for example, time, cost, quality and service.
- Value can be used in several contexts – in B2B relationships it tends to be economic in nature, but other aspects such as the emotional, environmental and social may also be considered as having a value quotient.
- Value is measureable/quantifiable – economic value might be seen as revenue, or cost savings, but other aspects have their own forms of measures: for example, the ability to exploit intellectual property right (IPR).

CPOs can map the way in which the customer gets value to the way in which the seller charges for value. For example, in the construction industry the value of a surface coating may derive from the area covered, while the price is far more likely to be quoted in volume.

Value management relies on multiple streams of information from inside and outside the organization – both internal and external perspectives are necessary. Today procurement holds information regarding customers,

FIGURE 9.1 Procurement's value proposition

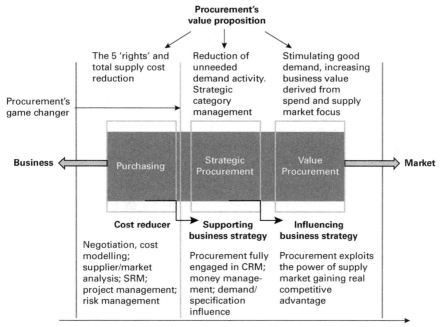

Increasing value and development of supply-side capabilities and business impact

competitors, demand, offers, costs and production constraints. These data are all used in value management and this places procurement in a strong position to make this aspect of business their own (see Figure 9.1).

Procurement leaders are faced with a dichotomy: cost (savings) versus value (creation); and this requires CPOs to think hard about how well they understand the market. If CPOs are to be truly market facing – and for too long their focus has been internal clients and stakeholders – then there is a real need to bring the balance of their focus to some sort of equilibrium. It will be because of this equilibrium between the business and the market that the long-heralded co-creation of value can take place. This is where the next big windfalls will come from, the next big gains and the next competitive advantages. Value procurement will be category management's legacy.

It is no longer enough to build a supply management capability that is efficient, demand-driven and transparent. Procurement must offer the organization something that is value adding – a new supply management where the strategic scope of procurement's value is delivered via innovation, a networking function that is focused.

So how does this change the game?

We have been wondering for some time: has the big business idea of the last 30 years gone rancid? The idea being that you drive cost out of the organization in order to make it more profitable and to maximize shareholder value – only to drive risk in. Why do organizations continue to get this so wrong, pursuing the will-o'-the-wisp of cost reduction with measures that end up increasing them? This preoccupation seems to have tainted the cream on the top of most business models.

It is quite clear to us that the procurement function is going through something of an evolution, as the strategic impact of it comes to the fore. Organizations are increasingly moving away from the discrete function of the past; the doers (buyers) are being replaced by enablers (value adders). Enablers are deemed more useful to the organization and stay embedded in strategic business units.

Another interesting aspect is that more and more we are seeing profits replace cost savings. Consequently, the cost-savings focus is giving way to a strategically aligned emphasis on profitability. Moreover, as the discrete procurement function moves into a new modus, the battles to ensure that cost savings are reflected in their budgets will fade and the emphasis on cost savings only will have less weight than timeliness and quality.

If we reflect on the above it points to the 'doers' – those who excel at cutting deals in the back office – finding themselves and their role outsourced to third-party services organizations. Procurement then will be freed up to operate on a strictly strategic remit, perhaps embedded in other SBUs or operating as a loose network. Certainly they will be market/supplier-facing. They will be there when required, constantly moving and reinventing their roles as needs shift.

The commentary in much of the business press these days relates to the desire for the emergence of a new supply management to meet modern business needs. Procurement's horizon has clearly widened since the 1980s and has seen procurement transform from tactical to strategic. But the notion of 'strategic' remains hemmed inside the function, almost a prisoner of its own history. It requires a change in mindset and the development of a cultured understanding of the (strategic) value-adding capability of procurement – and, with it, the realization of what strategic can mean gets much broader.

Procurement needs to become more commercially focused, as its new highly strategic role requires that: 1) it understands the workings of the financial supply chains; 2) that it stimulates good demand and increasing business value derived from spend (and supply markets) rather than simply reducing spend magnitude.

These changes bring with them new issues:

- As outsourcing takes off, many current procurement and supply-side activities, the ones that do not get pushed elsewhere in the business, will be outsourced as organizations adjust and 'slim down'.

- Increasingly third-party service providers call the shots as the quantity and quality of third-party procurement services increase. Their performance, across many spend categories, will surpass what can be achieved in-house; and as these operational activities move outside the business, often in extended supply chains with little transparency, this will have very real consequences.

   Naturally, there will be several areas of business management that will be materially impacted. At the top of the list will be corporate governance and risk. A cursory glance at today's business landscape reveals why business leaders must ensure that activities in their extended and more complex supply chains are acceptable. This applies to both core and non-core suppliers in equal measure. For example, the scandal in the UK in 2013 where pork DNA was found in products supplied to the prison service in foodstuffs for Muslim prisoners.[2] Another good example is that of the professional services industry, where we are seeing a global debate on the Big 4's (Deloitte, PwC, Ernst & Young, KPMG) grip on the audit market and the pressure to create more competition.

   There is also need to re-evaluate where business risks lie. Risk since 2008 has changed in nature. Today there is much more emphasis on fragility and, as such, the financial and reputational standing of organizations is subject to global market volatility. As businesses have replaced internal operations with external suppliers, risks associated with them are also externalized. Some recent examples of the impact of this include:

   - the Deepwater Horizon incident in the Gulf of Mexico in 2010;

   - the Aston Martin, Shenzhen Kexiang Mold Tool Co counterfeit plastic debacle, uncovered in 2014;

   - the collapse of the Bangladesh garment factory in 2013.

Added to these issues, an increase in collaboration brings with it potential problems regarding the ownership of intellectual property (IP). Since the 1990s the move from closed to open innovation models has facilitated innovation-oriented cost-saving strategies. Today, suppliers invest heavily in R&D, so it follows that relationships are established to facilitate this innovation to flow into the business – and equally for the suppliers to understand the needs of the businesses they service in order to guide and tailor innovation.

With the dawn of the 'extended enterprise' there are tangible changes regarding IP ownership and exploitation. Manufacturing has been led by the 'make versus buy' paradigm for many years and in so doing creating what is known as shallow depth of manufacture. Whilst the manufacturers intend to stay there, services organizations are increasingly engaged in outsourcing. Clearly as IP development moves into the supplier base any future exploitation of IP will depend on where it sits, and who owns it.

Suppliers are one of the main engines of income, and, as suppliers, take on bigger chunks of things they already do for their customers, for example by developing end-to-end solutions if they do not already exist. Where solutions do already exist, then customer enterprises must become much more receptive to sourcing them, with suppliers moving out of their comfort zones to drive customer performance.

Clearly the foregoing demonstrates that there are new sources of value for businesses to explore. Collaboration creates value. Developing structures to support shared purpose, ideas and insights is inherently value-creating. In turn this demands a shift in how the supply base is viewed. Suppliers can be enablers too, who will deliver value. For example, networks for innovation – a transition from the dyadic 'buyer and supplier' relationship to 'integrated supplier networks' – will enable greater coordination of innovation road maps across connected businesses and industries.

With developments such as these, organizations share risks and rewards. As supply management professionals get better at segmenting, defining and measuring value, they will begin to incorporate both gain- and risk-sharing into commercial relationships with suppliers. Ultimately this kind of relationship also facilitates 'motivational contracting'. As well as sharing risks and rewards in contracts, supply management professionals will accept greater risk in commercial relationships with critical suppliers by leaving out all the demotivational stuff that inhibits supplier innovation.

The evolution of procurement's value proposition

The focus of much of this book has been to establish the notion that new practice is needed within business with regard to its use of supply management and its position in the business. Today's uncertain and volatile markets make agility and change inevitable as well as essential.

Supply management mind and skill sets must change. Many business leaders have ambitions to improve profitability by reducing costs. But to do so, they must also reshape their supplier relationships, aligning their supply chain with a more progressive strategy and securing a competitive advantage. So what are the new realities?

Moreover procurement professionals need to get savvy. Their professional credentials will be measured by their ability to influence, persuade and provide vision. Their mindset must be strategic, global, collaborative and, above all, commercial (see Figure 9.2).

No strategy – whether it is business-as-usual or a radical shift – can now be implemented without listening to and working with stakeholders and suppliers. We have seen how they fulfil the majority of a corporation's needs. How well they are mobilized will determine how well the organization can execute on its strategy. Procurement professionals have to be able to connect, network and trade.

In Chapter 5 we looked at the impact of technological applications on business. Today everything starts with an E! Procure-to-pay, sourcing, contract management and other automated solutions are integrated up and

FIGURE 9.2 The evolution of procurement's value proposition

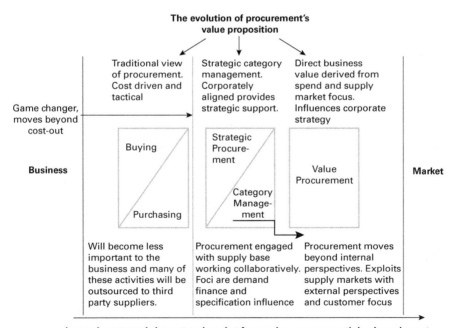

Increasing strategic impact and market focus raise procurement's business impact

down supply chains, fully adopted, providing greater transparency and real-time insight.

More and more we see people working 'on the go'. A new internet-savvy and technically confident generation is entering the workplace using smartphones, tablets, embedded chips and other devices to create a mobile work environment for procurement professionals and suppliers alike. This coupled with the internet-of-things will change the shape and dynamics of supply chains and our working lives. We are seeing it now; it will only get bigger and faster.

To be in the swim we must connect and collaborate. For some considerable time we have been talking about dynamic supply chains and how networks are the way forward; but actually manifesting that in our day-to-day work-life has been difficult. Now, we have an opportunity where in 10 minutes you can find second- and third-tier connections in global networks, with people who know people you know. Buyers and sellers are increasingly relying on digital trading networks and communities that allow them to quickly and easily discover each other, connect and collaborate.

Business intelligence has become critical to the sustainability of corporates wishing to compete in global markets. Open pricing for goods and services is becoming increasingly transparent due to the internet, e-sourcing, global trading networks, online communities and procurement's intrepid scrutiny into still-cloaked categories. Might negotiation become a lost art? We are beginning to see too some consensus develop around risk and complexity and how to model risk. This is helping to develop more standardized, readily available third-party information and networked communities where people pool data for operational risk assessment.

The emergence of intelligent data is reversing procurement's reliance on looking backward at money spent or supplier past performance. The increased use of 'big data', the cloud and analytics enables procurement to work with information, data and models that predict – providing knowledge at your fingertips! With analytics comes more visibility regarding spend, risk and performance, which will be available when you need it. Ready access to accurate, timely, structured internal and external business intelligence will create unprecedented capability regarding information manipulation in support of decision making.

The CPOS enigma

There is probably no paradox more prominent in economic theory than the 'paradox of value' or the 'water-diamond paradox', which appears in a passage concerning the meanings of value in Adam Smith's *The Wealth of Nations*. There is an argument equally as recognized amongst historians of economic theory regarding the existence of *any* paradox – one that Smith himself saw in his discussion of meanings of value or the twin concepts 'value in use' and 'value in exchange'. Value is very difficult to define. Things are often given great 'value' when in truth they are worthless – diamonds in the desert have little if any value compared to water. Water is life sustaining, diamonds are not. Conversely, in a city water is plentiful and has little value (in exchange for money) whereas diamonds have tremendous value (in exchange for money) but their value in use remains the same as in the desert. In this instance let's suspend belief and accept that the 'paradox' is 'that value in exchange may exceed or fall short of value in use'.

It would seem that in business for some time a paradox has existed regarding the role and value of procurement to the organization it serves. Many have simply wanted to resign the function, apparently populated by dullards and failures, to the back rooms of corporations because they are of little worth other than saving the business a few quid. However as Warren Buffet famously said in 2008: 'Price is what you pay; value is what you get.'[3] If you treat or perceive someone or something as if it has little or no value, don't cry when it is gone. As has been alluded to already in this book, the global economic downturn that followed the October financial crash of 2008 emphasizes this. Procurement has a greater value to business than had been traditionally appreciated.

The fact that this is as much a misrepresentation as it is a myth seems to have passed most people by until relatively recently. It is very nearly 50 years since Peter Drucker coined the term 'knowledge worker', and never have employees who think for a living been more important or more in demand in organizations around the globe. Perhaps it seems obvious: but an organization full of *thinkers* is quite different from an organization full of *doers*.

With the introduction of the assembly line, theories of management focused on predefining the ideal outcome and creating performance measures that pushed employees to reach that goal. Efficient managers were those who set the course and very carefully defined, monitored and drove performance. Yet the new challenge in management is quite different. Organizations are less like finely tuned machines – operations with predictable processes and outcomes that can be predirected – but increasingly complex systems, living in vibrant and evolving ecosystems.

What is apparent here is that when the procurement function began it was a low-level tactical, mainly clerical role in most organizations and hence seen as delivering little or no value and, in some cases, being of little value

FIGURE 9.3 Cost versus value: the balance between business focus and market satisfaction

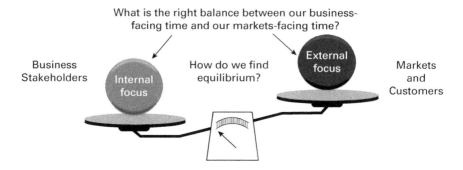

Cost (reduction) versus Value (creation) – procurement's balancing between the business and the markets

What is the right balance between our business-facing time and our markets-facing time?

Business Stakeholders

Internal focus

How do we find equilibrium?

External focus

Markets and Customers

either – anyone can do 'buying'. So perhaps there is a paradox here and it is that procurement's value in exchange (as an outsourced service) may exceed or fall short of its value in use.

The dilemma, or enigma, depending on how you wish to look at it, is: what is modern procurement's value to the business? From the perspective of the CPO it must relate to the now long-standing debate between cost (reduction) versus value (creation). Or, more to the point, risk (management) versus value (creation). CPOs must create equilibrium in their focus between the business and the market it serves, by understanding the right levels of focus of their procurement team on their internal clients and stakeholders and the external market and customer base (see Figure 9.3).

As important as the foregoing is, they must also understand the threats to the viability and sustainability of the enterprise as a result of discontinuity, innovation and obsolescence, and they must be capable of applying a 'commercial twist'.

Delivering commercial twist

Commercial twist relates to the 'elasticity' of the business model being deployed at any one time. CXOs in their efforts to chart the future course of their businesses will have several simultaneous objectives, which will require them to align their strategies to cope with rapidly changing business contexts.

They need to be able to execute those strategies effectively ensuring their supply chains are sustainable, flexible and responsive through their networks and collaborations. As mentioned above, CPOs must create equilibrium in their focus between the business and the market. They must be tuned in so that when conditions change as a consequence of any discontinuity they must be able to twist the commercial 'ribbon' at the point of change so that the enterprise can ride the wave (Figure 9.4).

Delivery of procurement's new value proposition must be seamless, without operational interruptions or performance slips. It will be a strategic balancing act and one that requires strong leadership crossing all lines of business and reporting into the board.

Rigid adherence to the tried and trusted, standard procedures or misplaced tradition, can mean that current needs are not well met and innovation stifled. There is a clear and present need for ongoing, active management of commercial focus balanced across the business. Agility makes a huge difference, not least in maintaining an understanding of business need as circumstances change.

Perhaps here procurement as well as other business decisions should be based on *risk* versus value rather that *cost* versus value, as clearly the stakes are higher: it is the difference between surviving and thriving. Procurement acts as an enabler to the business; it draws innovation from the supply base and plays the role of 'assembler-of-innovation-communities-and-then-gets-out-of-the-way'.

The two case studies below provide insights into some of the typical challenges being identified in deploying true value procurement. The first comes from an interview with a senior executive at a major oil and gas company. We have reproduced the transcript to provide key insights from

FIGURE 9.4 Commercial twist: the balance between risk versus value

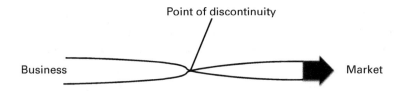

this discussion. The second relates to how Honda of America placed such an emphasis on strategic cost management that they were able to make it a concern for every part of the business.

CASE STUDY A Getting over the category management model

The following comments are taken from an interview with a senior executive at a major oil and gas company:

No question – people get too hung up on the notion of world-class procurement, and it has a number of tools on a tool belt. But the next real wave is on understanding the business well enough to apply all the tools that will drive the most cost-effective model. The obsession with leveraging has got in the way of that. I have come into some meetings where they have consolidated their supply base to extended relationships – and went from 12,000 suppliers to 3,000. But as they got into service area, you are never going to get the world down to a set of true *global* contractors – because they will end up subcontracting. So all this consolidation of the supply base has resulted in three tiers of subcontracting – and they [the contractors] can't manage it – and the real cost is now hidden.

People need to start with the right questions: what is a fit-for-purpose supply base and a fit-for-purpose set of procurement analysis tools to drive a sustainable organization? How do I optimize the cost between my organizations and eliminate the duplication of capability? That takes the due diligence associated with segmenting my suppliers, and understanding where it is necessary to play the market.

I have seen this done effectively in pockets. For example, a large consumer products company went through dynamic bidding to allow competitors to dynamically bundle their commodities – and they go out 180 days. They tell them very simply: you guys bid and bundle the need to optimize cost. All they are doing is supplier qualification, but they spend a lot of time qualifying the capability of suppliers. Then they have a real market that can deliver the quality of products. For commodities, it is all about driving a point in time to optimize a commodity for that specific point in time. Beyond 180 days, you are not optimizing commodities. So for commodities it becomes a question of 'at what level do we leverage?', and 'at what frequency?' That is a cost optimization problem.

At the next level of the segmentation business, it becomes a question of how to optimize the capability to get it into my business, and the issues revolve around product and distribution costs. And then at the third tier, the question is how do I drive full integration and harmonize capability between the two companies? (I have yet to see that work very well.) It is thus critical to have a structured supplier qualification process. I see so much happening where qualification is happening on sourcing and where people aren't doing the due diligence.

Category management isn't being done effectively in most places. The team isn't big enough, and in most cases is just shooting intuition, not based on true market intelligence. The real issue is how do I get my head around this whole area of focus to build effective supplier relationships and drive value-add? And how do I divide it up into those chunks that are management? This requires a different level of skill set and a different level of bundling.

Companies I've worked with have tried to drive a standard approach across all of upstream – using a central team to design a world-class solution. But these teams are hitting operations – and finding that their solution is not always appropriate in every operation. And it is grinding to a halt, especially for small, medium and large operations, as a single model may not work. What is the right operating model for procurement and getting that segmentation right is the difference between doing it well or not.

What I find is people try to apply the same tools in every application – and it doesn't make sense and it turns the business off. People respond with: 'In the part of the world where I work there are very different business drivers and this won't work!' Category management doesn't work when you overlay a global geographic component; it adds a whole new dimension.

The greatest success is where you have people who can apply a level of proficiency. Like in the United States – becoming an integrated consultant to help shape the business strategy, not just support it when it has already been solidified.

It requires you to change the way of thinking in category management – and do we even do category management – and a three- to five-year plan around business strategy and how it is evolving – and when you get into markets like ours it takes a very different way of looking at it.

What we are finding now is that the old-school thinkers are trying to drive world-class procurement organization – and it isn't required in all the business based on the dynamics of the business and the value chain. It is like trying to drive the wrong behaviours – and there is friction – and we have put some people accountable for the functional excellence around all the business units – and the friction is the guy at the top causing more problems by driving standardization that doesn't always make sense, and I think: it is good to have someone but they need to listen to the tools and how to package the tools – and the same 10 to 15 tools.

CASE STUDY B   Honda of America's emphasis on strategic cost management permeates every part of its business[4]

Honda was built upon a cost management culture from the time the company began. The company founder sought to move into the automotive industry from a motorcycle base, despite government blockades, and found that the automotive supply base in Japan was unwilling to support his business. As such, he developed his motorcycle component suppliers into automotive component suppliers through supplier development, financial support and, most importantly, relationships and trust. This loyalty to suppliers, under any circumstances, still exists today. Honda will not 'fire' a supplier unless the supplier requests them to do so. They will support and invest in suppliers who are going through difficult periods, but expect the same leeway when economic times become difficult in the automotive industry. This long-term view towards co-destiny has paid off. Moreover, like a strict but loving parent, Honda demands a lot from their suppliers, including multiple visits to their site to drive improvement with a refusal to take 'no' as an answer. This concept of supplier development, integration and ongoing socialization and trust is a core and integral component of the Honda business model.

Honda's business model has always been focused around a six-year plan, which is highly dependent on a small group of committed suppliers who are involved upfront for the entire six years. The second component of their model is 100 per cent understanding of all components of product cost, with a high level of precision. The third component of their model concerns lean supplier development engineering, with a large population of field engineers working closely with key suppliers on every aspect of their production process. The fourth component is based on flawless new product launch. Honda is a firm believer in extreme attention to detail in every aspect of component, subsystem and system development.

The 'Same Part, Same Place, Same Process' mentality emphasizes that multiple visits and meetings take place with a supplier during prototype development and ramp-up, to ensure that products coming off of a supplier's line are of 'first product' quality and ready to go to market when production conditions occur. Finally, one of the most important components of Honda's business model is *communications.* The quality, frequency and content of every communication that takes place between Honda and its dealers, suppliers and stakeholders is reviewed, and is systematically controlled in every aspect of their business model. Communications are the foundation for inter-organizational relationships.

Measurement systems support all cost management decisions. Initial metrics in the design include the price that the final product could be introduced at in the market. The price/value relationship for Honda's customer is a focal point of debate and discussion. What price at the retail level can provide the required profit at the manufacturing level? A production cost is established at a high level as a target, and then R&D, manufacturing and supply chain work on how to achieve it, separating manufacturing and supply cost to make that unit.

They then break it down component by component, on how to build up to the target price. Certain types of quality characteristics are set in stone (five-star crash ratings, eight airbags and so forth). There is then an ongoing effort by suppliers and supply management to share ideas and innovation with R&D teams early on to discover how to reduce expense, along with adding more value and features. Price is the first differentiator, followed by quality. Target cost elements are based on activity-based costing procedures, derived from historical analysis conducted by key R&D groups who are capable of estimating realistic manufacturing and supplier expenses. These are broken down into budgets developed by category teams. Trade-offs are always a point of discussion at category team meetings. This is a stressful and rigorous process, as multiple teams each work on their own target costs, all seeking to meet the market price.

Cost engineers (procurement) at Honda are aligned by the specific types of suppliers they work with, and are dedicated to this role with the objective of becoming global experts. For example, a cost engineer can visit any given supplier of stampings, and produce a lengthy report documenting the level of capability associated with that supplier, based on one visit. There is a high level of capability and knowledge regarding what to look for, which is designed into the culture.

On a regular basis, all of the procurement groups meet at a quarterly meeting to discuss integrated global supply management strategy. At this meeting, the discussion focuses on opportunities for commonality and standardization, coordination with marketing's export strategy, new product planning, cost management, and technology transfer issues within the supply base.

An important part of this strategy meeting also focuses on development of a truly 'global' supply base. All divisions and business units come together on a regular basis to discuss and share global platform development, common supply strategies and ongoing cost management objectives. Opportunities for learning, and identification of lessons learned, are a major part of this effort.

Honda continues to measure cost against attributes such as customer value, ensuring that its new vehicle costs do not rise even though global material costs are rising, and also to add features that ensure customers have a safe, innovative and fulfilling driving experience.

Some conclusions

For the introduction of this new approach cultural change is essential. Cultural change starts with a change in behaviour of the people employed within the organization. They need to know how strategic goals and operational performance are aligned with internal activity – in terms of challenging business rules and long-held beliefs and ways of working, improving policies and processes, allowing supplier-led innovation into the business, encouraging cross-functional working and so on.

Only then will they start thinking strategically about how the value procurement with all its component parts can empower them – as well as delivering efficiencies and lower costs to the business. The goal is to bring a high level of commercial rigor to how people go about their daily working lives.

Having a long-term perspective

Annularity has dominated the business mindset and calendar for some considerable time. Principally due to the focus on shareholder value maximization and all that that entails. But business is different now due to globalization and the consequent volatility in markets, which has evaporated much of the certainty of the preceding 30 years of business philosophy and practice.

Perhaps a long-term perspective of the effectiveness of value-driven procurement strategy is now what is called for. Value procurement is perhaps the vehicle to deliver business needs, and a longer-term view will ultimately pay rich dividends. All too often, attention moves on to the routine and the humdrum and important initiatives are forgotten.

Today's deeper and broader supply base has made operations more complex; and yet it is not clear that businesses have the capabilities in place to manage these new ways of working effectively, even if some profess that they do. This again begs for a focus on the longer term but with an agile mindset to accommodate the twists in the ribbon and ensure business continuity.

The need for top-level support

We are clear that a new mindset is needed. A new way of looking at the role that procurement can play, how it is perceived, led and what it can contribute to business objectives and customer satisfaction. That said, procurement needs top-level support to:

- manage the cost base commercially;
- provide operational advisory services to the business;
- influence and change behaviours, ways of working and business rules;
- execute sourcing and supplier management in a contemporary and professional manner.

Businesses that get these elements right can expect:

- a step-change in innovation;
- improved corporate governance and reduced risk;
- increased visibility and control;
- better alignment of day-to-day operations to corporate aims;
- improved cross-functional working;
- higher productivity;
- enhanced profitability.

The combination of a large externalized cost base with underexplored cost management strategies offers a compelling opportunity to unlock significant and sustainable improvements to performance, profitability and shareholder value.

Intelligent cost management

Managing cost in a progressive way can add value to a company's balance sheet and can identify numerous ways of boosting the underlying profitability of the business. The new commercially focused demands of modern businesses are rocking this traditional area of procurement strength.

Globalization has proven to be more about revenue growth than cost savings. Spend management is shrinking and the focus is on profits. Today your chief executive might well ask 'how much that price might cost the business'. As a procurement leader, could you give a competent as well as confident answer? Moreover, in this age of heightened scrutiny from stakeholders, can any business afford not to explore the opportunity than a holistic approach such as value procurement can offer?

'Make versus buy' begets complexity. So what to do? Who do we do business with in the fast-growing and culturally different organizations developing in the emerging economies? We still need to select suppliers, but in this new world it carries much more risk. Couple this with the inherent complexity in a globalized marketplace, and it becomes clear that doing business is increasingly difficult.

Risk versus value

Fragility and supply risk and converging global trends in often-turbulent economies mean that a new systemic approach to risk must be taken. In the past, business approached risk by calculating the potential impact of an event multiplied by the time it affected their operations – how exposed their business was to the uncertainty of something happening. Uncertainty was the source of the 'risk'.

However, the uncertainty of the (global) economic environment cannot be controlled; today, excessive complexity is the source of risk. Procurement must engender greater awareness around supply risk and also an expansion in perceptions of where risk lies. This must be set in the context of its contribution to business objectives and customer satisfaction.

Notes

1 For transaction cost economics see Williamson, O E (2005) *Handbook of New Institutional Economics, Transaction Cost Economics*, Springer, US, pp 41–65. For interactions method see Ford, D *et al* (2002) *Understanding*

Business Marketing and Purchasing, Thomson Learning, London. For relational method see Lamming, R C (1993) *Beyond Partnership: Strategies for innovation and lean supply*, Prentice Hall, Harlow; Hines, P *et al* (2000) *Value Stream Management: Strategy and excellence in the supply chain*, Financial Times/ Prentice Hall, Harlow; Christopher, M and Towill, D R (2002) Developing market specific supply chain strategies, *International Journal of Logistics Management*, **13** (1), pp 1–14.

2 Report in the *Daily Telegraph*, 3 February 2013.

3 Chairman's letter to shareholders of Berkshire Hathaway Inc. 2008.

4 Handfield, R and Edwards, S (2009) Cost Leadership Best Practices, white paper, Supply Chain Resource Cooperative, NC State University.

Reflections and conclusions

10

The very ink with which all history is written is merely fluid prejudice. MARK TWAIN

The purpose of this book is not to supply answers but to lead the reader towards thinking. We have established that in truth there is no best practice – only good, better and, quite obviously, bad practice too. To some this fact is intuitive – but nonetheless it is worth pointing out.

We have looked at how procurement has evolved and what is open to procurement professionals today. We have examined the potential of the ACE model and how this can be used in conjunction with our model of procurement maturity to help the procurement leaders work out for themselves what practice developments can be made, and to see how they can advance their own procurement practice to achieve their aspirations whilst taking account of both capability requirements and requisite levels of execution if they are to reach the heights they are aiming for.

Reflections

We need to spend more time thinking

There is no 'best' practice, we just need to think more. But, you might ask, what is the point of thinking about things? We just need to get on with the job don't we? Well, do we? Is there a point to this thinking, this 'philosophizing'?

There are times that we should allow ourselves to be esoteric. We should contemplate the world and our place in it. Otherwise, how can we be sure that the world is really as we take it to be? How can we tell whether our opinions are objective or subjective?

These questions are not only baffling they also defy simple processes of solution. They are not like practical questions that relate to our everyday experience. They require reflection – we might wonder whether what we say is objective or just our own perspective, our own 'take' on a situation. By thinking in this way we confront questions of knowledge, objectivity, truth and what we mean by them.

This kind of thinking takes us beyond the snapshot decisions of everyday life. Thinking reflectively allows us to consider our ideas and concepts in a different way. In the end, it's not a matter of how much you know, but what you can do when the going gets tough. If there is disagreement of opinion, a successful outcome will depend on being able to reflect on your opinions and values whilst taking seriously the implications of other ideas.

What should we spend time thinking about?

Why bother with reflection? Reflection doesn't get the world's business done – it doesn't bake any bread or build houses, so why not put this reflective notion to one side and simply get on with our lives? Well, from one perspective we know that reflection matters because it is continuous with performance. How you think about what you are doing affects how you do it, or whether you do it at all. It might direct your work, or your attitude towards people who do things differently.

For example, many people think that to be a good business person we should only be interested in ourselves – especially in the buyer–supplier relationship. They feel that it is about power and we should only focus on looking out for our own advantage, never really caring about anyone else; here, apparent concern disguises hope of future benefit.

In fact, if we do think that this is how things should be then our relationships with others will suffer. Meaningful interactions will be affected, which has costs, and cooperative ventures become nigh impossible. This is the 'war against all wars' in the marketplace. By always looking out not to be cheated and claiming to be a 'hard nosed' business we incur heavy transaction costs, because we are looking at human motivation through the wrong lens and misunderstanding what is actually going on.

Some of the most forward-thinking CPOs we interviewed understand the importance of challenging our mental models and pushing ourselves to consider the greater good that can be created through consideration of the broader ecosystem. For instance, Tom Linton of Flextronics noted the following:

> The siloed approach of building 'control towers' is giving way to a new layer of capabilities. Some of us are realizing that supply chains are more vertical

than virtual, and even going back to the Japanese – becoming more virtually vertical. What this means is that we are becoming more reliant on partners and creating a virtual vertical integration – which means more connectivity between other companies.

As a result of the flattening of labour, we are actually becoming more regionalized as we become more global, and sourcing is becoming much more regional and local, because that is where we can begin to have the right types of relationships, communication and understanding.

Because what is happening is that unpredictability is becoming more predictable. Procurement is like quality [assurance] was 30 years ago. Except that now, if you are not socially and environmentally responsible and are not caring for those working under you to ensure that there is no violation of labour laws, you cannot survive. It is now fundamental as the world has become much more flat.

One of the most important books of the 2010s in my mind is Robert Wright's *Nonzero: The logic of human destiny.*[1] It starts with a premise that the world is moving to non-zero-sum, which means that we need to be adopting a non-zero approach to procurement. Think of the Eskimos – they worked together to kill a whale and they shared it with other tribes. In this manner, the tribes were able to survive a very difficult environment, by forming alliances and states and working together. Their tribes marched through time based on collaboration. So I think non-zero approaches to supplier management will continue. There will be a force at play: more collaborative ways to do business – but there also needs to be a balance: what is the supply chain you respect the most?

Troglodytes, the Enlightenment, a Pole, a Frenchman and an Italian

From cave dwellers and their needs to our complex world how much real difference is there? Maslow's 'hierarchy of needs' would in our estimation reflect that there is little real difference.[2] We've simply got more stuff now and a more complex world where we need to make more decisions about things; but the basics – food, shelter, warmth, procreation, love, art – all existed then.

During the Enlightenment, society encountered a move away from a world view shaped by centuries of religious ideology to one shaped by science. This period in Europe saw people such as Copernicus (heliocentric model of the solar system), Descartes (*cogito ergo sum*) and Galileo (mechanical science of nature) all fall foul of the teachings of Catholic orthodoxy. All three were prepared to live their beliefs, all of them wanted to develop their and our understanding of the world we live in. And they did this despite the fierce backlash from both the Church and the state. In doing so they helped us to change the lens through which we view the world; but being different is hard and often gets a lukewarm reception, even from supporters.

Back to the five game changers

So let's turn our attention back once again to Chapter 4. Today we are witnessing increasing volume, speed and importance of flows across borders. Flows of people, ideas, greenhouse gasses, manufactured goods, dollars, euros, TV and radio signals, drugs, germs, e-mails, weapons and a good deal else. The world we live in is one that moves faster across more dimensions and with more complexity than ever before. Such rapid change is leading to new opportunities and we are increasingly facing situations for which we have no precedents. This requires hard thinking and new thinking: we need to change our mindsets in order to survive and thrive in this changing world!

One increasingly important idea regarding how we might work in this faster and more complex world is that of mass collaboration. As already stated, it is more than 50 years since Peter Drucker coined the term 'knowledge worker',[3] a recognition that the majority of workers no longer used their hands at work but instead use their brains. Again, this requires a realignment of our thinking.

Never have people who *think* for a living been more important – or more in demand. Today, a large part of the labour force is made up of people for whom complex problem solving is the primary component of their job, and increasingly people's jobs require significant abstract thinking and judgement skills. It is no secret that knowledge workers are proving to be a key source – if not *the* key source – of competitive advantage; and effectively leveraging knowledge workers is significantly more challenging than squeezing out productivity gains by improving processes.

It will come as no surprise, then, that an organization full of thinkers is quite different from one full of doers. Couple this with the changes brought by our increasingly globalized world and it is quite apparent why businesses will need to 'think up' new ways of utilizing the talent working with them – and the relationships they have in their supply networks – far more effectively in a far more competitive environment.

Reflections on the five game changers from a procurement perspective

Procurement professionals have to get savvy. Here the difference between the 'doer' (the buyer of old) and the 'enabler' (today's strategic procurement professional) is most pronounced. Procurement professionals today and in the future will need to be:

- professional;
- polished;
- intelligent;
- respected;
- influential;
- persuasive;
- visionary;
- strategic;
- sharp;
- global;
- collaborative;
- executive;
- business savvy.

All these terms reflect the discussion in Chapters 6, 7 and 8. These are the attributes of the future supply professional.

As discussed, the competition for talent is heating up. In fact, there is considerable opinion regarding the talent pipeline. Is it too sparsely populated to meet the demand for strategic market-facing professionals we need? Or are we ignoring the fact that the people are there but that we are just asking the wrong questions of them? The outcome will be intense competition to attract the best and brightest, but it is likely to be on their terms.

We need some sort of reality check regarding professional procurement and its value to the business. What some would like to believe is that due to the large depth of external value-add from procurement it delivers a substantial bottom-line impact. Others might say no, procurement is the graveyard of the enterprise. Some might say that due to the cross-functional nature of our role we draw the best talent, whilst others might say that procurement is in fact a professional silo.

Also, some believe that due to the strong commercial requirements of procurement we breed management material, whereas critics might say, 'Ah, but the CPO is often based in the financial community and reports to the CFO and not the main board.'

Reflections on the consequences of procurement maturity and its value to business

A cursory glance at the outputs of the overabundance of industrial journals and consultancy white papers and reports, as well as the myriad blogs and other commentary, reflect unequivocally what can be expected of contemporary procurement. Moreover, they articulate that those setting the pace in developing better procurement practice differ from conventional businesses along three dimensions: they hire better people, they set clearer performance aspirations and they create strong procurement cultures, which are aligned to the corporate strategy.

The result of this clarity of thought is clearly reflected in the results of the companies they operate in. These leading companies enjoy annual cost savings from their overall sourcing efforts that are nearly six times greater than the annual savings of low performers. Moreover, the winners are positioning themselves for broader strategic gains as the pressures of globalization intensify.[4]

So what does this all mean? As mentioned above, change is hard and requires a degree of bravery; a move away from orthodoxy and tradition is required. Some of the critical features of bringing this change include ensuring that procurement is aligned to and supports the corporate strategy:

- The way contemporary procurement professionals think, feel and conduct themselves in the workplace, individually and collectively must reflect an embedded commercial focus.

- Procurement's strategies and processes must be shaped around a desire to create explicit value, with the resources of the procurement function being managed in such a way that the function naturally and effectively interacts with other functions.

- Procurement's productivity must make a contribution to company success relative to cost, revenues, quality and execution speed.

Attracting and retaining the best and the brightest procurement talent

As already stated, there is a lot of speculation today regarding the demand for top talent in procurement. Indeed, many of the leading industrial journals have indicated that finding enough qualified talent is amongst the top management concerns of businesses.

Procurement's role is progressing from decision support to one requiring a predictive capability; increasingly there is demand for procurement professionals who can demonstrate that they are both commercially focused and analytically capable. It would appear that the emergence of these skills rests on three factors:

- The success that many procurement departments have had in increasing their influence on indirect spend in the business: as their influence has grown in respect to spend management, it seems that the requisite number of staff to manage that spend has not been recruited in line with the growth.

- The volatility of commodity prices: in an attempt to manage the risk, this uncertain environment has generated senior managers who have been looking to procurement to use its teams to round in on the issue. Yet it is not uncommon for CPOs to have people in their teams who (as discussed earlier) are woefully lacking the prerequisite skill sets to fulfil the need.

- Since the mid-1980s we have witnessed changes in both procurement and business yet the skill sets of many in the procurement function have remained tactical. This is because qualifications or learning have been either under-utilized or ignored, whilst the growing strategic influence of procurement has created a demand for something different.

Clearly some people can be retrained to meet these new demands. Whilst others, unable to adapt to today's more strategic skill sets, will need to find jobs elsewhere in the business or be transitioned out completely. These drivers have both increased demand and changed the fundamental requirements of what talented 'procurement' professionals means.

There is therefore an imperative, to get the right talent right now, to attract the right talent and quickly. We have listed below a few indicators that should be considered regarding the potential attractiveness of a business to smart candidates:

- Where are you based in relation to other top employers inside or outside your industry sector?
- Has your business been through hard times?
- Is the salary you are offering attractive in the current job market?
- Is the scale and scope of the role appealing enough to attract top talent?

- What kind of relationship do you have with your HR department?
- Can you articulate the skills and abilities you want well enough?
- Who is the final arbiter regarding the job specification?
- Who will choose the successful candidate?

Without a clear expectation of the type and quality of the people you want, and how you will position the role to attract them, you are setting yourself up to fail. In particular, the best procurement organizations want people who can make sound commercial decisions. The traditional transactional skills of procurement on which the function was built are changing with increasing importance towards people who are culturally aware. Look for people who are collaborative, innovative, diligent optimizers with strong leadership skills:

- Developing a strong relationship with your HR department is essential. One area where there is a great deal of room for improvement is in the dynamic between HR and procurement. If you want top people don't get out your standard job description template. To attract the best people to apply for your vacancy make the job description compelling; explain why the candidate should be excited about this opportunity. Then describe the duties, and only briefly mention the requirements. If it's not a challenging job, who will want to apply for it? Once you have done this, make your decisions quickly – candidates are most receptive to offers in the first week after their interview, don't let good candidates die on the vine.

- When it comes to your star players you need to accelerate their potential to rise within the business, or create opportunities for them to gain breadth. For example, if someone is very good at procuring a particular commodity, advancement may take the form of growing laterally as opposed to vertically – moving into different categories or leading special projects.

- It is better to recruit for talent, not background. It is critically important to differentiate between your requirements and your preferences so that you don't waste time searching for the 'nice-to-haves' rather than essential requirements.

To improve recruitment and retention levels in procurement, it is crucial to create a deeper working relationship between procurement and HR. Building strong partnerships that will allow talent management to succeed, functional and procurement executives need to go beyond their comfort zone and adopt a much more creative, candidate-centred approach to recruitment and retention.

Procurement managers can no longer rely entirely on HR, and must instead shoulder some of the responsibility for recruiting the best and the brightest. By investing time and resources, developing clear and appropriate job roles and setting out clear paths for professional growth and advancement you will find, develop and retain the talent your organization needs.

We are entering the era of the bimodal procurement professional

In contemplating writing this book we were intrigued by the slow progress of real change in supply management. Despite a plethora of readily available and high-quality commentary about contemporary procurement practice, which is frequently backed by solid experience and empirical data, many procurement organizations remain loath to move beyond the most basic level(s) of professional procurement practice.

It is now well documented that few if any companies can allow procurement to be managed in isolation from overall business systems. From previous work in this space, primarily with Bath School of Management,[5] we have produced evidence that suggests supply management requires greater integration, stronger cross-functional relationships and more senior management involvement.

The procurement profession needs to explore two perplexing questions:

- Is an alternative procurement mindset starting to emerge – one that recognizes there is no substitute for having deep procurement skills combined with a sense of ambition, accountability and self-responsibility? This personal credo must be aligned with specific organizational goals but, more significantly, it must be actively conscious of strategic issues as well as longer-term horizons.

- In what ways can this new mindset be nurtured and how can people make the transition?

This perspective, that a new modus is required in order to get some traction in businesses, is even more astonishing when one reflects that it is 30 years since Peter Kraljic published his seminal paper on procurement's future.[6] Today this serves to underscore the issue of change inertia in procurement.

But will contemporary businesses tolerate this inertia? We work in a world where aligned and agile procurement with a firm focus on profits rather than simply cost-savings is what is required; and whilst this may look something of a tall order, people must be found who can meet the challenge and excel. While some of these competent, confident, high achievers are already in the profession or will be recruited, above all they need to be nurtured and directed by competent leaders.

In procurement, competence must be based on an understanding of appropriateness. This means knowing what to do to deliver strategic goals operationally within specific supply chain and market circumstances. This requires people with a well-developed professional knowledge of the procurement tools and techniques at their disposal, supported by well-developed commercial acumen.

Commercial prudence is a prerequisite in the contemporary supply management professional. Competent and confident they will be able to work with both risk and reward in contracts, and accept and manage greater risk in relationships, they will be the 'intelligent client' able to motivate suppliers.

Technology too has created challenges – smartphones, tablets and embedded chips have initiated a mobile work environment in which the modern supply professional must feel comfortable. Added to this, in the era of 'big data' they have to be adept at handling and analysing data, able to see major trends and important takeaways at a glance.

Why risk has become the number one issue

For the foreseeable future one suspects that risk will dominate the thinking of CEOs and CPOs alike. As emerging economies place successful, fast-growing and culturally different companies into the global markets, the process of selecting suppliers will carry more risk, more complexity and become more fluid.

Research commissioned by CIPS anticipates big increases in companies' awareness around supply risk and also an expansion in their perceptions of where risk lies.[7] By way of example, if we look at two areas of the world where, in 2014, current tensions are creating situations that create greater volatility and increased risk – Russia's actions in the Ukraine and ongoing tensions in Asia – the foregoing becomes clear in reflecting global risk.

Weakening growth in China (as well as other emerging economies) combined with geopolitical tensions are the biggest risks to financial markets, and these two things are dangerously interconnected right now. The repercussions of the situation in Ukraine will reverberate well outside of the European context. In Asia, the sovereignty over various islands, islets and reefs is disputed. Some may see Putin's land grab as an inspiration to do something similar regarding their ongoing disputes over the Senkaku/Diaoyu, Paracel, Pratas and Spratly islands and the Macclesfield Bank and Scarborough Reef.

Procurement relationships in China

Stability in Asia is important to global markets, and yet there seems to be an unbridgeable gap between China and Japan. The two Asian powerhouses cannot see eye to eye on issues such as military armament, human rights, Taiwan, regional security and even the rule of international law. The relationship between Japan and the United States on the one hand, and the impact of this relationship on China, on the other, is increasingly competitive and the same applies to several other power balances in the region.

China in particular is becoming increasingly uneasy about its position within the current global order. After all, this creaking edifice has been set up, and is still largely dominated by, the West. This changing geopolitical landscape and the fragmentation of the international community is complicating global governance. The world lacks clear structures, while constantly changing coalitions of countries, international institutions, businesses, movements, and NGOs are trying to get to grips with a raft of risk-laden issues such as pollution, territorial conflicts, terrorism and attempts to govern the internet.

One of the topics we have been exploring is the interesting nature of social and economic relationships between buyers and sellers in China. This set of relationships does not fall under the typical theoretical rubrics that are conveniently applied in Western culture. Somewhere between the strong predicted relationships identified by transaction cost economics,[8] and social exchange theory,[9] there seems to be white space when it comes to understanding how buyer–seller relationships are governed. Nowhere is this more the case than in emerging economies such as China.

When one overlays the cultural artefacts that exist in Chinese culture and the roles of 'guanxi', there is comparably little research that specifies how such relationships unfold, and the types of outcomes that can be predicted. Recent research calls for a deeper set of explanations that translates the typical Western pragmatic business relationships into a Chinese context and provides substantive guidance for how to build effective business relationships that build trust in China.[10]

This recent research points to the fact that 'guanxi' is in reality an important cultural artefact that embodies the level of trust that exists in a relationship. The two forms of trust that develop include cognitive trust that emanates from the confidence one has in the partner's accomplishments, skills and reliability ('trust from the head') as well as the emotional trust that arises from the feelings one has in the partner's emotional closeness, empathy and rapport ('trust from the heart').

Both forms of trust are needed to effectively establish business ties in a Chinese buyer–seller relationship. However, we currently have little understanding of the relative importance of these forms of trust and how they are established through patterns of communication between buyers and sellers, under different conditions of power, which are oriented in Chinese high power distance culture.

This is made even more so when Western managers travel to China, and fail to understand what goes wrong when they attempt to build supplier relationships in China. To some extent, the nature of power plays an important role here. When power distance is higher, coercive power will be more effective in influencing others, while when collectivism or guanxi culture is more typical, non-coercive power will be more effective.

So, the predictive power of the power theory developed in the Western world will be weak in Chinese combined high power distance and guanxi culture. Other work by the authors of this book points to the challenges of finding supply management talent in China, which we discussed with John Zapko, vice president of global procurement at Lenovo:

Zapko: Without question, attracting talent, bringing it on board, being able to hire this talent and especially retaining talent around the world in some of our most important positions, not only at management levels, senior management levels, but also commodity management and the people that really focus on the procurement activity, driving the supplier-based management . . . negotiations, contracts. As we drive in this complex world, having that level of talent is really critical for us, and it is clearly the biggest challenge we have.

Authors: How do you create talent and why is it so important in a complex world? We've been hearing a lot about global complexity and the challenges in dealing with governments, with regulations. Why is talent so important in procurement as you work these issues?

Zapko: Global complexity is becoming more and more significant for us – as we drive our growth, in emerging markets especially, and as we drive our activity into those emerging markets, people that really understand the procurement role, with experience in delivering professional procurement activity . . . in a more complex environment in the merging market, where government regulations' specific uniqueness is around contract.

Our ability to manage new emerging suppliers demands key critical skills, which if we don't have we are seriously lacking. So when we find people with these skills and experience, whether built internally through activity, growth and development, or whether we hire it in – once we have it and once we're driving the advantages with it we really have to retain it. And so that becomes the major initiative for us as we work in this complex world.

Until recently, most of us assumed that countries derived their security interests from their economic interests. Vladimir Putin has made it clear that this may well be a rather naive hypothesis. A preoccupation with power will continue to play a prominent role in international relations and markets. This in conjunction with national pride and prestige could send tensions, and with them risk ratings, sky high.

Some commentators have begun to talk about the potential for war in Asia. Although a real war seems very unlikely, Graham Allison talks about the Thucydides Trap, which maintains that the likelihood of war increases greatly when a rapidly rising power competes with an established power. In the past 500 years, 15 such situations have occurred; in 11 cases, the result was war. Sometimes the complicated dealings between various allies made the situations more explosive.[11]

Will China decide to test the waters and, if they do, is the US really prepared to step in? For some time the US has provided safety guarantees to the Philippines and Japan, but what if the continuation of this guarantee leads to war? The commitment of the US has been in doubt before and this view will increase since the global financial crisis has reinforced the impression that the West is losing strength. In 2007, the US economy was four times the economy of China. In 2012, it was twice as large. Given the West's power-lessness to stop Russia's brazen push in the Crimea, might this make China reckless?

But it is not only China that is causing concern. Japan under Prime Minister Abe, who has a nationalistic bent, wants to rewrite the Japanese constitution to give Japan a 'normal' army. In many ways, such a change is defensible but it is worrying in combination with Abe's visits to the Yasukuni Shrine, and the fact that he is just paying lip service to the Kono and Murayama declarations.[12]

Geopolitical tensions tend to rise once countries are in choppy economic waters. Undoubtedly, Vladimir Putin will have considered Europe's weakened position before he decided to annex Crimea, especially as the members of the eurozone are focused on their own economic crisis. Some politicians might even decide to go the other way, playing the nationalistic card, making sure the country is united against a perceived outside enemy in order to divert attention from domestic issues. Japan may well have a period of economic turbulence ahead, due to an increase in its rate of VAT, disappointing wage settlements and lower than anticipated consumption data. If Japan's economic measures turn out to be a disappointment Abe might well turn to a 'nationalistic' agenda.

Today opinions differ about the economic prospects of China. Some think it will manage to deflate the credit and property bubble in an orderly fashion. In spring 2014, Beijing let the money market rates rise to show that it does not shy away from tackling excessive credit. But it is also propping up state-owned companies. This is far from ideal, but it could pave the way towards gradual deleveraging instead of the severe shock of a crash.

Some of the global financial institutions are less sanguine. They are concerned about excessive investment funded with excessive debt in China. A sudden collapse of asset values has been mooted as not unlike the 2008 crash in the US economy, with too many debtors unable to meet their interest and debt repayment commitments. Interest payments on outstanding debts run to 17 per cent of GDP (twice the percentage in the US in 2007). In 2004 every invested yuan yielded 1 yuan in GDP growth; at the time of writing in 2014 it is four times that and, as a consequence, growth could slow considerably. As with northern hemisphere countries in 2008, a growth slump would stoke unrest in other regional economies producing a similarly negative impact on the rest of the global economy.

So could an escalating Ukraine crisis impact global trade, increase energy prices and hit economic growth in Europe? Will conflicts in Asia have far worse implications for the world economy? Whilst war is unlikely, this could be the beginning of a period of mounting tensions with more geopolitical power games, a lack of decisive action by international institutions, a more cautious America and economic headwinds in Asia. All of which spells increased risk and supports the view proposed in this book that procurement professionals need to know much, much more than how to do a deal and reduce purchase costs.

Procurement must drive productivity to generate value for the business it serves

As industry faces the challenges to improve productivity, augment sales and reduce costs, there are greater expectations from business leadership for procurement professionals to develop and implement approaches that can assist businesses in addressing these challenges and to help them realize value.

These expectations and options for value creation have been examined in this book, looking at the role of contemporary procurement and its value proposition to the business. A broad theme has emerged from this examination, one in which procurement is moving from the role of strategic procurement to one of value procurement.

In its traditional role, procurement was focused on basic purchasing and sought to secure stable supply at the right price and quality while ensuring compliance. In this environment, the emphasis is on centralized processes and making transactions more efficient. Typically, the buying is local, and there is little or no category/strategic management.

Procurement evolved to strategic procurement, where the clear focus is on generating savings. Strategic procurement involves applying category management, aggregating global or regional volumes, establishing long-term agreements, and the introduction of automated tools and systems to generate the desired savings. In its next evolution procurement is focused on augmenting spend, by generating higher returns per pound, euro or dollar by focusing on demand management. Allied to this is process management, how goods and services are bought.

Organizations are seeking to move beyond this towards procurement's next iteration, by developing ways to optimize costs and generate value across businesses. We are now in the phase of going beyond procurement to drive company-wide productivity, which involves presenting the business with options to achieve that goal: we call this value procurement.

Value procurement is the realization of all of the benefits to be gained by the implementation of good procurement practice (as described in the model in Chapter 2). This encompasses everything from the foundations, the application of procurement's 'five rights',[13] through to the reduction of unneeded demand activity, complexity, immediacy and variability. Here the ultimate goal for procurement is the stimulation of 'good' demand and increasing value to the business derived from spend (and supply markets) rather than simply reducing 'spend' magnitude.

In the process of following procurement's evolution we uncovered six signposts to procurement's future value, which reflect the value received by the business, for example through innovation and growth; and to who the value is presented, which could be the supply base, the business or the customer. The six signposts described in Chapter 8 are:

- *No 1 – intelligent cost-reduction strategies*: new commercially focused demands are rocking this traditional area of procurement strength. Globalization has proven to be more about revenue growth than cost savings. Spend management is shrinking and the focus is on profits. Today CEOs might well ask the question 'how much might that price cost the business?' You will have to be able to answer it.

- *No 2 – a holistic focus around risk*: risk management has to become everyone's business as capacity and demand soar and complexity dominates our thinking. The process of selecting suppliers will carry more risk, more complexity, and become increasingly fluid. As converging trends make supply relationships even riskier as this decade progresses, innovative cross-organization solutions will need to be developed as contexts and challenges change. Supply management will need to anticipate scenarios and increase awareness around supply risk, plus an expansion in its perception of where risk lies.

- *No 3 – customer-centricity*: procurement must become more involved in determining what the customer wants and what the organization needs from suppliers to deliver it. Direct engagement with large business-to-business customers must become a key part of procurement's role. Essentially, managing value can help to deliver profitable growth; for example, innovation is focused on products and services that provide value to the customer. Procurement is expected to deliver innovation, often from the supply base and this is reflected in the end product or service. Any innovation that does not provide additional value relative to the best alternatives is in essence money wasted.

- *No 4 – sustainability and diversity challenges*: in today's business world we face an array of difficulties whose scope and complexity can make them intractable. Sustainability, once considered the preserve of the impassioned few, has become a burning issue to all in business. A key sustainability theme today is supplier diversity. Suppliers have an impact on the price and quality of an organization's products and services. They affect efficiency and ultimately they can affect the performance of an organization, including its relationships with key stakeholders. They can also help businesses meet corporate social responsibility (CSR) objectives, improving sustainability and reducing risk.

- *No 5 – embracing change*: flooded with more information than ever, supply managers need to be able to discern and act on the right intelligence. They also need to think about their visibility and impact within the business. This refers to both the impact that the organization's own purchasing choices has on its brand, as well as a need for procurement to build its own internal reputation within the organization.

  As we have already seen, procurement has a brand and PR challenge. Although information is freely available it would seem that less is being effectively captured, managed, analysed and made available to the people who need it. Procurement leaders must be purposeful and effective. Gaining the visibility and developing alliances internally does not appear to be attracting the attention it needs in terms of activities and programmes to achieve this.

- *No 6 – procurement's bright future*: much of the foregoing suggests that procurement's bright future may actually be a change of modus; one where the incumbents are more entrepreneurial, brand-conscious analysts with a bimodal capability – a group of enablers, operating under a name that is yet to be determined: but it will come.

Overcoming the barriers to value creation

One of the biggest challenges to procurement is how to effectively leverage its relationship with the supply base. From a procurement perspective, four issues act as barriers to developing value-based relationships with suppliers. The first is the never-ending focus on cost savings. This often shuts down any discussions about better ways of working. The second relates to how suppliers are measured. There is the challenge of 'control versus collaboration', and finally for many managers in business it is simply down to finding the time.

It would be naive to expect companies to ignore cost pressures. Most businesses are focused on lowering prices rather than dealing with the loftier goal of finding routes to develop intelligent cost-reduction strategies. With respect to metrics, although measuring supplier performance is critical, this fact frequently prevents more important dialogue, and certainly any dialogue about value-creating activities.

Moreover, for many organizations today the ageing systems they have in place are simply not flexible or mature enough to support supplier innovation. A further barrier is that many people in procurement simply do not have the knowledge or experience, let alone the time, to have more in-depth discussions with suppliers to identify opportunities for value creation or innovation.

One way to address this problem might be to move beyond the linear (dyadic) relationship between supplier and buyer. There needs to be a transformation so that both are working collaboratively to meet the needs of the customer. Possibly the best way to achieve this is via the development of a set of services that increases the buyer's and ultimately the customer's perception of value. From a buyer's perspective, this might be achieved through a new type of business relationship.

As C-level executives chart the future course of their businesses, they will have several simultaneous objectives. First, there is the need for strategic alignment with rapidly changing business contexts. Second, there is the need for effective execution of these strategies, to ensure that supply chains are sustainable, flexible and responsive. This will be achieved through the effective use of the networks, collaborative relationships and deep commercial focus at their disposal. Finally, delivery of value must be seamless, without operational interruptions or performance slips. It will in essence be a strategic balancing act and one that requires strong leadership.

The dilemma, or enigma, depending on how you wish to look at it, is what is modern procurement's value to the business? From the perspective of the CPO it must relate to the now long-standing debate between cost (reduction) versus value (creation). Or, more to the point today, risk (management) versus value (creation). CPOs must create equilibrium in their focus between the business and the market it serves by understanding the right levels of focus of their procurement team on their internal clients and stakeholders, and the external market and customer base.

In Chapter 9 we introduced the notion of commercial twist. This relates to the 'elasticity' of the business model being deployed at any one time. As mentioned above, CEOs in their efforts to chart the future course of their businesses will have several simultaneous objectives. As important as this is, they must also understand the threats to the viability and sustainability of the enterprise as a result of innovation and discontinuity, and they must be capable of applying a 'commercial twist'.

They need too to be able to execute those strategies effectively; ensure that their supply chains are sustainable, flexible and responsive; and create equilibrium in their focus between the business and the market. They must be tuned in so that when conditions change, as a consequence of any discontinuity, they can twist the organization at the point of change so that the enterprise can ride the wave.

Rigid adherence to the tried and trusted – standard procedures or misplaced tradition – can mean that current needs are not well met and innovation is stifled. There is a clear and present need for ongoing, active management of commercial focus balanced across the business and it is here that agility makes a huge difference, not least in maintaining an understanding of business need as circumstances change. Here the process of involving suppliers, buyers and customers to find and share, translate, understand, assess, select and implement, and communicate becomes the catalyst for value creation.

To conclude

The future of purchasing and supply management is an important concern and it is possible to identify some key themes predicting its future developments as a profession, function and process.

Key factors, such as globalization, technology and a greater need for the integration of business processes, are influencing the development of purchasing and supply. There is a need to understand better the changing identity, structure and processes of purchasing and supply within organizations, from a broad business perspective. There is also a need to better understand this role as it impacts corporate success, and the link between purchasing performance measurement and corporate performance.

More focus is required around risk and sustainable procurement, and other issues such as the increasingly complex contextual issues in procurement, and how patterns of change vary across different sectors. Whilst we have a reasonably good understanding of the key factors that need to be taken into account when considering the future of procurement, there are a lot of important innovations in today's function that have been initiated outside procurement, which raise important questions. One immediate question is whether, for example, there has to be a much greater cognizance of the need for interdisciplinary cooperation in thinking and service provision in the field of procurement at the highest strategic levels.

It seems that there is the possibility of a convergence of several disciplinary groups all attempting to develop their strategic contribution by moving into one 'domain': supply management. To understand the future role and contribution of procurement in dynamic business environments, it is essential that procurement leaders consider the views of specialists from other functions and senior managers, not just those within professional procurement.

To deliver its value proposition and meet the needs of business today implies a different role and set of responsibilities for procurement. At its disposal will be smarter systems, increasing responsiveness and limiting but not excluding the need for human intervention.

Procurement's future role will require investments in talent management and then the development of this talent. In considering these options, the next task is to evaluate the feasibility of implementation in terms of organizational readiness and capability proficiency. In making that assessment, we can use the ACE model identified in Chapter 5 to evaluate which options are feasible.

With the massive global economic shifts we have recently encountered, 'change or perish' pronouncements pile up. Supply management has at its disposal the necessary ingredients to make supply chains substantially better connected and more important to current strategic enablers. The growing understanding of CEOs of how critical the procurement function is to the company's success establishes the challenge and the opportunity to create change.

There is little doubt that procurement is increasingly gaining control over its main purpose: the sourcing of goods and services for the organization it serves. However, in this modern era, procurement professionals are facing a variety of broad challenges. All organizations are rapidly investing in new technologies to meet the challenges of business in the contemporary, global marketplace; however, procurement often lacks the skills required to take full advantage of these tools and circumstances.

As scrutiny of organizations' environmental and ethical practices increases, there is also a requirement for procurement to understand the implications of its corporate responsibility and sustainability. Efforts to make a bigger contribution to corporate strategy continue, but sometimes at the cost of misunderstandings between procurement and the rest of the business. And yet procurement has much expertise to offer, which can provide substantial financial benefits. Convincing colleagues across the business of this, and aligning not just goals but thinking about where the procurement can and cannot add value, is potentially the biggest challenge.

However, this is no reason for not trying to anticipate what may happen or for not trying to shape developments for the better. It is true to say that the only way to predict the future is by helping to shape it. There needs to be a constructive debate about where and what value procurement can bring to the business. Blind faith is not enough. This book represents our contribution to uncovering how procurement will deliver value to both business and society for them to thrive.

Notes

1 Robert Wright, in his book *Nonzero: The logic of human destiny* (2000), argues that biological evolution and cultural evolution are shaped and directed first and foremost by 'non-zero-sumness', ie the prospect of creating new interactions that are not zero-sum.

2 Maslow, A H (1943) A theory of human motivation, *Psychological Review*, 50, pp 370–96.

3 Drucker, P (1959) *The Landmarks of Tomorrow*, Harper & Row, New York.

4 Reinecke, N, Spiller, R P and Ungerman, D (2007) The talent factor in purchasing, *The McKinsey Quarterly*, 1.

5 Chick, G and Lewis, M (2009–10) 7 habits of highly effective CPOs, *CPO Agenda*, Winter, pp 50–54.

6 Kraljic, P (1983) Purchasing must become supply management, *Harvard Business Review*, 61 (5) September–October, pp 109–17.

7 Cousins, P, Squire B and Lawson, B (2008) Looking to the Future: Purchasing as Cost Reducer or Value Broker? A research report carried out for the CIPS Centre for Procurement Leadership by Manchester Business School, July.

8 In economics and related disciplines, a transaction cost is a cost incurred in making an economic exchange or the cost of participating in a market.

9 Social exchange theory is a social psychological and sociological perspective that explains social change and stability as a process of negotiated exchanges between parties.

10 See Rob Handfield's SCRC Supply Chain Blog, 12 December 2013, Unlocking the Secrets of Guanxi in Supply Chains.

11 Allison, G (2014) A good year for a Great War, Harvard, Kennedy School, Winter.

12 Yasukuni Shrine is a Shinto shrine in Chiyoda, Tokyo, Japan. It was founded by Emperor Meiji to commemorate individuals who had died in service of the Empire of Japan.

13 The five rights of procurement are: the right quality, the right quantity, at the right price, at the right place, at the right time.

PART B
Innovation debates
Creating your own value from procurement

Introduction to innovation debates

11

In this chapter, the intention is that you take subjects raised and opinion from the book and look to develop your own discussion regarding the issues. The issues we feel are most pertinent for further situational analysis are:

- talent: finding it, developing it, keeping it;
- building team competence frameworks for contemporary procurement;
- thinking about the future;
- dealing with 21st-century risk;
- sustainable procurement.

In designing your event or workshop you will want to explore a number of perspectives regarding the issue at hand. In the issues presented in the book we have drawn on particular insights generated from our own work with CPOs and procurement teams in a range of organizations.

You will need to develop a set of substantive questions to address in relation to the issue you are looking to explore. You will also need to plan out your event, for example working together and then splitting into syndicate working sessions. Each session should combine some formal input from a facilitator and be combined with structured discussions aimed at addressing your key questions.

Event styles

To help structure overall discussion (and presentation of thoughts and ideas) an event model that details how you will run the day should be developed (see below) and introduced to your delegates in advance.

What you are looking to do is capture from the attendees what they see as the hot issues in your business and how the procurement function can best align to support and generate value. But you do not need to be prescriptive in this. Your principal aim is to capture the views from the 'outside in' as you will have a fairly good understanding of the 'insider' view. Effectively we want to get people to talk about how they see the world changing, how they see the organization changing and how they feel that organizations can better leverage the supply side of business to create value.

You can 'seed corn' the discussion via the pre-event work you ask delegates to carry out or by inviting guest speakers.

Title/theme

Detail the overarching theme and any rider so that it is clear from the outset exactly what you will be doing on the day. As time can be precious it is useful to set your delegates 'things to make and do' in advance so that they come thinking about the issue.

This can be set around a cascade, for example:

1 What is happening in the world?
2 How does this impact our business?
3 How will this impact procurement?

Format

You need to consider in advance the format of the event. For example, you could invite one or two 'thought leaders' or experts to provide their view of how the world, business etc are changing and what their hot issues are. This will set off the discussion. Having a moderator or facilitator ensures that everyone contributes and that each theme moves on. We have prepared a workshop agenda template as an example of how the day might be structured (Figure 11.1). Additionally, ensure you have the room set up so that people can speak freely and easily; a cafe style is probably best as theatre-style has everyone facing in the same direction. Keep table sizes manageable so that interactive discussion is easy. Also monitor the tables to ensure that people are talking and that no individuals are dominating the discussions.

FIGURE 11.1 Workshop agenda template

EVENT TITLE: Event Date: Event Venue: Version 01						
Event Theme/Title						
Start Time	**Duration**	**End Time**	**Event Session**	**Content**	**Lead Person**	**Infra-structure**
9:00	0:15	**9:15**	**Coffee**			
9:15	0:15	**9:30**	**Welcome**	**Introductions, purpose of the day**	**Facilitator**	Laptop and projector
9:30	0:30	**10:00**	**ICE BREAKER: What do we think of when we think about X?**	**Short Introduction to the session. Followed by each of the delegates sharing views.**	**Openner followed by all**	Laptop and projector
10:00	0:45	**10:45**	**Presentation**	**30 minute presentation to set up an innovation debate.**	**Speaker**	Laptop and projector
10:45	0:15	**11:00**	**Coffee**	**Tables choose a scribe and a rapporteur**	**All**	

(continued)

FIGURE 11.1 Workshop agenda template (*continued*)

Start Time	Duration	End Time	Event Session	Content	Lead Person	Infra-structure
11:00	0:45	11:45	Group work and feedback session	Group discussion. Each table to feedback.	All	Pens, paper and Flip Charts
11:45	0:20	12:05	Presentation on impacts of change	15 minute presentation to set up pre-lunch session	Facilitator	Laptop and projector
12:05	0:10	12:15	Bio Break			
12:15	0:45	13:00	Group work and feedback session	Group discussion. Each table to feedback.	All	Pens, paper and flipcharts
13:00	1:00	14:00	Lunch			
14:00	1:30	15:30	Presentation with group work and feedback session	30 minute presentation on the XYZ	Speaker or Facilitator followed by All	Laptop and projector; pens paper and flipcharts
15:30	0:15	15:45	Tea			
15:45	1:00	16:45	Innovation Debate	How can we make XYZ happen	Speaker or Facilitator followed by All	Laptop and projector; pens paper and flipcharts
16:45	0:15	17:00	Closeout	Summary of day	Facilitator	

Moderator/facilitator

It is best to use a facilitator to moderate the discussion. You can invite a facilitator or do it yourself. You don't have to be very experienced in doing this but to be effective you must stick to a format. To moderate or facilitate a discussion can be daunting if you are not sure what you need to do. Often sessions wind up with people speaking beyond their allotted time, or with delegates feeling 'talked at' or not included. As the name suggests, innovation debates are just that: debates. They need to be interactive and you and any speakers you invite need to be engaging. So here are some things to consider:

- *Take nothing for granted.* If you are introducing people, make sure their names and titles are correct. Make sure you know how to pronounce their name. Establish in advance how you and the speaker(s) will be heard – from a podium or walking around with a wireless microphone.

- *Avoid formality.* Avoid 'formal' introductory remarks as it slows things down and creates a spurious context. It also makes it much harder to develop the interaction you will want. People may be shy and speaking in public can be embarrassing – so the more informal the event the better.

- *Start with an opening question.* If no formal introductions, you should let people know that this opening question relates to the 'big picture' view of the topic. By taking this approach you will remain in control and be able to create a more interactive environment from the beginning.

- *Shorter is always better.* Short, to-the-point questions are usually best. Longer questions require longer answers.

- *Follow-ups.* A great moderating technique is to 'follow-up' a comment with things like: 'What's your take on what X said?' or 'Can you give us an example?' In doing this you are looking to provoke candour and spontaneity in your delegates' responses.

- *Get people to talk to one another.* Try to get people to talk directly to each other. This isn't easy but an effective tool is to encourage interactive dialogue from the outset. But you must control it.

- *Get the delegates involved early.* If you're looking for participation, wait no longer than 20 or 30 minutes before bringing in the delegates. The longer you wait, the harder it is to get them involved.

- *If you don't get any questions, don't panic!* You can ask delegates or your speaker(s) questions to get things going. You can even press down on a friend in the audience and ask them what they think.

- *Final comments*. Allow each speaker a minute or two to respond to a final 'big picture' question. Some options: 'Are you optimistic about the future?' 'Where do you think we will be in five years?' 'What one point or theme should we take from this discussion?'

- *Thank people*. Make sure you thank those who contribute, by name if possible, and ask the delegates to join you in expressing appreciation with their applause. Thank the organizers (and sponsors if there are any) who helped to make the event possible, and let everyone know how much you enjoyed moderating the discussion and appreciated their active participation.

Timings

How much time you can spend on planning and executing an event will depend on several things:

- what level of authority you have;
- whether it will cost money: for speakers, room and equipment hire;
- what level of senior support you have for establishing the debate.

If we assume the above has been taken care of, we feel from our experience that a half-day session well managed is often best. The template in Figure 11.1 gives consideration to things such as timings, equipment needs, breaks and meals.

You should aim to record the session and feedback to the participants as well as those for whom you have established the event. You can record the event (electronically) to capture the richness of the discussion, but assure the participants that the event is under the Chatham House Rule (ie there will be no attribution).[1] If at a later stage you wish to attribute comments in a report you will need the person's express permission to cite them.

Finally, you must allow good time for people to get to the event and settle before the work begins.

The innovation debates

At the end of this section of the book you should be able to:

- establish a debate regarding the key current issues in professional procurement with a view to evoking change;

- express to colleagues – in your own organization and across the business – in a non-confrontational and inclusive way why these changes are necessary;
- define procurement in relation to related concepts such as risk and sustainability;
- evaluate the criticality of the challenges and how they affect procurement and the other SBUs in your organization;
- argue the need for these issues to become an integrated part of procurement rather than separate add-on issues;
- explain the underlying theoretical perspective and structure of the issues.

Talent: finding it, developing it, keeping it

Background

As the economy moves slowly out of recession, the demand for top talent in procurement continues to grow. Indeed, CPOs we have spoken to have indicated that finding enough qualified talent is amongst their top management concerns.

Contemporary procurement's role is progressing from decision support to one requiring a predictive capability. Procurement professionals must be commercially aware and analytical, focused, respected across the business, collaborative, influential, persuasive and visionary. In our view, the lack of emergence of these skills rests on three factors:

- Many procurement departments have had success in increasing their influence on indirect spend in the business, yet as their influence has grown in respect of spend management, it seems that the requisite number of staff to manage that spend has not been recruited in line with the growth.
- The volatility of commodity prices: in an attempt to manage the risk, this uncertain environment has generated senior managers who have been looking to procurement to use its teams to round in on the issue. Yet frequently the CPOs we speak to either do not have the staff numbers to do this, or have people woefully lacking the prerequisite skill sets mentioned above to fulfil the need.
- Since the mid-1980s we have witnessed change in both procurement and business in general; along the way the skill sets of many in the procurement function have remained at best tactical whilst the strategic influence of procurement demands something different.

Our view is that some can be retrained, while others – unable to adapt to today's more strategic skill sets – will need to find jobs elsewhere in the business or be transitioned out completely. These drivers have both increased demand and, in our view, changed the fundamental requirements of what 'procurement' talent means.

The imperative – to get the right talent right now

It is critically important to attract the right talent and quickly. As opportunities arise, evaluate them for potential attractiveness to candidates:

- Where are you based?
- Has your business been through hard times?
- Is the salary you are offering attractive in the current job market?
- Is the scale and scope of the role appealing enough to attract top talent?

You need to develop a clear expectation of the type and quality of the people you want and how to position the role in the job market.

Recruit for talent, not background

It is critically important to differentiate between your requirements and your preferences so that you don't waste time searching for the 'nice-to-haves' rather than essential requirements.

In particular, the best procurement organizations want people who can make sound commercial decisions. The traditional transactional skills of procurement – on which the function was built – are changing, with increasing importance being placed on people who are culturally aware. Look for people who are collaborative, innovative, diligent optimizers with strong leadership skills.

These people can offer decision makers with more choices and alternatives, higher-precision controls and levers to achieve desired outcomes. They will be capable of optimizing global networks of assets and talent, not only their own but also those of partners and customers.

How well do you know your HR department?

One area where there is a great deal of room for improvement is in the dynamic between HR and procurement. If you want top people don't get out your standard job description template. To attract the best people to apply for your vacancy make the job description compelling; explain why the candidate should be excited about this opportunity. Then describe the duties, and only briefly mention the requirements. If it is not a challenging job who will want to apply for it?

Then make your decisions quickly, candidates are most receptive to offers in the first week after their interview, don't let good candidates die on the vine.

Remember that procurement skills sets have evolved

Global experience is an increasingly important requirement. Today, if a candidate for a strategic position lacks global experience, keep looking. You need people who can:

- influence;
- network across the business;
- articulate procurement's value proposition;
- convince functional managers to involve procurement in their activities from the outset;
- communicate at all levels.

Today's game changers are those with the ability to influence others in a way that makes procurement effective, respected and accepted.

How to retain the best people

The best strategy for retaining star performers is to make sure you make good recruitment decisions to start with. Be sure to hire some people who are good at what they do, but who will top out at a level they are happy to stay at.

When it comes to your star players you need to accelerate their potential to rise within the hierarchy or create opportunities for them to gain breadth. For example, if someone is very good at sourcing a particular commodity, advancement may take the form of growing laterally as opposed to vertically – moving into different categories or leading special projects.

Conclusions

To improve recruitment and retention levels in procurement, it is crucial to create a deeper working relationship between procurement and HR. In order to build strong partnerships that will allow talent management to succeed, functional and procurement executives need to go beyond their comfort zone and adopt a much more creative, candidate-centred approach to recruitment and retention.

Procurement managers can no longer rely entirely on HR, and must instead shoulder some of the responsibility for recruiting the best and the brightest. By investing time and resources, developing clear and appropriate job roles and setting out clear paths for professional growth and advancement you will find, develop and retain the talent your organization needs.

Setting up your own event

At **www.koganpage.com/pvp** we set out how to set up an event in your organization or team to establish a debate regarding talent development and retention.

Please go to **www.koganpage.com/pvp** for a full set of PowerPoint slides covering the talent innovation debate.

Building team competence frameworks for contemporary procurement

Background

The capability of many high-performing businesses that align their activities with those of equivalent or complementary organizations is seen as a key factor in successful performance and sustained competitive advantage. The importance of relations with other organizations, such as suppliers and customers, is fairly obvious in contemporary businesses.

So it should come as no surprise that the effectiveness of teams and individuals in business functions such as procurement has become an increasingly important priority. We have already discussed the rising profile of procurement purchasing and of relationship management activities. These changes to the function's role and contribution to business strategy have implications for skill sets. There is widespread recognition that increasingly professional procurement practitioners are required to think and behave more commercially, with a strategic and analytical mindset. They must also think in terms of, and take decisions in, wider supply networks. Added to this, for their knowledge to remain relevant they need to learn more effectively, and proactively drive their personal development needs.

Today there is a plethora of opinion on this aspect of procurement, including blog posts, white papers and feature articles. However, most of it is disjointed and focuses on the functioning of procurement systems and how they perform rather than investigating competence requirements for equipping people to manage and operate in inter-organizational networks.

Innovation debate

This aims to address the following issues:

- What do businesses and their teams need to learn about operating in cross-functional roles in order to support effective strategic procurement?
- How can they facilitate the required learning?
- What are the factors that enable or limit learning?
- How can continuous functional and personal development be encouraged and promoted?

Currently the majority of strategic procurement people work in teams responsible for particular product/service categories. Moreover, within these category teams, people will focus on specific subgroups, so there is a natural tendency for the creation of supply networks as they often match up with supplier and customer categories.

This innovation debate will help you to look specifically at what generates value-adding supply management. What are the skill sets, the knowledge acquisition and personal characteristics implemented by the best? And how do these factors differentiate the best from the rest?

Clearly at the supply network level, it is in the compilation of '*the team*' that businesses need to focus on. They need to ensure that the team has the competencies necessary for the roles and activities demanded by strategic procurement.

What you can do next

You can establish an event at your organization to help you understand how you can work with both procurement and other stakeholders to build a high-performing procurement team; a team that communicates and collaborates inside and outside your business to engender procurement excellence.

In your event you need to ask your delegates to consider specific network management roles:

- network coordinator;
- relationship manager;
- innovation developer.

This will help to keep their focus on strategic procurement, rather than more traditional procurement roles. To develop your understanding of what differentiates high performers from satisfactory and poor performers, you might think about encouraging delegates to identify specific cases of teams and individuals, and characterize how and why they differed from others.

As already suggested, you should record your discussions and later analyse them to draw out themes that will help you to understand patterns of effective and ineffective performance. You can then develop categories reflecting the distinguishing features of each.

To help you establish your debate we have identified below what we found from the discussions we had with CPOs in writing this book.

Examine the key personal attributes

The key attributes are, unsurprisingly, relationship management and credibility. The best teams are confident and capable, which means that they can challenge others without being confrontational.

However, effective procurement and effective performance management roles are different; for example the skill sets required to be a good 'buyer' do not equate to what makes a good strategic procurement professional. They are very different.

Contemporary procurement professionals need to be good communicators; they need commercial awareness, ability to demonstrate their commitment to the role and a willingness to expend discretionary effort. Such individuals also have a propensity for continual personal and professional development. When it comes to their personal style they are inclusive and consultative and demonstrate flexibility in their approach to work. Typically they will have good planning skills, be technically capable and act with probity.

Key elements of the team

We feel that there are six major themes and associated attributes required to build a practical competence framework for strategic procurement professionals. All are critically important, requiring simultaneous action. We asked those we interviewed to rank them in order of priority, reflecting the need for and importance of each to them in establishing a high-performance team (Table 11.1). High-performance procurement teams operate with a broad remit and in cross-functional network roles. Each of these roles should be developed through a set of behaviours, as it is far more reliable to identify behaviours than attitudes when evaluating competence.

TABLE 11.1 Roles and attributes of high-performing procurement teams

Role	Attributes
Strategy development	A high-performing team will develop a strategy, which is supported by robust evidence, has clear objectives, and is championed by key stakeholders.
Strategy deployment	A high-performing team plans and executes its strategy, monitoring outcomes against plan and adjusting strategy, objectives or actions as necessary.
Relationship management	A high-performing team actively develops and manages relationships.
Setting out your stall	A high-performing team has a planned approach to developing its position in its network, but is flexible enough to take advantage of opportunities that arise.
Network knowledge	A high-performing team has a deep understanding of the network(s) within which it operates.
Knowledge and learning	A high-performing team actively promotes learning and enhances its expertise through developing knowledge and knowledge-sharing systems.

In Table 11.2 we have suggested what one might look for in a good relationship manager. You could use the outputs from your event to develop similar skill-set attributes. That said, at your event it might be a good idea to make your primary focus developing an understanding of team competence, as it is a team that performs the network management role. Whilst there is a need to identify the personal attributes of team members, the above is included on the principle that, though the attribute is individual, it is deployed by the individual for the benefit of the team.

Conclusions

The notion of developing a competence framework, as outlined here, is centred on team capabilities (as discussed in Chapter 6). To build on what we have suggested you could ask yourself how your organization's teams

TABLE 11.2 Desired relationship management behaviours

Relationship Management
Developed relationship skill set:
Builds and maintains both formal and informal relationships. Identifies relationship 'gaps' – and establishes direct relationships as appropriate. Assesses the quality of relations, and takes any necessary steps to improve them. Establishes effective communication channels. Maintains contact with other network players, has regular informal contact with key individuals. Knows how to demonstrate commitment and is willing to put in discretionary effort. Predicts and deals with sources and causes of conflict. Deploys excellent consultation skills. Is able to be inclusive and build consensus. Is persuasive. Is skilled at chairing/managing meetings.
Foundational relationship skill set:
Able to form and maintain relationships with people at all levels. Confident with aggressive/difficult people. Able to remain calm under pressure. Able and willing to challenge others without being confrontational. Able to deal with resistance and diffuse a difficult situation. Demonstrates tact and diplomacy. Is good at listening. Avoids complacency. A good communicator (in writing and orally; in formal and informal settings).

should perform various procurement roles in your inter-organizational networks. We suggest this as it may help you to move away from the humdrum silo mentality of many procurement organizations, where the needs of individuals to perform their jobs within their function are considered paramount.

We feel with some degree of confidence that teams wishing to be top performers need to promote continuous learning at the organization, team and individual levels because this will directly impact the shared conceptions of effective performance across the business and how it can be achieved.

Thinking about the future

Background

Running workshops on visioning how procurement might change has proved extremely valuable to us in our work. These sessions tend to be highly productive. Why they are so useful stems from the fact that the profession has evolved and that the strategic role of purchasing and supply management is now well established. People often work 'head down, butt up' and change tends to pass them by. So providing the time for an opportunity to think and discuss this change is a very good use of time.

Regarding the evolution of procurement and its now well-documented increased importance to the organization there were concerns voiced that if it were unable to meet the new demands of the organization – be they an embedded role or, more importantly, a fully 'commercial' arm of the organization – then it might disappear altogether. This was a very real concern and is reflected in the issues detailed below.

You could develop your event/session to start an ongoing process. The outputs from the event(s) could be utilized across your organization as part of a PR and awareness-raising strategy as well as a method of seeking the opinions of other professionals in your organization who are well placed to provide first-hand experience and issues-recognition regarding the needs of the business and how all parts can become better aligned to the corporate goal.

Below we outline some of the (more dominant) cross-cutting themes derived from writing this book, which you will recognize from your journey through it.

Skills and abilities

One of the chief concerns we have encountered relates to the scarcity of talented procurement staff. The perceived lack of knowledge and understanding here relates to general business acumen as well as knowledge of specific markets and sectors.

There seems to be a perennial debate around the need for procurement people to develop the qualitative/social (soft) skills. These are perceived to be a prerequisite in business and particularly those associated with relationship management, eg communication, collaboration, co-dependence and influencing. So strong was this message that we have dedicated it as a theme on its own below.

Specific skill requirements highlighted through our work included the desire for risk 'gurus' and visionaries. The need for commercial skills featured prominently too, as did flexibility, agility and resilience. There was also a heavy emphasis on the more quantitative/scientific skills. There is a real and immediate need for people who are able to analyse data to demonstrate quantitative skills and be competent in developing and deriving solutions from data sets. We call this the bimodal procurement professional.

A new definition of expert is required: people need to be students of the industry, sector, geography, and products and services that they are dealing with.

Evolution and organizational change

An examination of this theme from the book reflects the need for organizations to consider the profound change we have experienced since the mid-1980s; and the development of new business models and formats need to be considered as a result.

There are clearly organizations that need to be convinced of the worth of a total value outlook, as opposed to one centred on cost. Total value is a far more holistic approach. People development within organizations must be seen as an ongoing process for all from board members and senior management, to front-line staff. The organizational changes referred to above will only come about through lifelong learning.

Consideration ought to be given to the increased use of technology and how the more tactical aspects of procurement operations are increasingly outsourced to third-party service providers. A focus on exactly what can and cannot be outsourced in the future should be debated. For example, businesses might want to consider a loose network versus a tight function for the organization – which of these makes commercial sense.

Other consideration can be given to the likelihood of procurement and supply management becoming embedded in other strategic parts of the business as a fully integrated part of them, and the profound need for a strong commercial focus.

What could happen at the most senior end of the profession as the aspiration to be on the board remains? Will we see a Chief Procurement, Supply, or even Commercial Officer?

What might the function look like? Smaller, value-adding, with a broader remit, dealing with 'externalities' – all are topics that are relevant and open for discussion. What are the boundaries of procurement's 'territory'? Will procurement have cross-functional accountability and governance for supply chain – perhaps jointly owned? How will it manage relationships with increasingly dominant outsourcing providers – the notion of 'buying' buying?

Relationships

We have seen a very heavy emphasis placed on procurement's role in relationships: their nature – commercial or otherwise; their management; and their importance. Whilst supplier relationship management (SRM) is a perennial issue for procurement it is one that for many reasons – assurance of supply being the most critical – is one that procurement must master. Collaborations, co-dependence, interdependence and the changes in the balance of power – be it between East and West, the buyer and the supplier, or third-party service organizations: relationships are key to the value that procurement brings to the business it serves.

Collaboration

This is seen as the 'new' way, with the old adversarial relationships being outmoded and inappropriate. There is a new challenge for procurement to become an intelligent customer, the buyer of choice.

Risk

Risk awareness and whole supply chain insights have become aspects of the daily activity of those working in the procurement, and this is a clear value-adding aspect of the role. The notion of risk managers with 'guruesque' knowledge of your supply network and a mature understanding of both the opportunity and threat presented by risk scenarios are becoming de rigeur. Nowhere will this be more prevalent than in the area of outsourcing (of tactical procurement), where service providers will gain power and the risk associated with this will need clinical management.

Commercial focus

There is no doubt that the level of sophistication in procurement today is set to increase even more. Nowhere is this more apparent than the commercial focus anticipated by organizations from their procurement and supply management professionals.

As the strategic scope of procurement broadens and its capabilities are increasingly recognized within organizations – it will have an increasingly financial (commercial) focus. The management of the legal/contracting base to affect consortia and greater interdependencies will demand a commercial mindset and mastery of acquisition as well as procurement know-how.

Messages for your business

The future of purchasing and supply should be an issue of concern to you as a procurement professional, and to your business. The global nature of business and markets means that in different geographies and cultures different things will be important; there will be development of different ways of doing things well, many of which will not have been exposed to us yet. Embedded procurement, transferable tool kits and skill sets could be the end of the dedicated discrete function that procurement has been for some time.

The issues and themes we have identified above are clearly not the only areas of interest that could be or should be raised in a workshop or event – they are simply the most prevalent from our perspective. You might suggest that a group should be formed that will shape the future within purchasing and supply in your organization. This group might be responsible for recommending future paths, moving the debate forward, giving clear and distinct priorities regarding the discipline to the wider business. Whatever you choose to do, an open forum for discussion regarding the future of procurement is of value to the wider business.

Setting up your own event

At **www.koganpage.com/pvp** we show how to set up an event in your organization or team to establish a debate regarding visioning. This is not meant to be prescriptive, merely a guide to set the debate going.

Please go to **www.koganpage.com/pvp** for a full set of PowerPoint slides covering the visioning innovation debate.

Dealing with 21st-century risk

Background

Given the changes we have experienced throughout the world of business in the last decade, we feel it would be interesting to consider the following question in the context of contemporary procurement and supply chain management: taking into consideration globalization, increased logistics costs, increasing levels of risk and rising labour costs, could it be time for a 'practice product' recall?

It is a fair question. Where will future global sourcing benefits come from given the foregoing? Should we be considering 'embedded procurement', by which we mean something that is locally embedded – allied to our giving serious consideration to the limits of global sourcing strategies?

In this book we have focused on procurement and supply chain management. As we wrote at the beginning of Chapter 1, this is a subject that was unheard of in the 1970s and has now become a strategic imperative to all organizations. Supply chain/supply management as a concept was born at the beginning of the 1980s. If we look back at the early concepts and developments some of the associated trends are easy to spot:

- The 1980s was about the demands of just-in-time.
- The 1990s was all about outsourcing.
- The 2000s saw the emergence of the internet and e-solutions.
- The 2010s thus far has been about supply chain risk (benefits + impediments).

The last 30 plus years have shaped the business situation in which companies now find themselves – via globalization and rapid developments in the new information technologies. Dealing with 'wicked problems' – the unanticipated outcomes of the implementation of new ideas – has made the need for the proper management of the supply chain in its entirety fundamental for all organizations to survive in the business world.

So let's consider a few of these issues and how they might impact modern supply chain design:

- *Globalization*: an old force but one that will continue to develop producing longer and longer lead times and demanding the constant attention of the CEO.
- *Increasing logistics costs*: transportation costs continue to rise due to rising energy prices and, with greater global consumption, inventories have risen too.
- *Increased levels of risk*: the consequential 'wicked problems' of embracing strategies such as lean manufacturing, outsourcing and offshoring without consideration of any possible draw backs from this activity.

- *Rising labour costs*: low-cost countries were only ever a one-hit opportunity. Globalization has been happening for some 20 years. In China, local labour costs have increased on average by 20 per cent year on year.

- *The focus on sustainability*: once considered a fad, now Europe leads the world in developing green supply chains.

- *The increasing volatility of commodity prices*: potentially fatal for some organizations. Think airlines procuring fuel – do you go long or short term? How do you out-guess the market?

Whilst the sourcing dreams of globalized markets are obvious – such as bottom-line improvements, new capabilities, access to new markets and so on – it is the sourcing nightmares that keep CEOs and CPOs awake at night. Were the supply chain calamities from the earthquake in Japan predictable? Are we living beyond risk mitigation and living in a business world where risk must be weighed up on its probability and not our ability to avoid it? Do we need to think about risk and rational, regional, practical supply chains?

Folklore has it that Henry Ford could get the customer any type of Model T as long as it was black; and yet, as a consequence of the disaster in north-east Japan the Ford Motor Company found itself in the strange position of being able to supply vehicles in any colour except (metallic) black as a result of the catastrophe.

The earthquake and tsunami that hit north-east Japan rocked global supply chains – and who knew that so much of the world's production could be so devastated by disruption from a single region? So how did this vulnerability come about?

A trend that started in the automotive industry in the 1990s has become the norm across pretty much the whole industrial world: a radical supply model that outsourced, offshored and 'single sourced' from a single suppler often at a single plant – thought to be the cheapest location in the world.

It was in the mid-1990s that Inaki Lopez, who worked at GM and then VW, launched this revolution in automotive supply chains: because a revolution was needed at that time. Original equipment manufacturer (OEM) supplier relations in the automotive industry were often too cosy and OEMs had so many suppliers they could barely identify them all. So businesses began to seek the lowest 'global piece price'.

Additionally, tooling costs were saved by establishing capacity at only one supplier location. All previous considerations of how parts related to operations were dispensed with. The buyer–seller relationships vanished – but sensible considerations such as total cost, quality, logistics and partnering for mutual prosperity also disappeared too. Before long, even internal operations were held to the same pricing standards, and business process outsourcing grew along with offshoring. The rationale was that if you couldn't price match those from China/India/Brazil, then the business would put that aspect of work out for bids. This led to a rash of bankruptcies. First, smaller suppliers closed their doors (at huge cost to OEMs), to replace the lost supply of parts and materials. They were followed by larger ones. As a result, procurement, supply management and logistics became increasingly complex.

Other trends contributed too: more sophisticated software and transportation systems, for example, led to the rise of '3PL' specialists. Logistics and even supply chain strategy also became outsourced in the rush to reduce costs – and outsourcing begat outsourcing. In the end, yet another key competence of manufacturers was lost to specialists whose interests were their own, not the OEM's, and most certainly not the customer's.

That said, there is nothing inherently wrong with sourcing globally. But a single-minded focus on lowest piece-price with no regard to broader strategies leads to unneeded complexities; and, as we see from the example of the natural disaster that befell north-east Japan, unneeded and unanticipated risk.

The simplistic and predictable reaction might be to question just-in-time (JIT). But this is not the real issue here; the real issue is to question supply chain strategy and configurations. Sourcing from far-flung global locations high-cost modular componentry that quickly loses value every day it sits in the distribution system has become the industry norm. The catastrophe in Japan meant that organizations that operated on minimal buffer stocks contemplated operating with increased production and more stock, increasing buffer stocks or finished goods inventory to protect themselves in some cases against a 100-year interruption. This can only be seen as absurd.

'Tuxedo black' is Ford's name for a colour that is dependent on a unique pigment from a Merck plant close to the Fukushima Daiichi nuclear plant. At the time of the disaster it was not produced anywhere else in the world. Merck said at the time that the plant itself wasn't damaged but, due to radiation, engineers couldn't even re-enter the plant and that when they could it would take months to set things back in order and begin producing zirallic, Merck's name for the pigment.

The deeper problem is that most companies still don't know the full extent of their exposure to risk. Buyers know their suppliers, but usually not their suppliers' suppliers, or the suppliers of those suppliers – think of recent issues and dilemmas over child labour, unsafe buildings, counterfeit components and foodstuff etc.

Clearly the solution isn't just a matter of exiting areas of the globe that we now consider, for whatever reason, to be risky. Rather, the solution lies in rethinking how we design and operate our supply chains. In general, it makes absolute sense to produce close to where one sells; and in general it makes most sense to engineer close to where one produces. And it certainly makes most sense to procure as close as possible to where one produces for one's customers.

At the beginning of this section we asked if it is time to bring to an end 20 years of antithetical sourcing strategies. Single sourcing is dangerous – that much is obvious. Moreover, 100 sources all competing for the next contract based on piece price is also dangerous, but in a different way. When that single source is continents away from production facilities, the danger is naturally magnified.

A new sourcing model is needed in this decade of increased risk. The wisdom of 'dual supplier' strategies of many lean-thinking supply chain managers is clear – avoid both single source and 'numerous sources' situations. When W Edwards Deming advocated what he called 'single sourcing' he was promoting OEM–supplier relationships based on partnership, not zero-sum negotiation; and on cost of quality, not price of transaction. Toyota's traditional approach was to pursue dual sourcing for first- and second-tier suppliers. Unfortunately this did not always extend to often small third- and fourth-tier suppliers – thus Toyota especially suffered in the global supply crisis, as 80 per cent of its in-vehicle computer chips were being supplied by one facility in north-east Japan with no easy re-sourcing possible.

Anyone, anywhere, who wants their country to be a competitive manufacturing location needs to practise 'lean'. That is, total cost including the potential cost of disruption on long-distance supply chains (see the simple economic value model in Chapter 2) rather than the piece price, plus slow freight-cost calculation done by most manufacturing firms today. We know that in continental Europe, especially Germany and France, there exists a much more 'competitive' manufacturing location than most procurement managers seem to think, based on the continuing decisions to send manufacturing to locations far and wide. Moreover, China has visited Europe recently to invest in it.

Caution needs to be exercised here because any costing model will be based on assumptions, and while risk can be factored in, no risk model could have ever accounted for the disruption that began on 11 March 2011 after the Tōhoku earthquake and tsunami. It is far more practical to work from some simple principles of lean supply chain configuration, for example shorter lead times are better than long. Closer proximity between suppliers and customers is better – shipping regionally is better than shipping across vast and sometimes troubled oceans. Fewer inventories with more frequent delivery are better than large inventories that move infrequently. Single sourcing, especially single location sourcing, is generally bad – it is risky and doesn't leverage natural, healthy competition. Maintaining hundreds of suppliers for the same component is also bad – it generates complexity, confusion and costs of redundancy.

No one with a 'value-add' procurement mindset would challenge the concept of adopting a total cost view; so it is more than simple resistance to the basic idea that is the problem. Rather, companies are simply inexpert when it comes to executing a true total-cost strategy. As costs are broken down and allocated across functional lines, ownership and even understanding increasingly become murky.

Recent research by Holger Schiele and others has shown that buyers who want to shift sourcing from Europe to China fail to consider plenitudes of costs and consequences. Good-quality metal can cost more in China than in Europe (see Shanghai Metal Index versus London Metal Exchange).[2] Energy costs more in parts of China than in parts of the United States and Europe; and what about the time and cost of managers travelling to visit global locations, along with the communication challenges of late-night conference calls with difficulty understanding those on the other end of the phone? In the face of all this, one might ask what reductions in total cost could be realized if the time, effort and energy of sourcing across the planet were actually invested in the local supplier through kaizen?

The point here, to repeat for emphasis, is *not* that sourcing in China or Brazil is a bad idea – the emergence of China and Brazil as viable sources for the global production community is a positive phenomenon of historical importance. However, each sourcing decision needs to be made on its own merits. Or else we are perpetuating the risky nature of procurement when we could be using sound procurement knowledge and business skills to work with the positive aspects of risk.

So, in conclusion, in preparing for a workshop on working with risk in a 21st-century supply chain, what might you pull together to set up the debate? You could start with the position that lean thinking brings things together, and emphasize the connectedness of all parts, organizationally and physically, namely suppliers that are close to OEMs that are close to customers.

Clearly it is no easy task to unravel the complexity of 20 years of piece price optimization. But there is no harm in going back to the basics of starting with the customer, defining value and working backwards from there. Working together we can create supply chains that flow value from raw material to the customer with ever-shortening lead times, profiting both OEMs and suppliers.

Just as JIT is not the practice to challenge here, neither is the practice of sourcing globally. The problem is far greater than being unable to order your vehicle in tuxedo black. Sometimes we need a crisis to spark transformation. Now is the time to rethink and reconfigure supply chains so they are rational, regional, practical, low in total cost and risk, and high in fostering quality – in short, lean, yet risk-aware supply chains.

Setting up your own event

At **www.koganpage.com/pvp** we set out how to set up an event in your organization or team to establish a debate regarding risk issues in the 21st century. Once again, this is not meant to be prescriptive, merely a guide to set the debate going.

Please go to **www.koganpage.com/pvp** for a full set of PowerPoint slides covering the risk innovation debate.

Sustainable procurement

Background

A major challenge to procurement is the rapidly rising interest in sustainability. The age of the 'triple bottom line' is upon us, where the assumption is that profit should no longer be at the expense of people (the social dimension) and planet (the environmental dimension). The pressure is mounting on business to deliver economic returns from greener goods, and corporate social responsibility (CSR) is no longer something that can be dismissed as a fad for environmental fanatics or 'tree huggers'. The planet's resources are in decline and the climate is changing, placing increasing pressures on companies to reduce carbon emissions, recycle or reuse, and to develop green technologies. Sustainable development is here to stay and only shows signs of gaining even greater momentum for the foreseeable future.

In today's business world we face an array of difficulties whose scope and complexity can make them intractable. Sustainability has become a burning issue to all in business. And yet if we think carefully through the trends affecting procurement and supply chain management today, and focus on using resources productively, sustainability needn't be one of these difficulties.

As the boundaries of our economy expand, we become ever more reliant on longer and more complex supply chains. As a consequence we see the debate becoming more complicated, especially around sustainable procurement, and never has it been more important for us to understand what is going on, why it happens and what works in a commercial environment.

Where once these discussions centred on the need for green or ethical practices – instigated by CSR policies – things have moved on. The impact of the 2011 tragedy and ongoing crisis in Japan has brought home what many had already started to realize: that without robust sustainable procurement practices, many organizations are in danger of severe disruptions to their business.

Managers are increasingly looking to improve the social and environmental impacts of their supply chains but say they feel blocked by forces beyond their control. Efforts to boost the sustainability of supply chains are hampered by cost, complexity, lack of information and know-how, and the sense that some of their principal stakeholders are not deeply concerned about the issue. Many sceptics focus on financial factors. This may be a response largely due to the weak economy. It also shows that people are not convinced by academics, consultants and others who argue that improving sustainability will not necessarily cut into profits, and may in fact help the bottom line. And yet it seems that a consensus of opinion reflects concern about sustainability and supply chain performance.

Sustainable procurement takes into account a range of environmental, social and economic consequences of a whole range of production methods and services such as design, non-renewable material use, manufacturing processes, service delivery, logistics and transportation options, maintenance, recycling and disposal, and not forgetting each tier of the supplier base. The driver is not 'just' CSR any more, but a range of influences from statutory, through to political and social, and of course commercial. Implementing processes that truly meet the demands of good sustainable procurement practice means that each level of supplier is required to do the same.

There are four core areas that impact on the sustainable debate. These are:

- *Ethical and sustainable trading*: where once it seemed the world had unlimited resources, now it is all too obvious that increasing populations and ecological challenges means the world is no longer able to replenish those valuable resources.

  To date, retailers and other directly consumer-facing businesses have borne the brunt of societal and business scrutiny, with criticism of unethical employment practices amongst suppliers hitting the headlines for companies such as Primark and Nike. Not understanding how suppliers conduct their business can lead to reputational damage that is hard to shake off, and increasingly business customers as well as consumers are looking deeper into the provenance of products.

- *Waste*: landfill is no longer an option and costs of disposal are increasingly expensive. By cutting waste, production costs are reduced and processes become more streamlined.

- *Carbon emissions*: according to the Carbon Disclosure Project supply chain report 2011, 50 per cent of an average organization's emissions come from the supply chain. So, if organizations do not put their house in order, they will soon be forced to by legislation. For instance, the Carbon Reduction Commitment's Energy Efficient Scheme in the UK is the first mandatory carbon trading scheme and targets those producing higher emissions.

- *Energy use*: declining reserves of fossil fuels, and rising costs of those fuels, means that everyone has the responsibility to make best use of those resources.

Though the frequency of dialogue around sustainable procurement is increasing, the activity itself is not new. Sustainability goals can be met merely through adhering to good and efficient procurement practices. Those organizations that have these practices in place will harvest the benefits of future-proof efficient supply chains. Those that don't will be exposed to the catastrophes and unpredictable forces outside their control.

Mitigating the risk of supply chain failures and fluctuating prices for raw materials, and being aware of political, environmental and cultural changes in the global environment, gives businesses an advantage. Those businesses putting sustainability at the top of their corporate agenda will have a competitive advantage, as well as an increased chance of survival when the going gets really tough. It also helps businesses to attract the best staff possible, with candidates increasingly looking to work for organizations with the highest ethical and sustainability standards.

Many organizations have already understood this message and are making proactive efforts to protect their businesses and the environment. Young's Seafood recognized the effect that unsustainable fishing would have on any long-term goals, as fish stocks dwindled and the quality of those catches plummeted. Their implementation of the 'Fish for Life' sustainable fish procurement policy made several demands of their suppliers to provide evidence of adherence to strict management protocols approved by Young's, as well as showing a commitment to constant improvement.

By making these demands themselves, Young's found that their own business also had to change, and they had to implement some key developments. They stopped purchasing North Sea cod because of the poor condition of fish stocks. Their obligations also developed into other areas of the business, such as policy, where they lobbied for more robust management of European fisheries – so their sustainable approach has far-reaching consequences.

Adnams, the Suffolk brewer, took something that started as an impetus for a CSR policy and developed it into a cost-saving initiative. Their lightweight bottles saved on raw materials and eventually transportation costs, as the lighter-weight bottles took less energy to deliver. Their East Green beer, marketed as 'the first carbon-neutral beer produced in the UK', uses locally produced high-yield quality barley. Their choice of hops is a variety that is more pest-resistant, reducing the need for chemicals, and so protecting the environment and reducing costs. Their energy-efficient brewing methods have enhanced their brand, as well as any promise that remaining CO_2 emissions will be offset.

All in all, businesses must have a positive impact on people, profit and the planet: the 'triple bottom line'. The need to measure and prove effectiveness, and the influence of sustainable procurement, is vital. For this reason, the CIPS Sustainable Procurement Review tool was recently launched, to enable businesses to measure the sustainability of their supply chain and for suppliers to demonstrate this to customers. The tool helps to benchmark purchasing performance and progress towards putting sustainable procurement at the heart of their organizations and in understanding their own standards and procedures across all aspects of environmental, social and economic policy.

Procurement and supply chain management professionals have a huge role to play in how this debate rumbles on. Supply chains are a key component in organization structure and so influence the health of every economy. A recent survey of our members found that 55 per cent now have a sustainability policy, with the pressure from public sector customers and stakeholders being the most popular reason as to why one was implemented. One in five stated that their driver was the need to conserve natural resources. Procurement professionals are increasingly aware of the benefits of sustainable procurement, not just to meet the needs of regulations, but as a strategic contributor in planning for future innovation and profit.

In the global economy, businesses are becoming much sharper at developing and coordinating suppliers in the battle for sustainability. Sustainable procurement is a commercial necessity, not a diversion, but of course has wider benefits to the environment and communities across the globe. Those who ignore this increasingly risk being left behind. The message is: become sustainable or go out of business.

Sustainability presents a risk to companies that are unprepared for it, but also an opportunity for companies willing to embrace the challenge. But companies cannot tackle sustainability by themselves: implementing sustainability requires systemic change, especially radically overhauled supply models. Paradoxically, the trend towards outsourcing, particularly to low-cost countries such as China or India, has exacerbated the sustainable procurement and supply chain management challenge. One of the negative results of global sourcing has been that companies have lost sight of what goes on within their extended supply chains – and low-cost country sourcing sometimes comes at an unexpected price.

Consider for one moment the problems of the BP oil spill in the Gulf of Mexico in 2010: it shows that companies cannot simply blame their suppliers when environmental disasters happen in the supply chain. Similarly, the collapse of a garment factory in Bangladesh in April 2013 killing over 1,100 factory workers; this was a supplier of Western fashion companies and retailers looking for low-cost sourcing. Companies such as IKEA and Apple have had to completely rethink their purchasing strategies due to damaging reports of ethical sourcing problems such as the use of child labour and suicides in supplier factories.

Again, a key message of this book is that a company is no more sustainable than the suppliers it sources from, putting purchasing right at the heart of sustainability implementation. New innovative purchasing strategies and methods are required not only to avoid the risks of unethical purchasing, but also to fully take advantage of the opportunities posed by sustainability.

Should there be a sustainability shake-up?

Are you thinking about the next generation of sustainability-focused procurement professionals? Is your aim to alter the way business is done in every function and unit of the business?

Today's successful sustainability-focused procurement executives are pushing the boundaries of their job description, budget constraints and the limits of 'moral influence'. Their goal is simple: *to alter the way business is done in every function and unit of the company.* Their motivation: *the implementation of shared organizational and social values.*

From the organizations that we spoke to, it was apparent that procurement executives are frequently leading via provocative measures that help functional managers to identify their own opportunities to improve corporate social and environmental performance with their range of influence. This drives sustainability consciousness down to lower organizational levels, embedding it in the company culture and organizational processes. Through a form of 'acculturation', sustainability moves from 'personality-focused' to process driven – and the creation of organizational routines that stick.

When procurement lead on this issue they typically work at identifying like-minded allies in key functional positions and persuading them that it is in their own interest to take action by demonstrating the value in sustainability. They help managers to find value by 'commercializing social value' into their individual business decisions. Social value is an important corporate asset gained by relating with key stakeholder constituencies.

Social intelligence as a business asset

Traditionally sustainability initiatives have been externally focused, with the bulk of managers' time spent communicating initiatives and reducing the company's carbon footprint. Social intelligence is a valuable corporate asset. Knowledge of the millennial generation's greater expectations about social responsibility, for instance, can be key in attracting, motivating and retaining the next generation of employees.

Understanding activist and shareholder demands for transparency in political contributions can avoid damaging revelations about your company's lobbying policies. Insights into indigenous rights issues when making raw-material sourcing decisions can help to avoid potential conflicts, supply disruptions or reputational risks.

Social intelligence is gained through relating with influential stakeholders and, more importantly, it is recognizing that social intelligence is most valuable when it enhances day-to-day business decision-making – and this is key. Inaction on sustainability initiatives often stems not from a lack of interest among functional managers, but a failure to demonstrate the business value of applying social intelligence to decision processes. Implementation often follows quickly after the value is understood.

Fortunately, it is not a difficult challenge; we all read the papers or talk with our neighbours and co-workers to share our experiences, concerns and hopes for the future. Through this habit we obtain and share social intelligence, which we use to make decisions, such as choosing what car to drive, what school to attend or who to vote for.

Unfortunately, while business managers are encouraged to use 'commercial intelligence' in business decision-making, most leave their 'social intelligence' behind when they arrive at work. Maximizing the benefits of social intelligence requires that your actions are not haphazard, but guided by an overarching sustainability vision and strategy. To achieve this, and lead sustainability via procurement, you need to rethink the role of procurement.

This recent trend towards sustainability is by no means purely a theoretical phenomenon. National governments and international bodies such as the European Union (EU) and World Trade Organization (WTO) are debating the sustainability challenge facing the global economy and putting into place ambitious targets and action plans. Companies across all industry sectors must adapt to a rapidly changing world in which the need for sustainable economic, environmental and social development is at the core. Many companies have made significant changes to the way they operate, fully embracing the sustainability challenge, but others still view sustainability as something that does not really concern them and might 'go away' in the next few years.

The future of sustainable purchasing and supply management simply cannot be viewed as a fad, a transient phenomenon, because the world is running out of natural resources whilst the world population keeps growing rapidly. So, there is no choice but for the whole world to become much more sustainable.

It is by no means a certainty that procurement will play a central role in creating sustainable business models. However, as we have pointed out throughout this book, businesses are increasingly reliant on their supply chains for production of the products and services they market to their customers. Thus, procurement managers are in an important position to make these sustainability changes happen.

Sustainability must avoid becoming the responsibility of a few more or less isolated individuals within companies; instead it is important that it become integrated into each company's fabric: all their processes, including purchasing and supply chain management, should take into account the need for sustainability.

If procurement leaders and managers are to embrace this challenge they have to change the way they operate. This requires new ways of thinking about supply structures and processes and new skills and competencies. It follows that sustainability is not the responsibility of a few sustainability experts but a challenge that must be embraced business-wide.

On this and other issues addressed here, we hope that this book will play its small part in not only educating, but also changing the mindsets of current and future procurement professionals.

Notes

1 The Chatham House Rule: anyone who comes to the meeting is free to use information from the discussion, but must not reveal who made any comment. It is designed to increase openness of discussion.

2 Schiele, H, Hoffmann, P and Reichenbachs, M (2011) How to Manage Strategic Supply Risk: A Preferred Customer Perspective, Proceedings of IPSERA; see also: Schiele, H, Pulles, N and Veldman, J (2011) Recognizing Innovative Suppliers: Empirical Study of the Antecedents of Innovative Suppliers within the Buyer–Supplier Relationship, Proceedings of IPSERA.

REFERENCES

Allison, G (2014) A good year for a Great War, Harvard Kennedy School, Winter

Babbage, C (1832) *On the Economy of Machinery and Manufactures*, Charles Knight, Pall Mall East

Baily, P and Farmer, D (1977) *Purchasing Principles and Techniques*, Pitman, London

Bisson, P (2010) Why trends matter, *McKinsey Quarterly*, July

Booz & Co (2014) [accessed 11 August 2014] The New CPO, white paper [Online] http://www.strategyand.pwc.com/media/file/New_CPO.pdf

Bustillo, M, Wright, T and Banjo, S (2012) Touch questions in fire's ashes, *Wall Street Journal*, 30 November, p B1

Chandler Jr, A D (1977) *The Visible Hand: The managerial revolution in American business*, Harvard University Press, Cambridge, MA, p 58

Chick, G and Lewis, M (2009–10) 7 habits of highly effective CPOs, *CPO Agenda*, Winter, pp 50–54

Chick, G and Rushton, P (2013) Procurement's New Value Proposition to Business, Optimum Procurement Group

Christensen, C (1997) *The Innovator's Dilemma: When new technologies cause great firms to fail*, Harvard Business School Press, Boston

Christopher, M and Towill, D R (2002) Developing market specific supply chain strategies, *International Journal of Logistics Management*, **13** (1), pp 1–14

Collins, J and Porras, J (1994) *Built to Last: Successful habits of visionary companies*, Harper Business Essentials, New York

Cousins, P, Squire B and Lawson, B (2006) A Typology of UK Purchasing Functions, Manchester Business School, UK

Cousins, P, Squire B and Lawson, B (2008) Looking to the Future: Purchasing as Cost Reducer or Value Broker? A research report carried out for the CIPS Centre for Procurement Leadership by Manchester Business School, July

Cousins, P, Squire B, and Lawson, B (2008) The Role of Risk in Environment-Related Supplier Initiatives, SCMRG Manchester Business School

Droege, P (2008) *Urban Energy Transition: From fossil fuels to renewable power*, Elsevier, Oxford

Drucker, P (1959) *The Landmarks of Tomorrow*, Harper & Row, New York

Drucker, P (1974) *Management: Tasks, responsibilities, practices*, Harper Business, New York

England, W (1970) *Modern Procurement Management: Principles and cases*, 5th edn, Irwin, Homewood, IL

Fearne, A *et al* (2009) Sustainable value chain analysis: a case study of South Australian wine. A report prepared for the Government of South Australia, January

Fearon, H (1968) History of purchasing, *Journal of Purchasing*, February, pp 44–50

Ford, D *et al* (2002) *Understanding Business Marketing and Purchasing*, Thomson Learning, London

Ganguly, Joydeep *et al* (2011) A textbook transformation: how Biogen Idec overhauled its supply chain, *Supply Chain Management Review*, May/June, pp 28–35

Handfield, R and Edwards, S (2009) Cost Leadership Best Practices, white paper, Supply Chain Resource Cooperative, NC State University

Handfield, Robert (2013) The future of Procurement, Research Brief, published by KPMG Procurement Advisory Group, KPMG International, October

Handfield, Robert *et al* (2013) *Trends and Strategies in Logistics and Supply Chain Management*, BVL International, Berlin

HBR, Spotlight (2010) Is your supply chain sustainable?, *Harvard Business Review*, October

Henke Jr, J and Zhang, C (2010) Increasing supplier driven innovation, *MIT Sloan Management Review*, **51** (2) pp 41–46

Hines, P *et al* (2000) *Value Stream Management: Strategy and excellence in the supply chain*, Financial Times/Prentice Hall, Harlow

Kamath, R and Liker, J (1994) A second look at Japanese product development, *Harvard Business Review*, November–December, **74**, pp 154–80

Khun, T (1962) *The Structure of Scientific Revolutions*, University of Chicago Press, Chicago

Kotabe, M and Swan, K (1995) The role of strategic alliance in high-technology new product development, *Strategic Management Journal*, November

Kraljic, P (1983) Purchasing must become supply management, *Harvard Business Review*, September–October, pp 109–17

Lamming, R C (1993) *Beyond Partnership: Strategies for innovation and lean supply*, Prentice Hall, Harlow

Lee, L Jr and Dobler, D W (1971) *Purchasing and Materials Management: Text and cases*, 2nd edn, McGraw Hill, New York

Machiavelli, N (1532) *The Prince*, Oxford World's Classics

Malik, Y, Niemeyer, A and Ruwadi, B (2011) Building the supply chain of the future, *McKinsey Quarterly*, January, pp 62–71

Maslow, A H (1943) A theory of human motivation, *Psychological Review*, **50**, pp 370–96

Maurer, J (2011) Relationships between foreign subsidiaries, DOI 10.1007/978-3-8349-6249-2_2, Gabler Verlag | Springer Fachmedien Wiesbaden GmbH

McKinsey Global Survey results (2008) Understanding supply chain risk, *McKinsey Quarterly*, October

McKinsey Global Survey results (2010) The challenges ahead for supply chains, *McKinsey Quarterly*, December

McKinsey Quarterly (2011) How women can contribute more to the US economy, *McKinsey Quarterly*, April

Miles, R and Snow, C (1992) Causes of failure in network organizations, *California Management Review*, Summer

Milman, D (1980) *Way of the Peaceful Warrior: A book that changes lives*, New World Library, CA

Nooteboom, B, Berger, H and Noorderhaven, N (1997) Effects of trust and governance on relational risk, *Academy of Management Journal*, **40** (2), pp 308–38

Oglethorpe, D (2008) Procurement and Climate Change: Urban Myths, Uncomfortable Truths and Unintended Effects, a report for the Chartered Institute of Purchasing & Supply, October

O'Neill, J (2001) Building better global economic BRICs, *Goldman Sachs Global Economics Paper*, No 153, 28 March 2007

Pagell, M and Wu, Z (2009) Building a more complete theory of sustainable supply chain management using case studies of 10 exemplars, *Journal of Supply Chain Management*, **45** (2), pp 37–56

Paul, D *et al* (1998) Case study: a leveraged learning network, *Sloan Management Review*, Summer

Porter, M E (1985) *Competitive Advantage: Creating and sustaining superior performance*, Simon & Schuster, New York

Reinecke, N, Spiller, R P and Ungerman, D (2007) The talent factor in purchasing, *McKinsey Quarterly*, **1**, pp 6–9

Rogers, P, Jalal, K F and Boyd, J A (2008) *An Introduction to Sustainable Development*, Earthscan, London

Schiele, H, Hoffmann, P and Reichenbachs, M (2011) How to Manage Strategic Supply Risk: A Preferred Customer Perspective, Proceedings of IPSERA

Schiele, H, Pulles, N and Veldman, J (2011) Recognizing Innovative Suppliers: Empirical Study of the Antecedents of Innovative Suppliers within the Buyer–Supplier Relationship, Proceedings of IPSERA

Taylor, F W (1911) *The Principles of Scientific Management*, Harper & Row, New York

Taylor, P (2011) Supply chain is a strategic discipline, *Financial Times* Special Report, January

The Hackett Group (2010) An Evolution of Value and Capability, Conference Presentation

The ILM (2009) Index of Leadership Trust

Williamson, O E (2005) *Handbook of New Institutional Economics, Transaction Cost Economics*, Springer, US

Wright, R (2000) *Nonzero: The logic of human destiny*, Knopf Doubleday, New York

Zheng, J *et al* (2007) An analysis of research into the future of purchasing and supply management, *Journal of Purchasing & Supply Management*, **13**, pp 69–83

FURTHER READING

Abery, J and Lenders, R (2009) Global Chief Procurement Officer Survey 2009: Responding to the Challenges of Economic Meltdown: a report prepared by CapGemini Consulting

Alfalla-Luque, R and Medina-Lo'pez, C (2009) Supply chain management: unheard of in the 1970s, core to today's company, *Business History*, **51** (2), March, pp 202–21

Allt-Graham, J (2008) Beyond Purchasing: Next Steps for the Procurement Profession; a report prepared by KPMG

Atsmon, Y and Magni, M (2011) China's confident consumers: a survey highlights how fast the market is changing, *McKinsey Quarterly*, November

Bauman, Z (2006) *Liquid Fear*, Polity, London

Bonini, S and Miller, E (2009) Tackling socio-political issues in hard times, *McKinsey Quarterly*, September

Bosshart, S, Luedi, T and Wang, E (2010) Past lessons for China's new joint ventures, *McKinsey Quarterly*, December

Bughin, J, Hung Byers, A and Chui, M (2011) How social technologies are extending the organization, *McKinsey Global Institute*, November

Carroll, T (2010) The Smarter Supply Chain of the Future: Insights from the Global Chief Supply Chain Officer Study, IBM Corporation, October

Chick, G and James, K (2006) The Coming Imperatives for the world of Procurement, The Chartered Institute of Purchasing & Supply, September

Chick, G and Lewis, M (2007–08) More than just the goalkeeper, *CPO Agenda*, Winter, pp 39–42

Chick, G and Martindale, N (2012) 80:20 Vision: Procurement and Supply Towards CIPS centenary, The Chartered Institute of Purchasing & Supply

Chui, M, Löffler, M and Roberts, R (2010) The internet of things, *McKinsey Quarterly*, March, **2**, pp 1–9

Chui, M, Miller, A and Roberts, R (2009) Six ways to make Web 2.0 work, *McKinsey Quarterly*, February, pp 1–7

Constantine, B, Ruwadi, B and Wine, J (2009) Management practices that drive supply chain success, *McKinsey Quarterly*, February

Cross, R, Parise, S and Weiss, L (2007) The role of networks in organisational change, *McKinsey Quarterly*, April

Dobbs, R, Lund, S and Schreiner, A (2010) How the growth of emerging markets will strain global finance, *McKinsey Quarterly*, December

Eddy, J, Hall, S and Robinson, S (2006) How global organisations develop local talent, *McKinsey Quarterly*, **3**, pp 6–8

Glatzel, C, Großpietsch, J and Silva, I (2011) Is your top team undermining your supply chain?, *McKinsey Quarterly*, January

Glatzel, C, Helmcke, S and Wine, J (2009) Building a flexible supply chain for uncertain times, *McKinsey Quarterly*, March

Hardt, C, Reinecke, N and Spiller, P (2007) Inventing the 21st century purchasing organisation, *McKinsey Quarterly*, October

Horn, J, Singer, V and Woetzel, J (2010) A truer picture of China's export machine, *McKinsey Quarterly*, September

Lee, H (2010) Don't tweak your supply chain – rethink it end to end, *Harvard Business Review*, October, pp 61–69

Lynch, G (2010) Managing risk, *Supply Chain Management Review*, March/April, pp 30–35

Naisbitt, J (1984) *Megatrends: Ten new directions transforming our lives*, Warner Press Grand Central Publishing, New York

New, S (2010) The transparent supply chain, *Harvard Business Review*, October, pp 76–82

Nizen, C and Deringer, H (2007) Demanding better supply management, *Business Strategy Review*, Spring, pp 47–50

Peck, H (2008) Opening the Way to Successful Risk Management in Purchasing and Supply; a report for the Chartered Institute of Purchasing & Supply, March

Sawchuk, C and Mitchell, P (2009) Attracting and retaining top procurement talent: difficulties finding and keeping 'A' players are growing even as global economy slows down, *Procurement Executive Insight*, 6 February

Slone, R, Mentzer, J and Dittmann, P (2007) Are you the weakest link in your company's supply chain?, *Harvard Business Review*, September, pp 116–25

Squire, B and Chu, Y (2010) Supply Chains at Risk: A Delphi Study, EPSRC

Swink, M (2010) Does supply chain excellence really pay off?, *Supply Chain Management Review*, March/April, pp 14–21

INDEX

CPSIA information can be obtained
at www.ICGtesting.com
Printed in the USA
LVHW101818191118
597645LV00006B/77/P